Salinger's Glass Stories

as a Composite Novel

J. D. Salinger in 1979   Photo: Michael McDermott

Salinger's Glass Stories

as a Composite Novel

by

Eberhard Alsen

The Whitston Publishing Company
Troy, New York
1983

Copyright 1983
Eberhard Alsen

Library of Congress Catalog Number 82-50411

ISBN: 0-87875-243-9

Printed in the United States of America

For Peter and Maria

You have the right to work, but for the work's sake only. You have no right to the fruits of work. Desire for the fruits of work must never be your motive in working. Never give way to laziness either.

Perform every action with your heart fixed on the Supreme Lord. Renounce all attachment to the fruits. Be even-tempered in success and failure; for it is this evenness of temper with is meant by yoga.

Work done with anxiety about results is far inferior to work done without such anxiety, in the calm of self-surrender. Seek refuge in the knowledge of Brahman. They who work selfishly for results are miserable.

Bhagavad Gita, II, 47-49

TABLE OF CONTENTS

ACKNOWLEDGEMENTS

I am grateful to the Fulbright Commission and the Research Foundation of the State University of New York for grants which gave me the time to write this book. I also wish to thank professors William Bysshe Stein of the State University of New York at Binghamton and Kenneth Hamilton of the University of Winnipeg for supporting the project.

Chapters 4, 9, and 10 have been published in slightly different form in the *English Record, Studies in Short Fiction,* and *Renascence*. I wish to thank the editors of these journals for their permission to reprint this material.

As far as the ideas in the book are concerned, I would like to acknowledge my indebtedness to the students in my undergraduate and graduate courses who helped me develop my interpretations of the Glass stories. Of special note are the contributions of George Lohmann of SUNY Cortland and Wolfram Hochstetter of the University of Tübingen.

But my most important debt is to Swami Adiswaranada of the Ramakrishna-Vivekananda Center in New York. The instruction in Vedanta philosophy that I received in his seminars and the conversations about Hindu scriptures that I had with him have been invaluable to me in coming to understand the Glass philosophy.

Finally, I also want to thank Alfred Weber, Dennis O'Connor, Del Janik, Alice Kaminsky, Robert Rhodes, Lynda Taylor, Carol Murphy, Marlea Crandall and many other friends and colleagues who have helped me with their typing, proofreading, criticism, and encouragement.

Ithaca, New York   E. A.
20 Aug 83

PREFACE

Between 1948 and 1965, J. D. Salinger published a series of stories about several members of an extraordinary family. Most of them focus on the two eldest sons, on the poet and God-seeker Seymour Glass, who is the spiritual guide of his younger siblings, and on the story writer and college teacher Buddy Glass, who is the chronicler of Seymour's life. The first of these stories, "A Perfect Day for Bananafish," is Buddy's account of the events leading up to Seymour's suicide, and to date the last story, "Hapworth 16, 1924" is a long letter from camp by the seven year old Seymour as transcribed by Buddy Glass some four decades later.[1]

During the years that the Glass stories continued to come out in irregular intervals, Salinger's readers speculated that he would eventually pull them together into a novel. After all, the appearance of his first novel, *The Catcher in the Rye* (1951), was also preceded by the publication of a number of stories about its protagonist. Salinger added fuel to these speculations when he collected four major Glass stories in two volumes, *Franny and Zooey* (1961) and *Raise High the Roof Beam, Carpenters* and *Seymour—An Introduction* (1963). In the comments he made on the dust jackets of these books, he mentioned that he had several new stories coming along and that the "Glass series" was "waxing" and "dilating" in his mind. And in 1965, when "Hapworth 16, 1924" was published, Salinger's narrator and alter ego, Buddy Glass, further stirred his readers' hopes by mentioning in a preface that he had been working on a story about a party at which he, Buddy, and Seymour were signed up for the radio quiz show "It's a Wise Child." But this story still has not been published. Rumor has it that Salinger submitted the story to the *New Yorker*, that it was actually set in print, but that he withdrew it at the last moment.[2]

Salinger's readers gave up their hopes of ever seeing the

Glass series completed when he announced in a 1974 interview that he would not publish any more. "There is a marvelous peace in not publishing," Salinger said. "It's peaceful. Still, publishing is a terrible invasion of my privacy. I like to write. I love to write. But I write just for myself and my own plea-sure."[3] This may strike us as an excessively flinty, even churlish statement until we realize that what disturbs Salinger's peace is not the experience of publishing his work but that of reading the criticism of his unskilled and unsympathetic readers. For while his early fiction, especially *The Catcher in the Rye* (1951) and *Nine Stories* (1953), has been widely praised for its narrative compactness and its success in recording the Rhythms and Cad-ences of Colloquial Speech, his later, maddeningly irregular stories with their extravagant style, their rambling development, and their increasing religious preoccupation have been harshly condemned. Faced with this lack of appreciation and under-standing, Salinger apparently decided that in order to preserve his peace of heart, he would share his work only with a few close friends to whom he is reported to send occasional samples for comments.

We are therefore left with a series of stories which give the impression of an incomplete puzzle. But since we have all the major pieces, we can arrange them in various ways to see how they best fit together. And as we do this, we find that the ser-ies has a wider latitude of meaning in its uncompleted form than it could possibly have if Salinger had arranged the stories in a fixed pattern. The Glass series thus constitutes a unique phen-omenon in contemporary fiction, for each story is designed to work both as a self-contained account and as a part of a composite novel which the reader must assemble himself if he wants to see any part of its rich overall meaning.

Although much has been written about the Glass series, little attention has been paid to the form of the stories and what it reveals about their meaning. Most interpretations have con-centrated on thematic elements and based their conclusions on outside information from companion stories. Particularly rare are analyses of the narrative structures of the later experimental stories "Zooey," "Seymour—An Introduction," and "Hapworth 16, 1924." Even less has been written about the form of the whole series as a composite novel.

Moreover, most critics have been too unsympathetic to the religious and aesthetic ideas in the Glass stories to study them in any depth. And although the vital relationship between art and religion in the Glass series has been recognized by a few commentators, this relationship has been explained chiefly in terms of Zen Buddhist ideas. The trend of treating Zen Buddhism as the major component of the Glass philosophy has continued to this day, even though Salinger protested against it in "Seymour—An Introduction" when he made Buddy Glass insist on his own and Seymour's "essential Zenlessness" and point out that their "roots in Eastern philosophy" were planted "in the New and Old Testaments, Advaita Vedanta, and classical Taoism."

This study hopes to contribute to a better understanding of Salinger's later fiction by concentrating on those aspects of its form and meaning that have not yet been adequately explained. It will offer close readings of the six Glass stories as self-contained accounts; it will describe the way in which the shape of the stories has changed over the years; it will explain the major religious and aesthetic ideas mentioned by the Glasses; and it will present an interpretation of the overall meaning of the Glass series as a composite novel.

The six stories that will be examined are the ones that Salinger has identified as the major parts of the series, either in comments on the dust jackets of his two Glass volumes or in statements by Buddy Glass. They are: "A Perfect Day for Bananafish" (1948); "Franny" (1955); "Raise High the Roof Beam, Carpenters" (1955); "Zooey" (1957); "Seymour—An Introduction" (1959); and "Hapworth 16, 1924" (1965). Brief consideration will also be given to four early pieces from *Nine Stories* which can be regarded as preliminary studies: They are "Down at the Dinghy" (1949); "For Esmé—With Love and Squalor" (1950); "DeDaumier-Smith's Blue Period" (1952); and "Teddy" (1953).

The thematic relationships among the six major stories suggest two obvious sequences in which to read them. One is the order in which they were published, which is also the order in which Buddy claims to have written them; and the other is the order suggested by the chronology of the events in the stories. Arranged one way, the stories focus on Buddy's struggle to understand Seymour by writing about him; arranged the other way, they focus on Seymour's quest for God.

The first part of this study therefore treats the Glass series as a *Künstler-Roman,* a novel about an artist's quest to understand his mission and to find the right form for his work. The analyses of the stories in this section will be close readings that pay special attention to what their form reveals about their meaning and about Buddy's development as a writer. This part of the book will conclude with a summary of the changes that occurred in the style and narrative structure of the stories between 1948 and 1965, and it will outline the philosophy of composition implicit in the later stories.

The second part treats the Glass series as a religious novel. It begins with a detailed chronology of Seymour's life and an examination of the Eastern roots of the Glass philosophy. After the role of Zen Buddhism, Christian ideas, classical Taoism and Advaita Vedanta Hinduism in the series has been explained, the six major stories will be discussed as stages in Seymour's lifelong quest for God. The purpose of this section is to explain why his siblings consider Seymour their spiritual guide, even though his quest ended in suicide.

The concluding chapter will bring together the findings of the two parts of the book and offer a thesis about the overall meaning of the Glass series. It will show that the two major thematic concerns of the composite novel coalesce into a statement about life as art and art as religion.

As may already have become apparent from these introductory remarks, the purpose of this study is not to evaluate but to explain. My attitude toward the Glass stories is not that of a detached critic but that of an undetached rhapsode. Like Plato's Ion, I believe that in order to come to an understanding of a work of literature, one must respond to it primarily with one's heart, not with one's head. And the Glass stories invite this kind of response, for like the Chinese and Japanese poetry that Seymour and Buddy love so much, they have the capacity to please, enlighten and enlarge the sympathetic reader to within an inch of his life.

My fondness for Salinger's stories has not only made me re-read them many times but it has also made me read widely in the works of literature and philosophy to which the Glasses keep referring. As a result, I have become interested in Eastern thought, particularly in Vedanta philosophy which, I believe, forms the basis of the eclectic religious and aesthetic ideas in the stories. To understand these ideas better, I immersed myself in Vedanta literature and took courses at the Ramakrishna-Vivekananda Center in New York, where Salinger himself studied in the early fifties.

Finally, my delight in the Glass stories has also made me read everything that has been written about them. This has been, for the most part, a rather irritating experience because most of the criticism on the Glass stories is either unsympathetic or uninformed. Only few commentaries have been a pleasure to read. Among those whose ideas I found enlightening are James Bryan, Kenneth Hamilton, Ihab Hassan, Arthur Mizener, and Dennis O'Connor. But rather than discuss the ideas of commentators and critics, no matter how delightful or irritating, I will concentrate on the ideas of the Glasses.

My emphasis on the texts of the stories themselves and on their unique aesthetic and religious ideas has resulted in readings that are in some ways radically different from those of previous commentaries, particularly as far as the meaning of Seymour's life and death is concerned. My interpretation argues that Seymour should not be seen as a saint, which is how most previous readings have treated him, but as a God-seeker whose quest failed. His quest failed because he pursued it in such a self-directed and single-minded fashion that he estranged himself from common humanity. But he recognized his mistake, even if he could not rectify it, and he passed his insights on to his siblings. These insights contain the religious meaning of the composite novel.

My interpretation of the aesthetic meaning of the Glass series also differs from that of previous commentators, for I do not think that Buddy's development of a writer has led him into a dead end and that the last two stories, "Seymour" and "Hapworth" are failures. Instead, I see these two most difficult parts of the Glass series as the result of Buddy's work gradually ripening into a form that truly expresses his aesthetic and religious beliefs.

But the chief purpose of his book is not to press a specific interpretation but to increase the reader's enjoyment and understanding of the Glass series. For while these stories continue to please and enlighten the amateur reader—as I find out again and again when I discuss them in introductory college courses—they will yield even more delight and insight to the skillful reader who re-reads them carefully, examines their interrelationship, and studies their vision of life.

NOTES

[1] "Hapworth 16, 1924" has so far only been published in the *New Yorker*, June 19, 1965, pp. 32-113.

[2] James Bryan, "Salinger and His Short Fiction," Unpubl. Diss. University of Virginia: Charlottesville, 1968, p. 75.

[3] Lacey Fosburgh, "J. D. Salinger Speaks About His Silence," *New York Times*, November 3, 1974, pp. 1, 69.
More recently, in a conversation that was surreptitiously taped by an unscrupulous reporter, Salinger said very definitely that he has "*no* plans to publish." See Betty Eppes, "What I Did Last Summer," *Paris Review*, 80 (August 1981), 233.

PART I

BUDDY'S STORIES

CHAPTER 1

Buddy—An Introduction

When we read the six major Glass stories in the sequence in which they were published, we will at first get the impression that they have only a very tenuous thematic connection and that the differences among them outweigh their similarities. This impression is due to the fact that during the seventeen years between the publication of "A Perfect Day for Bananafish" (1948) and "Hapworth 16, 1924" (1965), the stories became increasingly more extravagant in their style, more rambling in their narrative development, more bulky in their shape, and more esoteric in their content. These changes, so we learn from some of the self-reflexive comments of the narrator Buddy Glass, are the result of Buddy's development as writer, of his movement away from the rules of the traditional short story and toward a form of fiction that better suits his subject, the life and death of his eldest brother, the artist-seer Seymour Glass. By writing story after story about Seymour (and burning most of them as unfit for publication), Buddy tries to reconcile his admiration for Seymour's aesthetic and religious ideas with his bewilderment about Seymour's suicide. In the process of working out this problem, Buddy gradually comes to an understanding of his own purpose in life and of the relationship between art and religion.

Seen this way, the Glass series can be read as a composite novel about an artist's coming to terms with his calling, as a *Künstler-Roman* along the lines of Johann Wolfgang von Goethe's two *Wilhelm Meister* novels or James Joyce's *Portrait of the Artist as a Young Man*. That Buddy is indeed a figure such as Goethe's Wilhelm Meister or Joyce's Stephen Dedalus is suggested by Salinger himself in his dust cover notes for *Franny and Zooey* (1961) when he calls Buddy Glass his "alter ego." Moreover, there are some striking parallels between

Salinger's biography and the life of Buddy Glass. Both were born in 1919, both grew up in Upper Manhattan, both dropped out of college to become professional short story writers, both served in Europe during World War II, and both derive their world view from Eastern philosophy.[1] But the most important parallel between Buddy Glass and J. D. Salinger is that Buddy claims authorship of most of Salinger's works, particularly of *The Catcher in the Rye*, "Teddy," and the Glass stories.[2] Thus Buddy's growth as an artist reflects that of Salinger, just as the growth of Wilhelm Meister and Stephen Dedalus reflects that of Goethe and Joyce.

But the Glass series is unique as a *Künstler-Roman* because it was not written in retrospect, after the author's own development as an artist was already completed, but it was written in six installments over a period of seventeen years while the author's own development was still going on. The changes in style, structure, themes, and world view of the six Glass stories therefore are objective correlatives that illustrate Salinger's changing views of life and art. And the Glass series presents these changing ideas in terms of Buddy's growing understanding of his older brother's aesthetic and religious teachings. Because of the way in which this *Künstler-Roman* grew, because of the radical differences in the shape of its six parts, and because these six parts are not arranged in any specific order, the overall meaning does not only lie in Buddy's statements about what he learned from Seymour concerning the relationship of art and religion, it also lies in the form of the stories themselves, both as self-contained narratives and as a composite novel.

The form of the Glass series reveals a view of fiction and of art in general that is unusual because it is essentially religious in nature. I will explain this view of art by presenting close readings of the six major Glass stories, by tracing the way in which their form and content changed over the years, and by devoting a separate chapter to the philosophy of composition that they illustrate. This philosophy of composition is one which Buddy Glass developed over a period of seventeen years while he was struggling to come to terms with the artistic and religious legacy of his brother Seymour. To clarify Buddy's growth as an artist under the posthumous influence of Seymour, I will first pull together all the information about his life that is scattered throughout the stories.

* * *

Webb Gallagher "Buddy" Glass is born in 1919, the second child of the vaudeville performers Les and Bessie Gallagher Glass. In addition to his older brother Seymour (born 1917, died 1948), Buddy has five more siblings: Beatrice, "Boo Boo" (born 1920), Waker (born 1921) and Walter (born 1921, died 1945), Zachary, "Zooey" (born 1930), and Frances, "Franny" (born 1935).[3] When Buddy is four years old, he shows himself to be so precocious that his brother Seymour, himself a child prodigy, designs for him a reading program in masterworks of world literature and religious writings. The following year, in 1924, their parents send Buddy and Semour to a summer camp in Maine because they are worried about all the time that the boys are spending in libraries and because they want them to have some interaction with regular children.

When Buddy goes to Camp Hapworth in 1924, he is only five years old but has already decided that he wants to be a short story writer. And during the first sixteen days at camp, he writes six new stories. While he is at Camp Hapworth, Buddy also reveals that his precociousness is in part due to his photographic memory. He demonstrates this gift when he wins a bet by memorizing an entire book, *The Hardwoods of North America,* in less than thirty minutes. His photographic memory not only explains his ability to read prodigious amounts of material in a short time (he later admits that he seldom reads fewer than two hundred thousand words a day and often closer to four; the equivalent of two to four full size novels), but it also explains the ease with which he acquires foreign languages. At the age of five, he is already proficient in French, Italian, and Spanish; and in later years he picks up six more languages: German, Latin, Greek, Japanese, Pali, and Sanskrit.

Buddy's and Seymour's unusual mental powers become nationally known between 1927 and 1934, when they both appear as regulars on the radio quiz show "It's a Wise Child." In later years, the other five Glass children also perform on that show on a regular basis, and the proceeds from their employment allow Les and Bessie to send them all to college.

Three years after he leaves "It's a Wise Child," in 1937, Buddy enters Columbia University where Seymour is already teaching in the English department. During his senior year at Columbia, Buddy takes a course in short story writing from a Professor B. (Whit Burnett?), but Seymour convinces him not to be to content with the type of "rattling good story" that Professor B. makes him turn out.[4] That same year, when he turns twenty-one, Buddy leaves his parents' home on Riverside Drive and shares a small apartment with Seymour on 79th Street, a block from Madison Avenue. Later on that year, when Buddy and Seymour register for the draft, Buddy lists his profession as "writer." By that time, he has left Columbia without taking a degree and has begun to work as a free-lance author.

In February of 1942, Buddy is drafted and spends thirteen weeks of basic training at Fort Benning, Georgia. In June of that year, he goes to New York to attend Seymour's wedding to Muriel Fedder. After Buddy completes his military training, he serves in the European Theater of Operations. In 1945, shortly after the end of the war, Buddy visits Seymour in the psychiatric ward of an army hospital, somewhere in Germany. When he returns to the United States, Buddy at first resumes his work as a free-lance short story writer but then, in 1947, accepts a position as a college writing instructor.

In March of 1948, Buddy briefly sees his older brother in New York after Seymour has been released from the Army hospital and before Seymour and his wife Muriel leave for a vacation in Florida. At that time, Buddy reads a recent poem of Seymour's about a widower and a white cat. Later on that month, after Seymour has committed suicide, Buddy flies to Florida to bring the body back to New York. In the hotel room where Seymour shot himself, Buddy finds Seymour's last haiku poem, written in Japanese on the desk blotter. In May of that year, Buddy publishes "A Perfect Day for Bananafish," his version of the events leading up to Seymour's death.

Three years later, in 1951, Buddy has his first great success as an author when he publishes his novel, *The Catcher in the*

Rye. That same year, he writes a letter to his brother Zooey, advising him not to follow his head and take a Ph.D. degree but to follow his heart and become an actor. In that letter, he also mentions that he has begun to lecture to the faculty of his college, their wives, and a few oppressively deep-type undergraduates every Friday on Zen and Mahayana Buddhism. Buddy's interest in Eastern philosophy is further evident in the short story "Teddy" which he publishes in 1953 and in which he provides an introduction to Vedanta Hinduism. Two years later, in January of 1955, Buddy publishes "Franny," a story about the religious crisis of his sister. In November of that year, Buddy has another story published, "Raise High the Roof Beam, Carpenters," his account of the events on Seymour's wedding day, back in 1942. Like his earlier stories and his novel, "Carpenters" is still fairly conventional in its structure, but it is no longer the kind of "rattling good story" Professor B. taught him to write because its style and its narrative development are characterized by a self-reflexiveness that is absent in Buddy's early work.

In 1957, Buddy publishes "Zooey." Not a short story but a long "prose home movie," it details how Franny overcame her religious crisis with the help of her brother Zooey and some posthumous advice from Seymour. When this story comes out, Buddy is a "writer-in-residence" at a girls' junior college in upper New York State and lives alone in a small, unwinterized, unelectrified house without a telephone. His only contact with people outside of his classes occurs during his weekly lectures on the literature of Zen and Mahayana Buddhism. Buddy's comments in that story indicate that he has received some negative criticism on his fiction because of its religious preoccupation. Buddy says that this gives him pause but that he will not stop writing religious fiction.

Two years after "Zooey," in 1959, Buddy writes "Seymour—An Introduction," a long, unconventional narrative in which he serves notice that he is working on a series of interrelated pieces about Seymour. The "Introduction" shows that Buddy has moved even further away from the patterns of conventional fiction than he did in "Zooey" and that his religious concerns have deepened. Moreover, he provides a running commentary on the way in which he is composing the "Introduction," and this commentary shows that he has finally begun to understand Seymour's aesthetic ideas. In his self-reflexive comments, Buddy also reveals that he is still teaching at the same college in upper New York State and that he is still living the life of a recluse. He also mentions that his reclusiveness has led some literary gossip mongers to circulate the bogus information that he spends six months of the year in a Buddhist monastery and the other six in a mental institution. Although he still lectures on Zen and Mayhana Buddhism once a week, Buddy insists that he is not a Zen Buddhist or even a Zen adept but that his religious outlook has been shaped by the Old and New Testaments, classical Taoism, and Vedanta Hinduism. And then he uses Vedanta terms to label himself a "Karma Yogin, with perhaps a little Jnana Yoga thrown in to spice up the pot." This means that he is a person who worships God through his work, his writing, and also, to a lesser degree, through religious study. These comments indicate that by 1959, Buddy has come to accept Seymour's notion of the intimate relationship between art and religion.

In 1965, six years after he published "Seymour—An Introduction," Buddy is still teaching at the same small college in upper New York State and he is still writing about Seymour's life and death. While he is at work on a long story about the party in 1926, at which he and Seymour met the man who hired them for the radio show "It's a Wise Child," Buddy receives a package that contains an enormous letter by Seymour, written in 1924, when Seymour and Buddy were at summer camp. Buddy has never seen this letter before and is so amazed by its content that he decides to scrap the story that he was working on, to make "an exact copy" of the letter, and to publish it instead. And this letter, entitled "Hapworth 16, 1924," is an even more unconventional piece of fiction than the "Introduction" and "Zooey," both in its form and in its religious content. The letter apparently settles the last questions that Buddy still had about Seymour's aesthetic and religious ideas, for it is the last installment of the Glass series and the last time that Buddy Glass has been heard from.

NOTES

[1] For biographical information on Salinger, see John Skow, "Sonny: An Introduction," *Time*, 15 Sep 1961, pp. 84-90; reprinted in Anatole Grunwald, ed. *Salinger: A Critical and Personal Portrait* (New York: Harper, 1962), pp. 3-18; and the first two chapters in James Bryan, "Salinger and His Short Fiction," Unpubl. Diss. Univ. of Virginia, 1968, pp. 1-75.

[2] See *Raise High the Roof Beam, Carpenters and Seymour—An Introduction* (New York: Bantam, 1965), pp. 111-113, 176.

[3] For further information on the lives of the Glass family, see Chapter 9, "Seymour—A Chronology."

[4] In 1939, Salinger himself took a short story writing course at Columbia University. His instructor was Whit Burnett, the editor of *Story* magazine. See J. D. Salinger, "A Salute to Whit Burnett, 1899-1972," in Whit and Hallie Burnett, *Fiction Writer's Handbook* (New York: Harper, 1975), pp. 187-188.

CHAPTER 2

"A Perfect Day for Bananafish"

When J. D. Salinger published "A Perfect Day for Banana-fish" (1948), he apparently had not yet formulated his plan of a narrative series to be told by Buddy Glass. After all, he has Seymour kill himself at the end of the story, and this suggests that he had no further plans for him. Also, when Seymour next appears in "Raise High the Roof Beam, Carpenters" (1955), his character is noticeably different from that in "Bananafish." In "Seymour—An Introduction" (1959), Salinger makes Buddy Glass explain these differences by confessing that he, Buddy, wrote "Bananafish" and that he has been told by his siblings that "the 'Seymour' in the story and the Seymour in Real Life" are two different people. In fact, Buddy admits that "the young man, the 'Seymour,' who did the walking and talking in that early story, not to mention the shooting, was not Seymour at all but, oddly, someone with a striking resemblance to—alley oop, I'm afraid—myself" ("Introduction," p. 113).[1] When Salinger makes Buddy take the responsibility for the differences in the characterization of Seymour in "Bananafish" and in the later stories, he suggests that we ought to treat "Bananafish" as a story told by an unreliable narrator, as a story revealing Buddy's reaction to Seymour's suicide. But before we can interpret "Bananafish" in the light of the other Glass stories, we need first of all to determine what its text means by itself.[2]

* * *

Although "A Perfect Day for Bananafish" is a conventional short story, its form nevertheless has a number of unusual traits. One of them is that the protagonist, Seymour Glass, does not appear in the first and longest part of the story which consists of a phone conversation between Seymour's wife Muriel and her mother. This phone conversation concerns Seymour and thus provides us with an indirect characterization. Another unusual aspect of the story is its ending. Seymour's suicide comes as a surprise, and this makes us re-read the story in search for clues that might explain why Seymour kills himself.

At the first reading, the long phone conversation between Muriel and her mother develops a very negative picture of Seymour. Muriel's mother describes him as a mentally disturbed and potentially dangerous person. She begins the conversation by telling her daughter that she is "worried to death" about her, and she asks her three times: "Are you all right, Muriel?" She is very concerned when she finds out that Seymour did all of the driving from New York to Florida, and she asks: "Did he try any of that funny business with the trees?" We understand her concern when we learn that Seymour recently wrecked his in-laws' car, apparently by driving it into a tree. Why Muriel's mother is so concerned about Muriel's safety becomes even more clear when she reports that Muriel's father discussed Seymour's behavior with the family psychiatrist, Dr. Sivetski:

> "He told him *every*thing. At least, he said he did—you know your father. The trees. That business with the window. Those horrible things he said to Granny about her plans for passing away. What he did with all those lovely pictures from Bermuda—*every*thing."
> "Well?" said the girl.
> "Well. In the first place, he said it was a perfect *crime* the Army released him from the hospital—my word of honor. He very *definitely* told your father there's a chance—a very *great* chance, he said—that Seymour may com*plete*ly lose control of himself. My word of honor" ("Bananafish," p. 6).

Near the end of the phone conversation, Muriel's mother therefore asks: "Does he behave himself on the beach?" To this Muriel replies: "Mother . . . you talk about him as though he were a raving maniac—." And this is precisely the impression of Seymour's character that we are left with at the end of the first scene.

When the second scene shows us Seymour on a deserted part of the beach in the company of the four-year-old Sybil Carpenter, we are therefore afraid he may harm the little girl. However, we soon find that Seymour is not the dangerous psychotic that Muriel's mother has made him out to be. Instead he appears to be a sensitive man who has an unusual ability to communicate with children on their own level. This becomes apparent in the following conversation. Sybil asks Seymour:

> "Did you read 'Little Black Sambo'?" . . .
> "It's very funny you ask me that," he said. "It so happens I just finished reading it last night." He reached down and took back Sybil's hand. "What did you think of it?" he asked her.
> "Did the tigers run all around that tree?"
> "I thought they'd never stop. I never saw so many tigers."
> "There were only six," Sybil said.
> "*Only* six!" said the young man. "Do you call that *only*?"
> "Do you like wax?" Sybil asked.
> "Do I like what?" asked the young man.
> "Wax."
> "Very much. Don't you?"
> Sybil nodded. "Do you like olives?" she asked.
> "Olives—yes. Olives and wax. I never go anyplace without 'em" ("Bananafish," pp. 14-15).

Even when Sybil complains that Seymour should not have let another little girl sit on the piano bench with him, he handles her very well. He says: " '. . . you know how those things happen, Sybil. I was sitting there, playing. And you were nowhere in sight. And Sharon Lipschutz came over and sat down next to me. I couldn't push her off, could I?' 'Yes.' 'Oh, no. No. I couldn't do that,' said the young man. 'I'll tell you what I did do, though.' 'What?' 'I pretended she was you'." By the end of this section of the story, we are convinced that whatever Seymour's psychological problem is, it can't be very serious.

Hence we are surprised when Seymour behaves very oddly in the next scene. He says to a woman on the hotel elevator: "I see you're looking at my feet." And when the woman protests that she is only looking at the floor, he gets very upset: " 'If you want to look at my feet, say so,' said the young man, 'but don't be a God-damned sneak about it'." And after the woman gets out, Seymour says to the girl operating the car: "I have two normal feet and I can't see the slightest God-damned reason why anybody should stare at them. . . ." At the first reading, it is hard to understand why Seymour should be so upset. But then, Muriel's mother did mention that he spent some time in the psychiatric ward of an Army hospital.

Even if we take into account that all is not well with Seymour, we are utterly confounded by the last scene. A first reading of the story simply does not reveal anything so seriously wrong in Seymour's life or personality that it would explain why he takes a pistol from his suitcase, sits down on the unoccupied twin bed, looks at the sleeping Muriel, "aimed the pistol, and fired a bullet through his right temple." In order to understand Seymour's motivation, we must therefore consider the story from the beginning.

When we re-read the story in our search for clues that would explain why Seymour kills himself, we will find that the first part of the story, the phone conversation between Muriel and her mother, not only provides a characterization of Seymour but also of Muriel. And when we examine this characterization, we will discover a serious conflict between Muriel's and Seymour's personalities and values. This conflict is revealed when Muriel tells her mother that Seymour calls her "Miss Spiritual Tramp of 1948." What he means by this becomes clear when we analyze Muriel's values.

From the first paragraph of the story on it is apparent that Muriel's values are superficial and material ones. Muriel is very much concerned with her own and other people's appearances. As the narrative begins, we see Muriel in her hotel room waiting for her mother's phone call and doing a number of things that all have to do with her appearance:

> She washed her comb and brush. She took the spot out of the skirt of her beige suit. She moved the button on her Sak's blouse. She tweezed out two freshly surfaced hairs in her mole. When the operator finally rang her room, she was sitting on the window seat and had almost finished putting lacquer on the nails of her left hand ("Bananafish," p. 3).

But Muriel is not only concerned with what she herself looks like, she also judges others entirely by their appearance. She says about a psychiatrist's wife that she "was horrible" because she wore an "awful dinner dress" that did not compliment her figure because she was "all hips." And about some other guests at the hotel she says: "You should see what sits next to us in the dining room. At the next table. They look as if they drove down in a truck." Her lack of interest in anything that is not material or physical is perhaps best illustrated by her reading habits. Instead of reading poetry, as Seymour would like her to, she reads "an article in a women's pocket-size magazine, called 'Sex is Fun—or Hell'."

Seymour's values are not as well illustrated as Muriel's, but it is clear that they are intellectual and spiritual ones. This is suggested by his comment that Muriel is a "Spiritual Tramp" and by his interest in music and poetry. His interest in music becomes apparent when Muriel tells her mother that while everyone else was playing bingo, Seymour was playing the piano in the Ocean Room: "He's played the piano both nights we've been here." His interest in poetry is revealed when we learn that he had sent Muriel a book of German poems which he said were *"written by the only great poet of the century."* He liked these poems so much that he told Muriel she should get a translation or learn the language. And even while talking with the four-year-old Sybil Carpenter, Seymour cannot help quoting poetry. When Sybil mentions Sharon Lipschutz, Seymour quotes the third line from T. S. Eliot's *The Waste Land:* "How that name comes up. Mixing memory and desire."

Seymour's allusion to *The Waste Land* suggests that Muriel is not the only person whose lack of spiritual values troubles him. It seems that he sees the entire civilization as a spiritual wasteland, and his interaction with Sybil Carpenter shows that he does not even see any hope in children.

Sybil Carpenter is by no means the charming innocent child she may appear to be at a first glance. She is, in fact, a miniature Muriel. When we first see her, she is described as a small adult, for she is "wearing a canary-yellow bathing suit, one piece of which she would not actually be needing for another nine or ten years." Moreover, her mother feeds her the olives from her martinis and calls her "pussy," an endearment suggesting mature sexuality. In addition, Sybil has

two character traits that predict that she is not going to turn
into a very spiritual adult: She is cruel and she is possessive.
Seymour reveals her cruelty when he rebukes her for poking a
little dog with a balloon stick. He says that he likes Sharon
Lipschutz because "she never does anything mean to little
dogs in the lobby of the hotel."   And Sybil's possessiveness
comes out when she tells Seymour he should not let Sharon
Lipschutz sit on the piano bench with him: "Next time, push
her off."

   Sybil Carpenter not only makes Seymour think of *The
Waste Land* but she also inspires him to invent the bananafish
story, a parable which explains why he kills himself. Seymour
tells Sybil: "This is a *perfect* day for bananafish."   But Sybil
says that she doesn't see any, and Seymour explains:

> "That's understandable. Their habits are *very* peculiar. . . . They
> lead a very tragic life, . . . they swim into a hole where there's
> a lot of bananas. They're very ordinary fish when they swim
> *in*. But once they get in, they behave like pigs. Why, I've known
> some bananafish to swim into a banana hole and eat as many
> as seventy-eight bananas. . . . Naturally, after that they're so
> fat they can't get out of the hole again. Can't fit through the
> door" ("Bananafish," pp. 15-16).

And when Sybil asks what happens to the bananafish after they
eat so many bananas that they can't get out of the banana hole,
Seymour says: "Well, I hate to tell you, Sybil. They die."
"Why?" ". . . Well, they get banana fever. It's a terrible disease."

   In order to understand what this parable reveals about
Seymour's reasons for killing himself, we must first determine
who the bananafish are. Since both the bananafish and Seymour
die a self-inflicted death, we might jump to the conclusion that
Seymour must be the bananafish. But this does not make much
sense in view of the reason why the bananafish die. They die
because they eat too many bananas, because they are so greedy.
And there is no evidence in the story that Seymour is greedy.
In fact, his values are not material but spiritual ones. And the
gold color and phallic shape of bananas clearly suggest that
they represent physical, material values. Moreover, both in

the title of the short story and in the parable itself, the banana-fish appear in the plural, not in the singular. If the story were entitled "A Perfect Day for *A* Bananafish," then it would be quite clear that this bananafish must be Seymour. The plural, however, suggests that we are supposed to look for more than one bananafish in the story.

Since the bananafish are greedy for material things, it seems to me that they represent people like Muriel and Sybil Carpenter. The banana hole they swim into is the world of physical, material values, and the bananas are what people like Muriel and Sybil are greedy for. The color yellow represents sex. The banana fever is the effect of materialism on their spirit, and the death they die is a spiritual death.

Seymour's allusion to *The Waste Land* and his bananafish parable are indications of his despair about the lack of spiritual values among the people around him. He has been experiencing this despair for some time, as is evident from his earlier suicide attempt with his in-laws' car. Also, at the beginning of the scene with Sybil Carpenter, he makes a comment that suggests that he is again entertaining thoughts of suicide. When Sybil asks him if he is going in the water, Seymour answers: "I am seriously considering it. I'm giving it plenty of thought, Sybil, you'll be glad to know." And after he has talked to Sybil, Seymour gives it even more thought. He realizes that there is no hope for a spiritual regeneration of the wasteland, since even children like Sybil are already greedy bananafish. He therefore decides to kill himself.

When Seymour no longer sees any reason to live, his behavior toward Sybil suddenly changes. He abruptly cuts short their playing in the water: "We're going in now. You had enough?" Sybil says "No!" but Seymour responds with "Sorry," and pushes the float toward the shore. After Sybil has run back to the hotel, Seymour "put on his robe, closed the lapels tight, and jammed his towel into his pocket." The way he closes himself off in his robe and jams the towel in the pocket reveals his agitation and his feeling of antagonism toward the world around him. These feelings are even more apparent when he lashes out at the woman on the elevator who stares at his feet. She is described as "a woman with zinc-salve on her nose," and Seymour probably sees her as another appearance-conscious person, another bananafish. His hostility toward her suggests that it is people like she and Muriel who are responsible for his despair.

The final scene shows that it is indeed Muriel and what she stands for that drives Seymour to kill himself. For when he enters his hotel room, Seymour is met by the smell of "new calfskin luggage and nail lacquer remover," the smell of Muriel's banana fever. And before he kills himself, he looks twice at the sleeping Muriel. As he goes to get his pistol out of his suitcase, "he glanced at the girl lying asleep on one of the twin beds," and then once more "he looked at the girl," just before he "aimed the pistol, and fired a bullet through his right temple." The fact that he chooses to kill himself in his hotel room while looking at Muriel suggests not only that he holds her responsible for his death but also that he wants his death to have a profound effect on her. His comment that she is a "Spiritual Tramp" is an indication that he hopes to shock her into changing her values.

But no matter what effect Seymour intends his death to have on Muriel, his major concern is probably to escape from the world of the bananafish who consider him a misfit because he prefers playing the piano to playing bingo and because he prefers reading German poetry to reading magazine articles about sex. The day of Seymour's death is "a perfect day for a bananafish" because the bananafish can now continue to gorge themselves with bananas without Seymour pointing out to them that "they behave like pigs."

This reading of the story as a self-contained account shows that its meaning arises out of the conflict between the material values of people like Muriel and the spiritual values of Seymour. The resolution of this conflict, Seymour's suicide, suggests a very pessimistic message. The story implies that a person who can see more than others, who can see beyond appearances, will be so frustrated and alienated if he tries to live by his spiritual values that he might as well kill himself.

* * *

When we examine "A Perfect Day for Bananafish" in terms of what it reveals about Buddy's understanding of Seymour then we will find that when he wrote the story in 1948, he tried to blame Seymour's suicide on Muriel and other materialistic people like her. By explaining Seymour's death in this way, he tries to downplay his brother's psychological and spiritual problems. But Buddy not only tries to shift the blame by making Muriel and her mother appear so unsympathetic that we feel sorry for Seymour, he also falsifies Seymour's character. He admits to this falsification when he tells us in "Seymour—An Introduction" that his siblings have told him that the Seymour in "Bananafish" bears a striking resemblance to Buddy himself. In order to understand Buddy's reasons for misrepresenting his brother's character, we need to compare the characterization of Seymour in "Bananafish" and in later stories and we also need to determine which parts of the story can be considered incontrovertible "facts" within the framework of the Glass series (that is, which parts are corroborated by information from other Glass stories,) and which parts Buddy must have invented in order to develop his explanation of Seymour's suicide.

The major difference between the Seymour in "Bananafish" and the Seymour in the other stories is that the later Seymour is a much kinder person and has a much more charitable attitude toward unspiritual people. This makes Seymour quite different from Buddy. In the "Introduction," for example, Buddy reports that when Seymour told his siblings to take their galoshes off when entering the apartment, they knew he meant that "the floor would get tracked up if they didn't and that their mother, Bessie, would have to get the mop out" unnecessarily. But when Buddy told them to take off their rubbers, they knew he meant "that people who didn't take them off were slobs" ("Introduction," pp. 166-167). Seymour and Buddy differ even more in their attitudes toward people who do not share their spiritual values. As Seymour writes in his diary a few days before his wedding, Buddy would despise Muriel for her superficial marriage motives while Seymour finds these motives "humansize and beautiful." In fact, Seymour says that he "loves" and "needs" Muriel's "simplicity" and her "undiscriminating heart," the very qualities that Buddy despises in her ("Carpenters," pp. 66-67, 72-73). Buddy demonstrates his contempt for Muriel and her concern with her appearance in "Zooey" when he tells of his trip to Florida to bring home Seymour's body. He says he was met at the airport by "the Bereaved Widow . . . all in Bergdorf Goodman black" ("Zooey," p. 62). It is therefore hard to believe that Seymour should have called Muriel a "Spiritual Tramp," that he should have told Sybil Carpenter that Muriel is probably at the hairdresser's, "Having her hair dyed mink," and that he should have called a stranger on an elevator a "God-damned sneak" for staring at his feet. These comments, as Buddy's siblings were aware, reflect not Seymour's typical attitudes but Buddy's. They show that in writing the story, Buddy was less concerned with explaining why Seymour might have committed suicide but why he, Buddy, would have killed himself if he had been married to someone as superficial and materialistic as Muriel.

Moreover, the "facts" about Seymour that Buddy downplays and the incidents that he invents suggest that he is trying to hide what was wrong with Seymour. The facts about Seymour that Buddy downplays are that Seymour had just been released from a psychiatric ward of an Army hospital where he had received treatment for three years after the end of the war and that he had tried to kill himself before. These facts, which are corroborated in other Glass stories, indicate that a major reason for Seymour's suicide was his emotional instability.[3] But the most negative piece of information in "Bananafish" concerns not Seymour's psychological but his spiritual deterioration. It is the fact that he decided to shoot himself in his hotel room while sitting on a bed near the sleeping Muriel. This is a decision which seems to have been prompted by pure malice. It shows that Seymour was no paragon of spirituality when he died, and this is something Buddy cannot face.

To cover up Seymour's spiritual deterioration, Buddy invents incidents which make it seem as though Seymour was driven into suicide by the lack of spirituality in Muriel and others like her. He invents the phone conversation between Muriel and her mother and presents the two women as crass materialists who are only concerned with appearances. Similarly he invents Seymour's conversation with Sybil Carpenter to show that this four-year-old is already on her way to becoming as self-centered and materialistic as Muriel. And above all,

Buddy invents the bananafish story to drive home the point that most of the people in Seymour's life are motivated only by their desire for sex and money. He thus wants to make the point that a person with Seymour's values would prefer a physical death to the spiritual death of the bananafish. But this interpretation of Seymour's suicide, so the later Glass stories show, is clearly wrong. It reveals that in 1948, Buddy was still unable to acknowledge the negative aspects of Seymour's personality, that he worshipped his older brother and tried to continue thinking of him as a saint, despite his suicide.

The form of "A Perfect Day for Bananafish" also reveals that Buddy has not yet understood Seymour. When Buddy was getting serious about becoming a professional writer in 1940, he took a writing course from a professor B. He showed Seymour the stories he was then writing, and Seymour advised him not to be content with what Professor B. called a "rattling good story," that is, a story constructed according to the conventional standards of conciseness of style and compactness of structure. Instead, Seymour told Buddy: "ask yourself . . . what piece of writing in all the world Buddy Glass would most want to read if he had his heart's choice. The next step is terrible, but so simple. . . . You just sit down shamelessly and write the thing yourself. . . . Oh dare to do it, Buddy! Trust your heart. You're a deserving craftsman. It would never betray you" ("Introduction," p. 161). But Buddy clearly did not follow this advice eight years later when he wrote "Bananafish," for "Bananafish" is a "rattling good story" in the manner of the stories of such masters as Hemingway and Fitzgerald. In fact, the story illustrates Hemingway's "iceberg principle" according to which seven-eights of the story are underwater for every part that shows: Since the story is told from a totally objective point of view, it forces the reader to draw his own conclusions about what is going on in the minds of the characters. Also, in writing "Bananafish," Buddy is still addressing a general audience, for the form of the story seems to be dictated by what Buddy thinks the audience would most want to read and not what he himself would most want to read if he had his heart's choice.

Thus, at the same time Buddy writes "A Perfect Day for Bananafish," he has not yet understood the meaning of Seymour's life and death, nor has he understood Seymour's aesthetic ideas. Also, "Bananafish" is not a typical Buddy Glass story because Buddy does not yet dare to speak to us in his own characteristic garrulous-humorous voice, nor does he dare to let himself be carried to new insights by writing from his heart. And the reason why Buddy does not yet dare to follow Seymour's advice is that he has not yet forgiven him for his suicide.

NOTES

[1] The quotations in this chapter come from Bantam paperback editions of *Nine Stories* (New York, 1964); *Franny and Zooey* (New York, 1964), *Raise High the Roof Beam, Carpenters and Seymour—An Introduction* (New York, 1965).

[2] To my mind, the best interpretations of "Bananafish" are those of Ihab Hassan in *Radical Innocence* (Princeton: Princeton University Press, 1961), pp. 267-268; James E. Bryan, "Salinger's Seymour's Suicide," *College English*, 24 (1962), 226-229; and Charles Genthe, "Six, Sex, Sick: Seymour, Some Comments," *Twentieth Century Literature*, 10 (1965), 170-171.

Other noteworthy interpretations of the story are: William Wiegand, "J. D. Salinger: Seventy-Eight Bananas," *Chicago Review*, 11 (1958), 3-19; Samuel Bellman, "New Light on Seymour's Suicide: Salinger's *Hapworth 16, 1924*," *Studies in Short Fiction*, 3 (1970), 348-351; Gordon Slethaugh, "Seymour: A Clarification," *Renascence*, 23 (1971), 115-128; Frank Metcalf, "The Suicide of Salinger's Seymour Glass," *Studies in Short Fiction*, 9 (1972), 243-246; and Gary Lane, "Seymour's Suicide Again: A New Reading of J. D. Salinger's 'A Perfect Day for Bananafish'," *Studies in Short Fiction*, 10 (1973), 27-33.

[3] For a detailed account of Seymour's life, see Chapter 9: Seymour—A Chronology.

CHAPTER 3

"Franny"

"Franny" was published in January of 1955, nine months before "Raise High the Roof Beam, Carpenters." But it was probably written several years earlier, at a time when the plan of the Glass series had not yet taken shape, for it does not mention Seymour, nor does it mention that Franny's last name is Glass. Also, the story contains two pieces of information that are later contradicted in the story "Zooey" (1957). Franny tells Lane Coutell that she is taking a "Religion Survey" course and that she got the book, *The Way of a Pilgrim*, out of her college library after her instructor mentioned it to her. But in "Zooey" we learn that Franny had received religious training in Seymour's "home seminars" for many years. It is therefore highly unlikely that she would take an introductory religion course in college. And indeed, in "Zooey" she refers to the course not as a survey but as a "Religion seminar." Moreover, Zooey tells his mother that Franny did not get *The Way of a Pilgrim* and its sequel *The Pilgrim Continued His Way* from her college library but from Seymour's room, "where they've been sitting on Seymour's desk for as long as I can remember" ("Zooey," p. 101).[1] And finally, though "Franny" was published in January of 1955, its sequel, "Zooey," gives November of 1955 as the time of the story's action. These discrepancies suggest that Salinger had not yet decided to make Franny a member of the Glass family when he wrote the story.

It is my guess that Franny was written between "De Daumier-Smith's Blue Period" (1952) and "Teddy" (1953). "De Daumier-Smith" is the first Salinger story that deals with a religious theme, but like "Franny," it develops this theme in terms of Christian ideas and mentions Eastern religions only in passing. From "Teddy" on, however, Eastern philosophy forms the foundation of Salinger's fiction. Thus "Carpenters," published the same year as "Franny," makes no reference to Christian ideas but uses Taoist and Hindu concepts to develop its meaning.

The form of "Franny" also marks it as a transitional story. For one thing, it is more than twice as long as "A Perfect Day for "Bananafish," and its structure, while still quite conventional, is not as compact, nor is its language as crisp and concise. "Franny" thus foreshadows the loose style and rambling development of the later Glass stories. But above all, the story's narrative perspective is no longer the objective one of "Bananafish;" instead it is that of a subjective, omniscient narrator who quite clearly takes sides in the conflict between the two major characters. But before I deal with what "Franny" reveals when it is seen as a reflection of Buddy's development as a writer and of his struggle to understand Seymour, I will present a close reading of the story as a self-contained account.[2]

* * *

"Franny" is a textbook example of a well written short story. Structurally, it follows the traditional short story pattern. Its typography establishes five sections: an exposition, a three-part complication, and a brief resolution. These five parts function exactly as textbooks tell us they should function in a typical short story. The content does not present anything unusual, either. The plot consists largely of a conversation between Franny and her boyfriend, Lane Coutell. Their conversation illustrates their lack of true communication and reveals not only an external conflict between the spiritual values of Franny and the material values of Lane but also an internal conflict that Franny experiences. This inner conflict is Franny's struggle to transcend her ego. In the course of the conversation, Franny is sickened by both Lane's and her own self-centeredness. Her frustration about her inability to cope with this problem eventually leads to her physical collapse, and this collapse marks the climax of the story. The resolution shows how Franny plans to cope with her problem in the future.

The exposition initiates the story's external and internal conflicts by showing that there is something wrong in Franny's relationship with Lane. When we first meet Lane Coutell, he is re-reading Franny's last letter while waiting for her in a train station. This letter shows that Franny resents Lane's habit of analyzing everything she says and does. Franny writes: "Let's just try to have a marvellous time this weekend. I mean not try to analyze everything to death for once, if possible, especially me. I love you." After she expresses her irritation with Lane, the "I-love-you" sounds somewhat forced. And indeed, when Franny later talks about this letter to Lane, she admits: "I had to strain to write it." But Franny feels guilty about her negative feelings toward Lane, and for this reason she gives his arm "a special little pressure of simulated affection" and tells him "I've *missed* you." But then we read: "The words were no sooner out than she realized that she didn't mean them at all. Again with guilt, she took Lane's hand and tightly, warmly laced fingers with him." Franny seems to be forcing herself to like Lane, and this makes us wonder how long she is going to be able to suppress her negative feelings toward him. Thus the exposition foreshadows the open conflict that develops in the complication of the story.

The conversation that forms the bulk of the story takes place at Sickler's Restaurant. As the conversation begins, Lane talks endlessly about a Flaubert paper for which he has received an A. His bragging illustrates the kind of self-centeredness that Franny detests in people. After listening to Lane patiently for a while, Franny finally tries to change the subject by commenting on how she likes her martini and by asking Lane if she can have his martini olive. When Lane fails to see that Franny isn't really interested in his paper, Franny interrupts him again and says that he is "talking like a section man." A section man is a graduate assistant who sometimes takes over a professor's class and tries to impress the undergraduates by disparaging the work of great authors and by "ruining things for people." Franny says about section men: "I'm just so sick of pedants and conceited little tearer-downers I could scream." And then she explains that it isn't just Lane who makes her sick but everybody at college: "It's just that if I'd had any guts at all, I wouldn't have gone back to college at all this year. I don't know. I mean it's all the most incredible farce." What disturbs her most is that "everything everybody does is so—I don't know—not *wrong*, or even mean, or even stupid necessarily. But just so tiny and meaningless and—sad-making." The reason why she feels that way is that everybody "wants to *get* somewhere, do something distinguished, and all, be somebody interesting. It's disgusting—it is, it *is*. I don't care what anybody says." Lane can't understand why this bothers Franny. [All he cares about is "the possibility that this bug Franny had might bitch up the whole weekend."]

While Franny is trying to explain why she is so disgusted by everybody, she also becomes nauseated by her own attitude. When she compares Lane to one of the conceited section men, she feels "equal parts of malice and self-disapproval" and admits that she has "felt so *destructive* all week." She tries to collect herself by concentrating for a moment on a small blotch of sunshine on the tablecoth. She tunes out Lane and stares at it "with a special intensity, as if she were considering lying down in it." But this attempt to attain detachment fails, and she continues her attacks on people's self-centeredness. As she gets more upset with herself, she begins to lose color in her face and to perspire profusely. Finally she leaves the table, goes to the ladies' room, locks herself into a stall, and cries "for fully five minutes. She cried without trying to suppress any of the noisier manifestations of grief and confusion, with all the convulsive throat sounds that a hysterical child makes. . . ." Franny's grief is about the "sad-making" selfishness in others and in herself.

After her return from the ladies' room, Franny nevertheless continues attacking all the college types who "look like everybody else, and talk and dress like everybody else" and who do little else than brag and try to impress others. She would like to stop her harangue but she is unable to, despite the fact that "it sounded to her cavilling and bitchy, and she felt a wave of self-hatred that, quite literally, made her forehead begin to perspire again, in spite of herself." Franny's self-hatred is a symptom of her inner conflict. She is aware that she is not any better than Lane or anyone else, and she is frustrated about being unable to change her outlook.

The focus of the story shifts when Franny stops her attacks on others and begins to deal with her own shortcomings. She tells Lane that she quit the Theater Department and dropped the lead role in a play because she began to feel "like such a nasty little egomaniac." She explains: "I don't know. It seemed like such poor taste, sort of, to want to act in the first place. I mean all the *ego*. And I used to hate myself so, when I was in a play, to be backstage after the play was over. All those egos running around feeling terribly charitable and *warm*. Kissing everybody and wearing their makeup all over the place, and then trying to be horribly natural and friendly when your friends came backstage to see you." And she concludes: "I'm just sick of ego, ego, ego. My own and everybody else's. . . . Just because I'm so horribly conditioned to accept everybody else's values and just because I like applause and people to rave about me, doesn't make it right. I'm ashamed of it. I'm sick of it. I'm sick of not having the courage to be an absolute nobody."

Again Franny is perspiring, and at one point she even feels her forehead to see if she has a fever. She says: "I feel so woozy and funny. I don't know what's the matter with me." This time, Franny's condition is even worse than before she went to the ladies' room, and we expect her to leave the table again to have another cry. But this time she recovers, at least for a while, when Lane shows some concern for her condition and even asks her about a book he had earlier noticed her carrying.

Lane's question "What's the book?" marks the beginning of the story's climactic section. In this part of the conversation, Franny at first seems to feel better because she gets a chance to summarize for Lane the contents of *The Way of a Pilgrim*, a book by an anonymous Russian mystic which she says a professor had recommended to her. But when she realizes that Lane does not take the book seriously and calls its ideas "mumbo jumbo," Franny's condition gets worse again.

Franny's summary of *The Way of a Pilgrim* explains how she hopes to resolve her inner conflict and transcend her ego. The core of this book is the Jesus Prayer which Franny sees as the solution to her problems. Franny says about the book: ". . . it starts out with this peasant—the pilgrim—wanting to find out what it means in the Bible when it says you should pray incessantly. You know. Without stopping. In Thessalonians or someplace." After wandering around for some time, the pilgrim finally meets "a starets—some sort of terribly advanced religious person—and the starets tells him about a book called the 'Philokalia.' Which apparently was written by a group of terribly advanced monks who sort of advocated this incredible method of praying." The text of the prayer is "Lord Jesus Christ, have mercy on me," and "the starets tells the pilgrim that if you keep saying this prayer over and over again—you only have to just do it with your *lips* at first—then eventually what happens, the prayer becomes self-active . . . and the words get synchronized with the person's heartbeats, and then you're actually praying without ceasing. Which has a really tremendous, mystical effect on your whole outlook. I mean that's the whole *point* of it, more or less. I mean you do it to purify your whole outlook and get an absolutely new conception of what everything's about." And finally, "You get to see God. Something happens in some absolutely nonphysical part of the heart— where the Hindus say that Atman resides, if you ever took any Religion—and you see God, that's all." Franny is fascinated with *The Way of a Pilgrim* because she wants to change her outlook and she hopes to be able to do that with the help of the Jesus Prayer.

As Franny summarizes *The Way of a Pilgrim*, Lane is eating his frog legs and makes occasional comments that show his disinterest. Instead of responding to Franny, he tells his frog legs to "hold still," and then he interrupts her twice more. First he says, "I hate to mention it, but I am going to reek of garlic," and then he brings up his Flaubert paper again: "I hope to God we get time over the weekend so that you can take a quick look at this goddam paper I told you about." But Franny is so excited about *The Way of a Pilgrim* and the Jesus Prayer that she is unaware of Lane's lack of interest and asks: ". . . did you ever hear anything so fascinating in your *life*, in a way?" Lane finally responds and asks Franny: "You actually believe that stuff, or what?" Franny doesn't give a direct answer but explains that it can't be a coincidence that she keeps "running into that kind of advice—I mean all those really advanced and absolutely unbogus religious persons that keep telling you if you repeat the name of God incessantly, something *happens*." But Lane's condescending reply is: "What is the result that's supposed to follow? All this synchronization business and mumbo-jumbo. You get heart trouble?"

The climax of the story occurs after it becomes clear to

Franny that Lane is indifferent to her profound interest in the Jesus Prayer. She explains to him that the result of the prayer is that "You get to see God" and she admits that she doesn't even know "who or what God is" or even "if He exists." But instead of responding to this, Lane asks: "You want some dessert, or coffee?" And then he looks at his wrist watch and says: "God. We don't have time. We're lucky if we get to the game on time." But he does remember that their conversation about *The Way of a Pilgrim* isn't quite finished and tries to conclude by saying:

> "Well, it's interesting, anyway. All that stuff . . . I don't think you leave any margin for the most elementary *psychology*. I mean I think all those religious experiences have a very obvious psychological background—you know what I mean. . . . It's interesting, though. I mean you can't deny that. . . . Anyway. Just in case I forgot to mention it. I love you. Did I get around to mentioning that?" ("Franny," p. 40).

Nauseated by Lane's obtuseness and condescension toward her, Franny gets up to go to the ladies' room once more, but on the way she has to stop and steady herself against the bar. Then she weaves, faints, and collapses.

The story does not offer an explanation of Franny's collapse, but the conversation that leads up to it suggests that it must have something to do with her sudden realization of the profound difference between her own and Lane's values. This realization probably hit her because of the striking contrast between Lane's declaration of "love" and his insensitivity to her spiritual needs. The conflict between her physical attraction to Lane and her spiritual aspirations probably has something to do with why she felt so "woozy and funny" earlier. And her sudden recognition of the crassness of Lane's character is more than she can bear. Her fainting may be due not only to emotional strain but also to her wish to escape from her relationship with Lane and from the world of the Lane Coutells in general. She has apparently recognized the unbridgeable chasm between her own outlook and that of people like Lane. For while she is an idealist who is committed to the spiritual aspects of life, Lane is a materialist who only recognizes the physical dimension and tries to explain away anything spiritual.

Because of Lane's behaviour toward her, Franny withdraws from the physical into the spiritual world. This withdrawal doesn't resolve Franny's external conflict with Lane—after all, Franny never responds to Lane's condescending comments about her beliefs—but it does resolve her internal conflict between the demands of her physical and her spiritual nature. Her conflict with Lane has helped her decide which of these demands she should give in to.

In the resolution of the story, Lane once more reveals his crass materialism and demonstrates that his interest in Franny is chiefly physical. After Franny has been carried to the restaurant manager's office and barely regained consciousness, Lane tells her that they are not going to the football game but that she is to go to her rooming house: "'Then maybe after a while, if you get any decent rest, I can get upstairs somehow. I think there is a goddam back staircase. I can find out. . . . You know how long it's been?' Lane said. 'When was that Friday night? Way the hell early last month, wasn't it?' He shook his head. 'That's no good. Too goddam long between drinks. To put it crassly'." Franny doesn't respond to this. Instead she asks for a drink of water. After Lane has gone to get her a drink, she silently says her Jesus Prayer: "Alone, Franny lay quite still, looking at the ceiling. Her lips begin to move, forming soundless words, and they continued to move." It becomes clear now that Franny has decided to withdraw from the world. As she explained earlier, the Jesus Prayer is supposed to purify her outlook and give her an absolutely new conception of what everything is about. And maybe it will even allow her "to see God."

Thus the meaning of the story lies in Franny's attempt to use the Jesus Prayer to resolve her spiritual crisis. Her crisis represents the plight of all those whose spiritual aspirations put them in conflict with people who are as crass and self-centered as Lane Coutell. And although we may not be in sympathy with the way in which Franny wants to transcend the world of the Lane Coutells, the story does make us understand why people with spiritual values may wish to escape into mysticism.

* * *

Since neither Buddy nor Seymour is mentioned in the story, "Franny" does not seem to shed any light on Buddy's struggle to understand Seymour's legacy. But if we assume that the story was written by Buddy Glass and if we compare "Franny" to the other work that Buddy produced between "A Perfect Day for Bananafish" (1948) and the next Glass story, "Raise High the Roof Beam, Carpenters" (1955), then the story reveals quite a bit about Buddy's development as a writer and about his understanding of Seymour.

In "Seymour—An Introduction" (1959), Buddy mentions that he is the author of "A Perfect Day for Bananafish" and "Raise High the Roof Beam, Carpenters." He does not mention any of the nine other stories that Salinger published between "Bananafish" and "Carpenters," but he says that "there's seldom been a time when I haven't written about [Seymour]." He also tells us that some of his readers have asked him "whether a lot of Seymour didn't go into the young leading character of the one novel I've published" ("Introduction," p. 111), and he admits that there is an evanescent quality about the eyes of the "gifted" young boy in "Teddy" that has suggested to at least two members of the Glass family that Buddy was trying "to get at" Seymour's eyes ("Introduction," p. 176). These statements show that Seymour has been constantly on Buddy's mind but that, during the seven years between "Bananafish" and "Carpenters," he has not been able to write "directly about Seymour." In fact, Buddy says that he has "written and histrionically burned at least a dozen stories or sketches about him since 1948" ("Introduction," p. 182).

Thus "Franny" can be seen as an indirect story about Seymour which shares some elements of form and theme with "Bananafish" and some with the later Glass stories. If we compare "Franny" to "Bananafish," we will find that it develops a similar conflict, ends in a similar resolution, and has a similar conventional structure. And if we compare it to the later parts of the Glass series, we will find that it is the first Glass story to develop a religious theme and that its narrative technique foreshadows the subjectivity and rambling development of the later stories.

Even a casual reader will notice striking thematic similarities between "Franny" and "A Perfect Day for Bananafish." Like the Seymour in "Bananafish," the spiritual Franny is in conflict with materialistic people. Her principal antagonist, Lane Coutell, is much like Muriel because he values appearances more than essences and considers matter rather then spirit to be the ultimate reality. Franny has a very different outlook and can't get along with people like Lane. She therefore tries to withdraw from them. But because her problems are less severe than Seymour's, her withdrawal takes a milder form. Rather than killing herself, she retreats into the Jesus Prayer.

These similarities suggest that since he wrote "Bananafish," Buddy has made very little progress in his understanding of Seymour. After all, he develops Lane Coutell as an utterly repulsive, male version of Muriel and Franny as a very attractive, female version of Seymour. Because he makes us sympathize with Franny's attempt to withdraw from the world of the Lane Coutells, it seems that Buddy still believes that a person who wants to live a spiritual life in America is bound to find himself so hopelessly estranged from other people that he will be forced either into suicide or into some other form of escape. This is a notion which Buddy eventually gives up in the later Glass stories.

While the content of "Franny" suggests that Buddy has not yet learned anything positive from Seymour's suicide, the form of the story shows that he has at least made some progress as a writer. Even though "Franny" is a conventional short story, it is in some respects quite different from "A Perfect Day for Bananafish." In "Bananafish," Buddy is a totally objective narrator who seems to follow Hemingway's iceberg theory according to which the impact of a story comes largely from what is not obvious, from what one has to deduce about the characters' thoughts and feelings by observing the way they act and speak. But in "Franny," Buddy is a subjective, omniscient narrator who tells us what is going on in the minds of both Franny and Lane Coutell. And what he tells us about their thoughts and feelings is designed to make us dislike Lane and sympathize with Franny. Thus its narrative perspective links

"Franny" to the later Glass stories which are even more subjective.

But what most clearly shows Buddy's development as a
writer is the frankly religious nature of the story. In his "auth-
or's formal introduction" to "Zooey," Buddy says that people
have already begun to shake their heads about the religious
themes in his stories and that his persistence in writing stories
of this kind can only expedite the day and hour of his professional undoing. Buddy's awareness that the general public does
not like religious fiction suggests that he did not mention the
religious nature of Seymour's problems when he wrote "A Perfect Day for Bananafish" because at that time he was still very
much concerned with reaching a large audience. But when he
wrote "Franny," he had begun to be less interested in pleasing
the general reader than in trying to understand the nature of the
problems that drove Seymour into suicide, even if he was only
able to write about them indirectly by dealing with Franny's
very similar problems. This new attitude foreshadows Buddy's
later attempts to use the process of writing about Seymour as a
way to reach an understanding of his life and death.

NOTES

[1] The quotations in this chapter come from the paperback editions of
Franny and Zooey (New York: Bantam, 1964) and *Raise High the Roof
Beam, Carpenters and Seymour—An Introduction* (New York: Bantam,
1965).

[2] "Franny" has not received much attention as an independent story.
It is usually discussed in connection with its sequel "Zooey." The only
detailed explication of the story that I know of is a psychoanalytical reading
by Daniel Seitzman, "Salinger's 'Franny': Homoerotic Imagery," *American
Imago*, 22 (1955), 57-76.

Other useful commentaries are George Panichas, "J. D. Salinger and the Russian Pilgrim," *Greek Orthodox Theological Review*, 8 (1963), 111-126; rpt. in Panichas, *The Reverent Discipline* (Knoxville: University of Tennessee Press, 1974), pp. 373-387; David Galloway, *The Absurd Hero in American Fiction* (Austin: University of Texas Press, 1966), pp. 156-159; and Warren French, *J. D. Salinger*, rev. ed. (Boston: Twayne, 1976), pp. 139-143.

CHAPTER 4

"Raise High the Roof Beam, Carpenters"

"Raise High the Roof Beam, Carpenters," published in November of 1955, is the first story which shows that Salinger has begun to think of the Glass stories as a narrative series or composite novel. "Carpenters" not only introduces all the members of the Glass family, it also introduces Buddy Glass as the narrator of the series. And although the story is ostensibly about Seymour's wedding day, its real concern turns out to be Buddy's attitude toward Seymour's choice of Muriel as a marriage partner, both at the time that the events of the story took place in 1942 and at the same time that Buddy wrote the story in 1955. The story thus shows how Buddy's understanding of Seymour has changed since he wrote "A Perfect Day for Bananafish" in 1948.[1]

"Carpenters" also shows that Buddy has made considerable progress as a prose writer. The story is more than five times as long as "Bananafish" and more than twice as long as "Franny," and even though it has clearly defined beginning, middle, and end, it is constructed in such a way that we cannot tell until the end whether the protagonist is Seymour or Buddy. Moreover, the story relies heavily on a new narrative element that is to become a hallmark of Buddy's later fiction, on quotations from religious writings, from letters, from memoirs, and from diaries. But most importantly, it is the first Glass story that uses the first person point of view and thus gives us Buddy's very subjective analysis of the events he is reporting. And he gives this analysis for the first time in his very own distinctive, involuted voice, in a style which is very different from that in "A Perfect Day for Bananafish." Also, "Carpenters" shows a significant change in the way Buddy resolves the familiar conflict between spiritual and materialistic attitudes. These changes reveal a definite growth in Buddy's understanding of Seymour's ideas.

* * *

"Carpenters" is an account of the events on Seymour's wedding day, events which bring Buddy to the realization that Seymour, despite a number of disturbing character flaws, is still spiritually farther advanced than anyone Buddy has ever known. Since the focus of the story's interest is constantly on Seymour, we assume at first that Seymour is the protagonist. But since Seymour never makes a physical appearance in the story and since he does not go through any inner change or reach any new insight, we come to realize that the protagonist must be Buddy.

To illustrate the extraordinary character of his brother, Buddy opens the story with a Taoist tale that Seymour once read to his ten-month-old sister Franny in order to make her stop crying. I will quote it in full because it is essential to an understanding of Buddy's epiphany near the end of the story:

> Duke Mu of Chin said to Po Lo: "You are now advanced in years. Is there any member of your family whom I could employ to look for horses in your stead?" Po Lo replied: "A good horse can be picked out by its general build and appearance. But the superlative horse—one that raises no dust and leaves no tracks— is something evanescent and fleeting, elusive as thin air. The talents of my sons lie on a lower plane altogether; they can tell a good horse when they see one, but they cannot tell a superlative horse. I have a friend, however, one Chiu-fang Kao, a hawker of fuel and vegetables, who in things appertaining to horses is nowise my inferior. Pray see him."

> Duke Mu did so, and subsequently dispatched him on the quest for a steed. Three months later, he returned with the news that he had found one. "It is now in Shach'iu," he said. "What kind of horse it it?" asked the Duke. "Oh, it is a dun-colored mare," was the reply. However, someone being sent to fetch it, the animal turned out to be a coal-black stallion! Much displeased, the Duke sent for Po Lo. "That friend of yours" he said, "whom I commissioned to look for a horse, has made a fine mess of it. Why, he cannot even distinguish a beast's color or sex! What on earth can he know about horses?" Po Lo heaved a sigh of satisfaction. "Has he really got as far as that?" he cried. "Ah, then he is worth ten thousand of me put together. There is no comparison between

us. What Kao keeps in view is the spiritual mechanism. In making sure of the essential, he forgets the homely details; intent on the inward qualities, he loses sight of the external. He sees what he wants to see, and not what he does not want to see. He looks at things he ought to look at, and neglects those that need not be looked at. So clever a judge of horses is Kao, that he has it in him to judge something better than horses."

When the horse arrived, it turned out indeed to be a superlative animal.[2]

To Buddy it does not make sense to read this or any other tale to a ten-month-old infant, but Seymour tells him: "They have ears. They can hear" ("Carpenters," p. 4).[3] Seymour's reply to Buddy and his choice of the Taoist tale show that, like Po Lo in the tale, he believes in the superiority of intuitive over rational understanding. But the Taoist tale not only reveals Seymour's philosophy, it also helps explain his love for his bride Muriel and his relationship with his brother Buddy. But this does not become apparent until the end of "Carpenters."

In addition to the Taoist tale, the exposition of "Carpenters" contains information about the Glass family that helps us understand the major conflicts in the story. We learn, for instance, that the seven Glass children, Seymour, Buddy, Boo Boo, Walter, Waker, Zooey and Franny are all unusually talented and intelligent and that they all were, or are, regulars on the national radio quiz show "It's a Wise Child." We also find out that Buddy is the only member of the family who is able to come to New York for Seymour's wedding, because in 1942, the Glasses are, as Buddy says, "flung all over the United States." Zooey and Franny, the youngest children, are with their parents in California; Walter is in the Army, somewhere in the Pacific; Waker is in a conscientious objectors camp; and Boo Boo is in the Navy. Thus everyone but Buddy has a good excuse for not coming to the wedding.

Buddy also tells us in the exposition that the story will be "all but exclusively concerned" with Seymour. He does not tell us, however, that Seymour is not going to make an appearance in the story. It is precisely because of Seymour's physical absence that he is ever-present in Buddy's mind, for Buddy's

inability to understand his absence creates the two inner conflicts in the story.

Initially, though, it is an external conflict that advances the
plot development, the conflict between Buddy and the Matron of
Honor who is furious because Seymour has failed to show up for
his own wedding. But the core of "Carpenters" consists of two
related inner conflicts that Buddy experiences. He cannot understand why Seymour would want to be so cruel as to stand his
bride up at the wedding ceremony, and, what is more important,
he cannot comprehend why his brother would want to marry
someone like Muriel in the first place. The vast differences between the personalities of Seymour and Muriel become clear
early in the story when we learn that Seymour is an English professor, a poet, and a student of such Eastern religions as Buddhism, Taoism, and Hinduism, while Muriel is described by Seymour's sister Boo Boo as "a Zero . . . but terrific looking." It is
only when Buddy comes to understand why Seymour loves her
that the meaning of the story is revealed.

The external conflict in the story arises because of the
attacks that the Matron of Honor makes on Seymour's character. She has never met him and bases her opinions entirely on
what she has heard form the bride's mother. She reports that
Mrs. Fedder has labelled Seymour a "latent homosexual" and a
"schizoid personality" because he has asked Muriel to postpone
the wedding until "he feels steadier." The Matron of Honor
therefore says that Seymour is "a raving maniac of some crazy
kind" and should be "stuck in some booby hatch." To support this opinion, she refers to an incident from Seymour's
childhood. She explains that the crooked smile of Charlotte
Mayhew, a well-known actress, is due to the fact that this "Seymour person apparently hit her, and she had nine stitches taken
in her face." Although Buddy becomes "vastly upset" during
the Matron of Honor's diatribes, he manages to keep quiet
for a long time. But he finally blows up when the Matron of
Honor refers to the Charlotte Mayhew incident a second time
and when she relates it to the fact the Seymour had been a child
prodigy and a regular performer on the radio quiz show "It's a
Wise Child." She says: "I mean you lead an absolutely freakish life like that when you're a kid, and so naturally you never
learn to grow up. You never learn to relate to normal people

or anything. That's exactly what Mrs. Fedder was saying. . . . Your brother's never learned to relate to anybody. All he can do, apparently, is go around giving people a bunch of stitches in their faces. He's absolutely unfit for marriage or anything half-way normal, for goodness sake. As a matter of fact, that's *exactly* what Mrs. Fedder said." To this, Buddy reacts vehemently. He reports:

> I said I didn't give a good God-damn what Mrs. Fedder had to say on the subject of Seymour. Or, for that matter, what any professional dilettante or amateur bitch had to say. I said that from the time Seymour was ten years old, every *summa-cum-laude* Thinker and intellectual men's-room attendant in the country had been having a go at him. I said it might be different if Seymour had just been some nasty little high-I.Q. showoff. I said he hadn't ever been an exhibitionist. He went down to the broadcast every Wednesday night as though he were going to his own funeral. He didn't even talk to you, for God's sake, the whole way down on the bus or subway. I said that not one God-damn person, of all the patronizing, fourth-rate critics and column writers, had ever seen him for what he really was. A poet, for God's sake. And I mean a *poet*. If he never wrote a line of poetry, he could still flash what he had at you with the back of his ear if he wanted to ("Carpenters," pp. 59-60).

The Matron of Honor probably does not understand what Buddy means when he claims that Seymour is a true poet, but she is intimidated and does not respond to his "polluted little stream of invective." Buddy thus puts his antagonist in her place and thereby resolves the exterior conflict of the story. But he does not resolve the questions that the Matron of Honor has raised about Seymour's cruelty toward his bride and about his inability to relate to "normal people."

The vehemence with which Buddy responds to the Matron of Honor is not only the result of his irritation with her and with Mrs. Fedder but also of his inner conflict, his inability to understand Seymour. After all, the Matron of Honor's indignation is justified. Buddy realizes this after she says about Seymour: "You can't just *barge* through life hurting people's feelings whenever you feel like it." Although Buddy despises Muriel and what she stands for, he cannot justify Seymour's cruel behavior toward her, and he admits that "a small wave of prejudice against the missing groom passed over me, a just perceptible little whitecap of censure for his unexplained absenteeism."

Buddy's slight irritation with Seymour's behavior turns into inner turmoil after the Matron of Honor brings up the injury that Seymour caused Charlotte Mayhew when he deliberately hit her in the face with a stone. This is an incident which has bothered Buddy all his life, as becomes apparent when Buddy feels compelled to lie about it to someone who can't even hear him. He tells the deaf-mute uncle of Muriel's father that Seymour threw that stone at Charlotte "because she looked so beautiful sitting in the middle of our driveway with Boo Boo's cat," and he claims that everybody understood that. But then he admits: "I'm a liar, of course. Charlotte never understood why Seymour threw that stone." Buddy here implies that he himself never understood Seymour's motivation, either. And this is why he gets so upset at the Matron of Honor. Buddy would like to see his older brother as a near-saint and does not want to acknowledge his negative character traits. When he is reminded of the Charlotte Mayhew incident, Buddy realizes that Seymour's failure to show up for his wedding may well be another one of his inexplicable acts of cruelty. He is therefore relieved when he learns that Seymour has "eloped" with Muriel in order to get married privately. But although this allays Buddy's uneasiness about Seymour's instability and cruelty, it does not resolve his inner conflict. Instead, it merely shifts Buddy's attention to the question of why Seymour loves someone as superficial as Muriel.

Buddy can't help feeling that the marriage of Seymour and Muriel is a ghastly mismatch. He has never met Muriel but he trusts his sister Boo Boo's judgment that Muriel is "a Zero." Reading about Muriel in Seymour's diary, Buddy finds that she is indeed as shallow as Boo Boo's comment suggests. Muriel's superficiality is well illustrated in Seymour's account of an evening they spent at the movies. They went to see *Mrs. Miniver*, a war movie with Greer Garson, and Seymour writes:

> She looked over at me when the children in the picture brought in the kitten to show to their mother. M. loved the kitten and wanted me to love it. Even in the dark, I could sense that she felt the usual estrangement from me when I don't automatically love what she

loves. Later, when we were having a drink at the station, she asked me if I didn't think that kitten was "rather nice." She doesn't use the word "cute" any more. When did I ever frighten her out of her normal vocabulary? Bore that I am, I mentioned R. H. Blyth's definition of sentimentality: that we are being sentimental when we give to a thing more tenderness than God gives to it. I said (sententiously?) that God undoubtedly loves kittens, but not, in all probability, with Technicolor bootees on their paws.[4] He leaves that creative touch to script writers. M. thought this over, seemed to agree with me, but the "knowledge" wasn't too very welcome. She sat stirring her drink and feeling unclose to me ("Carpenters," p. 67).

The passage points out the apparent incompatibility of Seymour and Muriel, and it explains why Buddy and Boo Boo have misgivings about Seymour's marriage.

But Seymour's diary not only shows that Muriel is superficial, it also shows that she is materialistic. Seymour says, for example, that when he leaves the Fedders' house after a visit, he feels as though he were carrying home with him symbols of Muriel's materialism. He writes: "Sometimes I have a peculiar feeling that both M. and her mother have stuffed my pockets with little bottles and tubes containing lipstick, rouge, hairnets, deodorants, and so on." Muriel's materialism becomes even more evident when Seymour describes her marriage motives:

Her marital goals are so absurd and touching. She wants to get a very dark sun tan and go up to the desk clerk in some very posh hotel and ask if her Husband has picked up the mail yet. She wants to shop for curtains. She wants to shop for maternity clothes. She wants to get out of her mother's house, whether she knows it or not, and despite her attachment to her. She wants children—good-looking children, with her features, not mine. I have a feeling, too, that she wants her own Christmas-tree ornaments to unbox annually, not her mother's ("Carpenters," pp. 71-72).

As we can see, Muriel's hopes and aspirations do not go beyond appearances and material things. Intellectual or spiritual values do not seem to matter in her life. We can also see that Seymour is fully aware of Muriel's materialism. But instead of finding it despicable, he finds it "absurd and touching."

Buddy, however, does not find Muriel's superficiality and materialism touching. He becomes very irritated by what he reads in the diary. And as if Seymour could foresee that Buddy would read his diary, he writes about Buddy's reaction to Muriel: "I think of him as I write about Muriel. He would despise her for her marriage motives as I've put them down here. But are they despicable? In a way, they must be, but yet they seem to me so human-size and beautiful that I can't think of them even now as I write this without feeling deeply, deeply moved." Seymour suggests that Muriel is in some ways more human and normal than he is because she does not constantly analyze her feelings and actions and instead simply follows her natural impulses. And he is attracted to her because, unlike Buddy, he is able to see her simplicity and naturalness as positive qualities which he himself lacks and needs.

Although these diary entries should reconcile Buddy to Seymour's choice of Muriel as a marriage partner, they don't. Instead, Buddy becomes very upset by what he reads. This is apparent when he suddenly slams the diary shut, flings it away "with an almost vicious wrist movement," and storms out of the room, "closing the door excessively hard." Then he goes to the kitchen and pours himself "at least four fingers of Scotch" while "giving out small, faintly audible whimpers." And because he is a non-drinker, he swigs the Scotch down like medicine, "in one deadpan toss."

Buddy's inner turmoil increases when one of Muriel's relatives looks at a picture of Charlotte Mayhew from "It's a Wise Child" and observes: "This child could *double* for Muriel at that age. But to a T." Buddy is stunned and tells us: "I could not quite take in this information whole, let alone consider its many possible ramifications." He does not say why he finds Muriel's resemblance to Charlotte so meaningful, but it probably suggests to him an explanation of Seymour's attraction to Muriel. Seymour may be drawn to Muriel, for example, by a desire to atone for the injury he caused Charlotte. Whatever the ramifications are that impinge on Buddy's mind, they make him even more uneasy about Seymour's marriage to Muriel.

In order to ease his mind, Buddy decides to read the rest of Seymour's diary. And when he does, he finds out why Seymour needs Muriel. In an entry written a day before the wedding, Seymour reports that he begged Muriel "for the last time to go off alone with me and get married. I'm too keyed up to be with people." This confirms what the Matron of Honor had heard from Mrs. Fedder. She had mentioned that Seymour told Muriel on the day before the wedding that he was "too *happy* to get married and that she'll have to *postpone* the wedding until he feels steadier." The diary explains that Seymour is so excessively happy because he feels that his marriage to Muriel will make a tremendous change in his life, that it will mark a new beginning. Seymour writes: "I feel as though I'm about to be born. Sacred, sacred day." Then he mentions that he has been "reading a miscellany of Vedanta all day" and he summarizes what Vedanta Hinduism considers to be the essential responsibilities of the married state: "Marriage partners are to serve each other. Elevate, help, teach, strengthen each other, but above all *serve*." And Seymour concludes his comments about marriage by exclaiming: "The joy of responsibility for the first time in my life!"

After reading this diary entry, Buddy experiences the epiphany that resolves his inner conflict. He reports:

> I read the entry through just once, then closed the diary and brought it back to the bedroom with me. I dropped it into Seymour's canvas bag, on the window seat. Then I fell, more or less deliberately, on the nearer of the two beds. I was asleep— or, possibly out cold—before I landed, or so it seemed ("Carpenters," p. 91).

This passage contains the climax of the story. It shows that Buddy, who had become increasingly more upset and agitated as the story progressed, is now no longer in turmoil. The tension gone, he can fall asleep. When he wakes up, he is reconciled to Seymour's choice of Muriel as a marriage partner and he even thinks of sending them a wedding present.

Buddy's inner change, his acceptance of Seymour's reasons for marrying Muriel, reveals the meaning of "Carpenters." What it is that reconciles Buddy to Seymour's choice of Muriel

will become clear if we relate Seymour's marriage motives to the
Taoist tale that Buddy quotes at the beginning of the story. The
central idea in that tale is expressed by Po Lo who had sent Chiu-
fang Kao to select a horse. Po Lo says that Kao's judgment is
much better than his own because "What Kao keeps in view is
the spiritual mechanism. In making sure of the essential, he forgets the homely details; intent on the inward qualities, he loses
sight of the external." After quoting the Taoist tale, Buddy
compares Seymour to Kao and says: "Since the bridegroom's
permanent retirement from the scene [that is, since Seymour's
death], I haven't been able to think of anybody I'd care to send
out to look for horses in his stead." Buddy thus admits that his
older brother can indeed see more than anyone else he knows.

This raises the question of what the essential inward qualities of Muriel's are that Buddy cannot see. The diary shows that,
to Seymour, her superficiality and materialism, which Buddy
finds so objectionable, are merely external details. Her essential
qualitites, in Seymour's view, are her "simplicity," and her "undiscriminating heart," that is, her uncomplicated approach to
life and her willingness to trust her natural impulses. These are
the aspects of Muriel's personality that Seymour loves, worships, and needs because his sophistication and erudition have
estranged him from normal people. But Buddy has been unwilling to admit that. He accepts it only after he reads the last
diary entry in which Seymour points out that he needs to be
elevated, helped, taught, and strengthened by Muriel just as
much as she by him. Buddy now realizes that Seymour does
indeed need Muriel's simplicity and undiscriminating heart just
as Muriel needs his intellectual and spiritual values.

Thus, on its most basic level of meaning, "Raise High the
Roof Beam, Carpenters" makes a statement about the relationship between intellectuals like the Glasses and normal people
like the Fedders. This statement concerns two related problems,
the alienation of the intellectuals and the anti-intellectualism of
the average middle-class Americans. Unlike other works in American literature that deal with this theme, "Carpenters" blames
the intellectuals and not the middle-class Americans for these
problems. Buddy Glass represents the traditional elitist attitude
of the American intellectuals, their unwillingness to have anything to do with those whose values they consider less sophis-

ticated and less spiritual than their own. Seymour, on the other hand, represents the attitude that the story wants the intellectuals to adopt. Seymour has come to realize that his preoccupation with intellectual and spiritual matters has estranged him from average humanity, and he has decided to marry Muriel Fedder because he knows that he needs to be strengthened by her just as much as she needs to be elevated by him. The marriage of Seymour and Muriel therefore points out the vital service that the intellectuals and the normal people can render one another. For their mutual benefit, they should become partners and, in Seymour's words, elevate, help, teach, strengthen, but above all, *serve* each other.

* * *

When we read "Raise High the Roof Beam, Carpenters" as a self-contained account, we can't tell whether Buddy reaches his understanding of Seymour's motives for marrying Muriel on the day of the wedding in 1942 or on the day that he writes the story in 1955. And for a basic understanding of the story, it does not matter. But when we read "Carpenters" as a part of the Glass series, and particularly as a stage in Buddy's struggle to come to terms with Seymour's legacy, then we will find that while he accepts Seymour's decision to marry Muriel in 1942, he does not understand it until 1955, when he writes about it.

Buddy's account of the events on Seymour's wedding day shows that in 1942 he was "vastly upset" not only about the Matron of Honor's attacks on Seymour but even more about Seymour's choice of a marriage partner. A non-drinker, Buddy has to anesthesize himself with a large dose of Scotch to be able to bear the thought that in marrying Muriel Seymour is going to give up his spiritual values and even have himself "slightly overhauled" by a psychiatrist. Buddy is only reconciled to Seymour's decision when he reads the last entries in Seymour's diary and learns that Seymour is not going to give up his spiritual quest after all but will simply pursue it in a different way. But Buddy still can't appreciate Muriel's simplicity and her undiscriminating heart. After all, six years after the wedding day, when he writes "A Perfect Day for Bananafish," Buddy blames Seymour's death on Muriel's superficiality and materialism, and three years after that, in a letter to Zooey, he still feels very hostile toward Muriel and suggests that after Seymour's death she was less concerned with her loss of her husband than with looking her fashionable best as "the Bereaved Widow . . . all in Bergdorf Goodman black" ("Zooey," p. 64). Thus it is not until Buddy writes "Carpenters," eight years after Seymour's suicide and thirteen years after his wedding, that Buddy has come to accept that Seymour did indeed need to marry Muriel because he had become too estranged from normal people for his own spiritual good.

Although Buddy has come to see why Seymour needed Muriel, he still cannot understand Seymour's cruelty in deliberately hurting Charlotte Mayhew. But at least he is no longer as troubled by it as he was in 1942, when he felt compelled to lie about the incident to Muriel's deaf-mute great-uncle. Buddy is now able to admit that Seymour was no saint, for he does not attempt to explain away the Charlotte Mayhew incident or Seymour's cruelty toward Muriel and her family on the day of the wedding, and he even chooses to reprint a passage from Seymour's diary which shows that even before he met Muriel Seymour tried to commit suicide by slashing his wrists. The content of the story thus reveals that Buddy has developed a much more balanced view of Seymour's character than he had when he wrote "A Perfect Day for Bananafish."

The form of "Carpenters" shows that Buddy has also achieved a much better understanding of Seymour's aesthetic ideas. Even though the story still has a conventional beginning, middle, and end and seems to be addressed to a general reader, it is evident that in writing it, Buddy is coming close to writing the kind of story that Seymour wanted him to write. For one thing, Buddy plays with conventional story structure by constructing the plot in such a way that it isn't clear whether Seymour or he, Buddy himself, is the protagonist. This gives the story a double focus which is a typical element of all of the later Glass stories. For another thing, "Carpenters" is much more loose in its narrative development than previous stories. Instead of staying on the beaten path of the plot, Buddy again and again veers off to explain, ruminate, and quote apparently irrelevant stories, letters, memos, and diary entries. While these apparent digressions make "Carpenters" a longer piece than any previous Glass story, they are vital narrative elements that allow Buddy to give us insights about Seymour that he could not develop as well with more conventional means.

But above all, "Carpenters" is the first story in which Buddy Glass speaks to us in his own, unmistakable voice. In "Franny," Buddy had already gone beyond the crisp, concise style and objective point of view of "Bananafish." But even though he wrote "Franny" from the point of view of a subjective, omniscient narrator, he developed the plot largely in terms of Franny's dialogue with Lane, and in the few passages of narrative summary and authorial comment he still used relatively simple sentence patterns. In "Carpenters," however, Buddy not only speaks in the first person but also comments on the process of composition as he tells his story. This self-reflexiveness, together with a whimsically complex prose style is characteristic of all the later Glass stories.

The most typical trait of Buddy's prose style is that the flow of his sentences is constantly interrupted by modifying words, phrases, or clauses. The following is a typical example:

> Once the bridal car was at least physically removed from the scene, the tension on the sidewalk—especially around the mouth of the canvas canopy, where I, for one, was loitering—deteriorated into what, had the building been a church, and had it been a Sunday, might have been taken for a fairly normal congregation—dispersing confusion ("Carpenters," pp. 13-14).

By constructing many of his sentences in this way, Buddy gives his prose the unhurried quality of amused detachment. But the many modifiers not only slow down the pace for the reader, they also make him consider objects, people, situations, and ideals from more than one angle. It is almost as though, through this particular stylistic device, Buddy is urging the reader not to take anything at face value but to look beyond the appearances of all things. Buddy's style can thus be said to reflect his and Seymour's vision of life.

Although the narrative technique and style of "Raise High the Roof Beam, Carpenters" show that Buddy's storytelling has changed significantly since he wrote "A Perfect Day for Bananafish," the story also shows that Buddy still does not quite dare to follow Seymour's advice to follow his heart and write spontaneously. This is apparent in the exposition when Buddy implies that he reproduced the Taoist tale because it holds the key to the meaning of his story. It is therefore clear from the beginning that Buddy knows what the point of the story is going to be, that he has come to his insight concerning Seymour's wisdom in marrying Muriel before he began to write the story and not in the process of writing it. This also explains the conventional structure of "Carpenters." Buddy obviously plotted it out in advance rather than letting it take its own shape. "Carpenters" therefore does not yet illustrate Seymour's belief that writing becomes a process of discovery if the writer only dares to write without aiming to express a preconceived idea.

NOTES

[1] Most interpretations do not pay sufficient attention to the structure of the story and talk about Seymour as the protagonist. See for example William Wiegand, "Seventy-Eight Bananas," *Chicago Review*, 11 (1958), 3-19; Ihab Hassan, *Radical Innocence* (Princeton: Princeton University Press, 1961), pp. 279-281; and Arthur Schwartz, "For Seymour—With Love and Judgment," *Contemporary Literature*, 4 (1963), 91.

Zen Buddhist interpretations which disregard the form of the story altogether are those of Frederick Gwynn and Joseph Blotner, *The Fiction of J. D. Salinger* (Pittsburgh: University of Pittsburgh Press, 1958), pp. 45-46; Sam Baskett, "The Splendid/Squalid World of J. D. Salinger," *Contemporary Literature*, 4 (1963), 48-61; and Bernice and Sanford Goldstein, "Some Zen References in Salinger," *Literature East and West*, 15 (1971), 83-87.

[2] See Lionel Giles, trans. *Taoist Teachings: Translated from the Book of Lieh-Tzu* (London: Murray, 1947), pp. 105-107.

[3] The quotations from the Glass stories in this chapter come from the Bantam paperback editions of *Raise High the Roof Beam, Carpenters and Seymour—An Introduction* (New York, 1965) and *Franny and Zooey* (New York, 1964).

[4] Seymour (or Salinger) slips up here, since *Mrs. Miniver* is not in "Technicolor." It is in black and white.

CHAPTER 5

"Zooey"

"Zooey" (1957) is a sequel to "Franny." It is the story of Zooey's efforts to help Franny overcome her religious crisis. But the form of "Zooey" is quite different from that of "Franny." More than three times as long, more rambling in its development, and more irregular in its structure, "Zooey" is a further step in Buddy's development away from conventional short fiction. Moreover, it is addressed to a more restricted audience than previous Glass stories, and this shows that Buddy is now beginning to follow Seymour's advice to write the kind of story that he himself would most want to read. "Zooey" also reveals that Buddy has made further progress in his understanding of the meaning of Seymour's life and death, for it is the first story that contains explicit criticism of Seymour. In fact, the story makes the point that Seymour, despite his best intentions, had a very negative influence on his siblings. By examining the nature of this influence, Buddy comes to a partial understanding of what went wrong with Seymour's quest for God.[1]

* * *

The most unusual thing about the form of "Zooey" is its unconventional structure. In an "author's formal introduction," Buddy Glass explains that what he is about to offer "isn't really a short story at all but a sort of prose home movie," and he hints at the nature of its structure when he says that it is "a compound, or multiple, love story, pure and complicated" ("Zooey," pp. 47-49).[2] It is a home movie because it takes place entirely at the home of the Glasses and because it deals with a family problem, the nervous breakdown of Franny Glass. It is a compound or multiple story because it has two protagonists who both come to a realization involving their love for God. Because of this structural peculiarity, it seems at first as though the story contains much material that is irrelevant. It therefore takes us a while until we realize where the story's plot is going.

The plot develops two parallel concerns, Zooey's attempts to help Franny overcome her religious crisis and his recognition that he has a similar problem. In four long conversations—two with his mother and two with Franny—Zooey analyzes in great detail what his and Franny's problems are and how they ought to deal with them. As he leads Franny to the realization that helps her overcome her crisis, Zooey himself experiences a moment of insight, and the two strands of the plot converge in Franny's and Zooey's simultaneous epiphanies.

In the first scene, Zooey sits in the bathtub and re-reads a four-year-old letter from Buddy. This scene presents much background information, but it does not yet introduce either of the story's two main concerns. Instead, it introduces us to all the members of the Glass family; it explains that the seven Glass children were all child prodigies and appeared on the national radio quiz show "It's a Wise Child"; and it reveals that Franny and Zooey began to receive religious instruction from their older brothers Seymour and Buddy at a very young age. Most of this information is contained in Buddy's long letter. But the major concern of this letter is Zooey's unwillingness to continue his academic career beyond his M. A. degree. Buddy supports Zooey's plan to become an actor rather than a Ph.D., and he tells him: "*Act*, Zachary Martin Glass, when and where you want to, since you feel you must, but do it *with all your might*." Buddy's letter doesn't seem to have anything to do with the story until we realize that Zooey is re-reading it because he is looking for advice that might help him deal with Franny's crisis.

The second scene also contains much material whose relevance isn't immediately apparent, but it does finally introduce the story's major topic, Franny's nervous collapse. In this scene, Zooey is studying a TV script which reveals the lack of imagination of the people Zooey is working with. Then Bessie Glass comes into the bathroom and begins her first conversation with Zooey. The subject is Franny's condition. Mrs. Glass mentions that ever since Franny showed up at the apartment on Saturday night, she has been "laying there by the hour crying her eyes out if you say boo to her, and mumbling heaven knows *what* to herself." Bessie is worried about Franny because, as she tells Zooey, she hasn't been able to find out "when that child intends to go back to college and finish her *year*." Also, Franny has eaten practically nothing since she arrived on Saturday night. She is so overwrought, Bessie believes, because she has "been reading too many religious books." Bessie has been trying to get hold of Buddy for advice because he is "the one person that's supposed to *know* about all this funny business," but she has been unsuccessful. Therefore she asks Zooey to talk to Franny. Zooey tells her that he did talk to Franny "for two solid hours last night" and that he doesn't believe that "she frankly wants to talk to any goddam one of us today."

During the second conversation between Zooey and his mother, Zooey gives a detailed analysis of the causes of Franny's religious crisis. This occurs after Bessie tells him that she knows what brought on Franny's crisis. She says: "I happen to know that that little book she carried all around the whole house with her yesterday is at the whole *root* of this whole business." Franny's boyfriend, Lane Coutell, told Bessie that Franny got this book from her college library and that is is "a terribly religious little book—fanatical and all like that. . . ." But Zooey informs his mother: "That little book is called 'The Pilgrim Continues His Way,' and it's a sequel to another little book called 'The Way of a Pilgrim,' which she's also dragging around with her, and she got *both* books out of Seymour and Buddy's old room, where they've been sitting on Seymour's desk for as long as I can remember." And Zooey explains that "the aim of *both* little books . . . is supposedly to wake everybody up to the need and *bene*fits of saying the Jesus Prayer incessantly." The text of this prayer is "Lord Jesus Christ have mercy on me" and its purpose is to generate God-consciousness or enlightenment, because if one prays "long enough and regularly enough and *lit*erally from the heart, sooner or later you'll get an answer. Not exactly an *an*swer. A *response*." And this is, so we now understand, what Franny has been doing all weekend; for according to Bessie, she has "been *mum*bling to herself for forty-eight hours." And while Franny's quest for God-consciousness is certainly an honorable one, Zooey suspects that her quitting college, giving up her acting career, and retreating into the Jesus Prayer is not an act of strength, or renunciation, but an act of weakness, an escape motivated by Franny's inability to get along with normal, unspiritual people. He condemns such an escape, but he also sympathizes with it, for he shares Franny's problem. His own conflicts with others have not driven him into a nervous breakdown but they have given him an ulcer.

Zooey blames his and Franny's problems on the religious education they received from their older brothers, Seymour and Buddy. As he tells Bessie: "We're *freaks*, the two of us, Franny and I. . . . I'm a twenty-five-year-old freak and she's a twenty-year-old freak, and both those bastards are responsible. . . . I swear to you, I could murder them both without even batting an eyelash. The great teachers. The great emancipators. My God. I can't even sit down to lunch with a man any more and hold up my end of a decent conversation. I either get so bored or so goddam preachy that if the son of a bitch had any sense, he'd break his chair over my head."

Buddy's letter shows how Seymour and Buddy turned their younger siblings into freaks. Buddy explains that when they took over Zooey's and Franny's education as early as they did, they decided that it should not begin with a quest for knowledge but with a quest for no-knowledge, for pure conciousness, for the "state of being where the mind knows the source of all light." And to make them understand that, Seymour and Buddy taught them everything they knew "about the men—the saints, the arhats, the bodhisattvas, the jivanmuktas—who know something or everything about this state of being." Thus it was figures such as "Jesus and Gautama and Lao-tse and Shankaracharya and Hui-neng and Ramakrishna" who became Zooey's and Franny's heroes. As a result of this kind of education, both Franny and Zooey developed very high intellectual and spiritual standards, but they also came to despise everyone who had different values. Mrs. Glass sums up their situation when she says: "I don't know what good it is to know so much and be smart as whips and all if it doesn't make you happy." Zooey's ulcer and Franny's nervous collapse are signs that their spiritual training indeed hasn't made them happy.

Concerned about Franny's breakdown, Mrs. Glass wonders if Franny shouldn't see a psychiatrist, but Zooey rejects this idea. He explains that Franny's problem is primarily a spiritual and not a psychological one. Therefore, the only psychiatrist that could possibly help Franny would have to be "a pretty peculiar type. . . . He'd have to believe that it was through the grace of God that he's been inspired to study psychoanalysis in the first place. He'd have to believe that it was through the grace of God that he wasn't run over by a goddam truck before he ever got his license to practice. He'd have to believe that it's through the grace of God that he has the native intelligence to help his goddam patients at *all*. I don't know any *good* analysts who think along those lines. But that's the only kind of psychoanalyst who might be able to do Franny any good at all." With psychoanalysts out of the question and Buddy holed up where he can't be reached, Zooey therefore decides to talk to Franny once more to see if he can help her.

In the story's longest scene, Franny and Zooey compare notes on their inability to get along with people. Zooey tells Franny that he has an ulcer because the people at the television studio make him so mad. He is thinking of running away from this problem by going to France and making a movie there: "I'm tired as hell of getting up furious in the morning and going to bed furious at night . . . because I sit in judgment on every poor ulcerous bastard I know. . . . there's something I do to people's morale downtown that I can't stand to watch much longer. I can tell you ex*act*ly what I do. I make everybody feel that he doesn't really want to do any good work but that he just wants to get work done that will be thought good by everybody he knows—the critics, the sponsors, the public, even his children's school teacher." After hearing about Zooey's conflicts with others, Franny realizes that their problems are very similar. She says: "I mean we're not bothered by ·exactly the same things, but by the same kind of things, I think, and for the same reasons. . . . You talk of undermining people's morale! I absolutely *ruined* Lane's whole day. I not only passed *out* on him every hour on the hour but here I'd gone all the way up there for a nice, friendly, *normal*, cocktaily, supposedly *happy* football game, and absolutely everything he said I either jumped on or contradicted or—I don't know—just spoiled." And it's not just her boyfriend Lane, it's also her professors and classmates whom

Franny cannot stop picking at. As she explains: "I actually reached a point where I said to myself, right out loud, like a lunatic, 'If I hear just one more picky, *cav*illing, unconstructive word out of you, Franny Glass, you and I are finished—but *fin*ished'." But this did not work, and Franny soon started criticizing people again: "And the worst part was, I *knew* what a bore I was being. I *knew* how I was depressing people, or even hurting their *feel*ings—but I just couldn't stop! I just *could not stop* picking."

Zooey now tells Franny what he had earlier explained to Bessie, namely that the reason why they are so critical of everybody is that Seymour and Buddy "funnel-fed" them with religious philosophy practically from infancy: "We're freaks, that's all. Those two bastards got us nice and early and made us into freaks with freakish standards, that's all. . . . On top of everything else . . . we've got 'Wise Child' complexes. We've never really got off the goddam air. Not one of us. We don't talk, we hold forth. We don't converse, we expound." And what is worse, so Zooey says, they both should know better. But still they both rail "at *things* and people" rather than at themselves.

As long as Zooey talks bout his own inability to get along with people, Franny responds well. But as soon as he begins to zero in on her, she becomes upset again and begins to mumble the Jesus Prayer. Zooey tells her: "There's something about the way you're going at this prayer that gives me the *willies*, if you want to know the truth. You think I'm out to stop you from saying it. I don't know whether I am or not—that's a goddam debatable point—but I *would* like you to clear up for me just what the hell your motives are for saying it." But rather than giving her a chance to respond, Zooey tells Franny that she is saying the prayer for the wrong reasons. He suspects that she is saying it to escape from people she despises, that she is "greedy for spiritual treasure," and that she is using the prayer "as a substitute for doing whatever the hell [her] duty is in life, or just [her] daily duty."

But Zooey's most important objection to Franny's saying the Jesus Prayer is that she does not understand Jesus. He tells her: "When you don't see Jesus for exactly what he was, you miss the whole point of the Jesus Prayer. If you don't understand Jesus, you can't understand his prayer—you don't get the prayer at all, you just get some kind of organized cant." And he explains to Franny that the supreme message of Jesus is "that we're carrying the Kingdom of Heaven around with us, *inside*, where we're all too goddam stupid and sentimental and unimaginative to look." Therefore, "The Jesus Prayer has one aim, and one aim *only*. To endow the person who says it with Christ-Consciousness. *Not* to set up some little cozy, holier-than-thou trysting place with some sticky, adorable divine *person*age who'll take you in his arms and relieve you of all your duties and make all your nasty *Weltschmerzen* and Professor Tuppers go away and never come back." And it is because of her mistaken view of Christ that Franny has "a tenth-rate nervous breakdown" at her parents' apartment. As Zooey says, ". . . that's one of the reasons why you're having this little nervous breakdown. And *espec*ially the reason why you're having it at home. This place is made to order for you. The service is good, and there's plenty of hot and cold running ghosts. What could be more convenient? You can say your prayer here and roll Jesus and St. Francis and Seymour and Heidi's grandfather all in one."

And when Zooey gets even more abusive, Franny breaks down in tears. This happens after Zooey tells her: ". . . you listen to the conversation of a bunch of nitwit college students, and you decide that everything's ego, ego, ego, and the only intelligent thing for a girl to do is to lie around and shave her head and say the Jesus Prayer and beg God for a little mystical experience that'll make her nice and happy." At this point, Franny shrieks, "*Will you shut up please?*" But despite Franny's tears and sobs, Zooey continues for a while because he has become involved in his argument that Christ-Consciousness can only be achieved when one accepts that the world is not "full of dolls and saints and no Professor Tuppers." But then he suddenly realizes that he is making Franny feel worse and not better. Therefore he apologizes and gives up his second attempt to help her.

Zooey makes a third attempt when he calls Franny on the telephone and impersonates Buddy. At first he is able to convince Franny that she is indeed talking to Buddy, and Franny promptly complains about how destructive Zooey has been in his two talks with her. Although Franny is doing most of the talking, she suddenly realizes that she is not speaking to Buddy but to Zooey. She tells Zooey that she has seen through his charade but she is sufficiently impressed by his persistence not to hang up on him.

In the telephone conversation, Zooey repeats the same ideas that Franny would not accept earlier, when they were talking face to face. But this time she accepts them because Zooey is less condescending and less critical. He says: "I suppose I more or less called to tell you to go on with your Jesus Prayer if you want to. I mean that's your business. That's your business. It's a goddam nice prayer, and don't let anybody tell you anything different. . . . I have no goddam authority to be speaking up like a *seer* the way I have been." But then he tells her: ". . . if it's the religious life you want, you ought to know right now that you're missing out on every single goddam religious action that's going on around this house. You don't even have sense enough to *drink* when somebody brings you a cup of conse-crated chicken soup—which is the only kind of chicken soup Bessie ever brings to anybody around this madhouse." In other words, the Kingdom of Heaven is not some remote place but it is inside us and others. Therefore Zooey tells Franny not to with-draw from people: ". . . the only religious thing you can do, is *act*. Act for God, if you want to—be *God's* actress, if you want to." This is what Zooey sees as Franny's duty in life and her daily duty. For the most religious thing one can do, according to Zooey, is to do one's duty with detachment, without concern for any rewards. This is why he tells Franny to continue her acting career and not to worry whether or not she receives applause: "An artist's only concern is to shoot for some kind of perfection, and *on his own terms*, not anyone else's." Thus Zooey's advice to Franny is similar to the advice Buddy gave him in his letter when he told Zooey to "Act. . . . but do it *with all your might*."

In the climactic section of the story, Zooey suddenly recalls that Seymour once told him something similar, but that he did not understand what Seymour meant. And it is by interpreting Seymour's advice and passing it along to Franny, that Zooey is able to make her give up the Jesus Prayer and pull out of her crisis. He tells her:

> "I remember about the fifth time I ever went on 'Wise Child.' I
> subbed for Walt a few times when he was in a cast—remember

when he was in that cast? Anyway, I started bitching one night before the broadcast. Seymour told me to shine my shoes just as I
was going out the door with Waker. I was furious. The studio audience were all morons, the announcer was a moron, the sponsors
were morons, and I just damn well wasn't going to shine my shoes
for them, I told Seymour. I said they couldn't see them *any*way,
where we sat. He said to shine them anyway. He said to shine
them for the Fat Lady. I didn't know what the hell he was talking about, but he had a very Seymour look on his face, and so I
did it. He never did tell me who the Fat Lady was, but I shined
my shoes for the Fat Lady every time I ever went on the air again—
all the years you and I were on the program together, if you remember. I don't think I missed more than just a couple of times.
This terribly clear, clear picture of the Fat Lady formed in my
mind. I had her sitting on this porch all day, swatting flies, with her
radio going full-blast from morning till night. I figured the heat
was terrible, and she probably had cancer, and I—don't know. Anyway, it seemed goddam clear why Seymour wanted me to shine my
shoes when I went on the air. It made *sense*" ("Zooey," pp. 200-
201).

At the other end of the line, Franny has to stand up because she
is so excited: "'He told me too,' she said into the phone. 'He
told me to be funny for the Fat Lady, once'." And Franny's
mental picture of the Fat Lady was similar to Zooey's, too: "I
didn't ever picture her on a porch, but with very—you know—
very thick legs, very veiny. I had her in an *awful* wicker chair
She had cancer,*too*, though, and she had the radio going full-
blast all day! Mine did too!" And then Zooey explains what
Seymour's advice meant: ". . . I'll tell you a terrible secret—Are
you listening to me? *There isn't anyone out there who isn't Seymour's Fat Lady.* That includes your Professor Tupper, buddy.
And all his goddam cousins by the dozens. There isn't anyone
*any*where that isn't Seymour's Fat Lady. Don't you know that?
Don't you know that goddam secret yet? And don't you know—
listen to me now—*don't you know who the Fat Lady really is?*
. . . Ah, buddy. Ah, buddy. It's Christ Himself. Christ Himself, buddy."

Franny doesn't respond, but "for joy apparently, it was all
Franny could do to hold the phone, even with both hands." Her
reaction shows that she is about to overcome her religious crisis.

After Zooey hangs up, she keeps holding the phone to her ear
and listens to the dial tone: "She appeared to find it extraordi-
narily beautiful to listen to, rather as if it were the best possible
substitute for the primordial silence itself. But she seemed to
know, too, when to stop listening to it, as if all of what little or
much wisdom there is in the world were suddenly hers." After
replacing the phone, she lies down on the bed, and instead of saying the Jesus Prayer, "she just lay quiet, smiling at the ceiling"
for several minutes, "before she fell into a deep, dreamless
sleep."

Thus Franny and Zooey reach their moments of insight
almost simultaneously, for Zooey's epiphany occurs while he is
telling Franny who Seymour's Fat Lady really is. The excited
way in which he talks suggests that he now realizes for the first
time what Seymour meant when he told him to shine his shoes
for the Fat Lady. By shining his shoes for the Fat Lady, or by
performing on the stage, or on radio, or on television, so Zooey
now understands, he is performing for Christ Himself. And now
Zooey knows where the solution to his and Franny's problem
lies. If they can remind themselves that despising people means
despising Christ and that loving people means loving Christ, then
they should be able to get along better with those whose values
are different from their own.

It becomes clear now why Buddy Glass refers to his "prose
home movie" as a "multiple love story, pure and complicated."
For the story is an account of two God-lovers coming to understand how they should deal with normal, unspiritual people. Because Seymour and Buddy had given them "a freakish education"
and equipped them with "freakish standards," Franny and Zooey
have come to despise those who are less spiritual than themselves.
But at the end of the story, both come to the realization that in
order to serve God, they must learn to serve people.

* * *

This reading of "Zooey" shows that Buddy's outlook has
changed considerably since he wrote "Franny." In "Franny,"
he presented the ideas of *The Way of a Pilgrim* as positive ones
and made us sympathize with Franny's desire to withdraw into

incessant prayer because she did not want to become as egotistical and materialistic as Lane Coutell and others like him. But in "Zooey," Buddy presents the ideas of the pilgrim books negatively and has Zooey accuse his sister of using the Jesus Prayer as a substitute for trying to get along with those whose values are different from her own. This changed attitude toward the pilgrim books reflects Buddy's new understanding of Seymour.

By illustrating Seymour's negative influence on his siblings, Buddy suggests that there was something seriously wrong with the way in which Semour pursued his quest for God. In his letter to Zooey, Buddy gives us an idea of the nature of Seymour's influence on Franny and Zooey when he mentions the "home seminars" in religion that he and Seymour used to conduct. By setting up Gautma Buddha, Hui-neng, Lao-tse, Shankaracharya, and Sri Ramakrishna as spiritual models for their siblings and by making them read their writings, Seymour suggested that the best method of spiritual development is the self-directed one of religious study and meditation. This is the path that Seymour himself followed in his quest for God.

But unlike Franny and Zooey, Buddy was aware that Seymour tried to give up his self-directed spiritual quest when he married Muriel. Franny and Zooey could not know that because they were in California with their parents when Seymour got married, and they did not see much of him after that, for Seymour was in the Army until shortly before his suicide. Even after Seymour's death, they did not find out about his change in spiritual direction because all the siblings "agreed not to say a word" to each other about Seymour's suicide ("Zooey," p. 67). And they could not have found out about Seymour's change in direction from Buddy's account of Seymour's wedding day either, because "Carpenters" was not published until Novemner of 1955, after Franny's nervous breakdown.

In his 1951 letter to Zooey, Buddy gives his younger brother the first indication that there was something wrong with Seymour's teachings. He admits now that his and Seymour's home seminars in religion did Franny and Zooey more harm than good, since he has heard a rumor that Zooey had a reputation in his college dorm "for sitting in meditation for ten hours at a time" ("Zooey," p. 67). And that makes Buddy worry. He therefore tells Zooey not to follow in Seymour's footsteps and get a Ph.D. degree but instead to go through with his plan of becoming an actor. Buddy writes: *"Act,* Zachary Martin Glass, when and where you want, but do it *with all your might."*

This advice reflects Buddy's understanding of the change in Seymour's religious outlook which went unnoticed by Franny and Zooey. Actually, Buddy knew as early as 1940 that Seymour had changed the direction of his spiritual quest and had begun to advocate the other-directed path of duty and service as a better way of making spiritual progress than the self-directed path of religious study and meditation. Seymour's change in direction became apparent when he decided to register for military service rather than spend the war years in a conscientious objectors' camp as did his brother Waker. That same year, Seymour also advocated his new outlook in a letter to Buddy in which he told him that his work as a writer is not his profession but his religion and that it is therefore Buddy's duty to give "his loot" whenever he writes, to always "write his heart out" ("Introduction," pp. 160-161). And eleven years later, in 1951, Buddy passes this advice along to Zooey when he writes to him and tells him to follow his heart, to become an actor, and to act with all his might.

Zooey follows Buddy's advice to act with all his might when he impersonates Buddy on the telephone and gives Franny the same advice that Buddy gave him. And even though Franny discovers very soon that she is not talking to Buddy but to Zooey, she is impressed by the inspired way in which Zooey now speaks to her. And so she listens when Zooey tells her not to withdraw from others because, since she is a born actress, the "only religious thing [she] can do is act." As he is telling Franny this, Zooey suddenly realizes what Seymour had meant when he once asked him to shine his shoes for the Fat Lady. Zooey comes to the insight that when Seymour told him about the Fat Lady, he had already renounced self-directed religious study and meditation in favor of service to others.

By making his story culminate in Zooey's insight, Buddy shows why Seymour had given up the kind of spiritual development that is advocated in the pilgrim books. But Buddy still can't tell us why Seymour's change in direction did not help him overcome his estrangement from others. After all, on the day of his suicide, Seymour was even more alienated than ever. And, what must even be more disturbing to Buddy, Seymour had been unable to make any further spiritual progress and had instead suffered a marked spiritual deterioration. This is suggested by the malice of his decision to shoot himself in his hotel room, right next to the sleeping Muriel.

Thus the content of "Zooey" indicates that, despite all of his insights about the change in the direction of Seymour's quest for God, Buddy still has not understood why Seymour's life ended in suicide. Similarly, the form of "Zooey" shows that Buddy still has not quite understood what Seymour meant when he told him to "follow your heart, win or lose." Nevertheless, the story reveals a new confidence in Buddy's handling of style and structure and in his attitude toward his audience.

Buddy's style is a further development of the style in "Raise High the Roof Beam, Carpenters." It is now deliberately extravagant, as for instance in his statement that his "author's formal introduction" is "comparable to a compulsory guided tour through the engine room, with myself, as guide, leading the way in an old one-piece Jantzen bathing suit." Commenting on his style, Buddy says that it is "a kind of esoteric, family language, a sort of semantic geometry in which the shortest distance between any two points is a fullish circle" ("Zooey," pp. 47, 49).

This description also fits the structure of the story. "Zooey" is almost ten times as long as "A Perfect Day for Bananafish," and its narrative development is extremely leisurely and full of repetitions. Zooey twice expresses the idea that he and Franny are "freaks," once to Bessie and once to Franny; and later on, he tells Franny twice that she should not withdraw into the Jesus Prayer but that the only religious thing she can do is to do her duty in life or just her daily duty. Also, the story contains a letter, an excerpt from a TV script, a diary entry, and quotations from a number of religious writings which slow down the narrative development but clarify the theme.

The structure of the story shows that Buddy is deliberately

going beyond the tradition of conventional short fiction. In fact, Buddy even tells us right at the beginning that the story "isn't really a short story at all but a sort of prose home movie," a kind of narrative which is not marked by "brevity of detail or compression of incident" as short stories traditionally are ("Zooey," pp. 47, 49).

Buddy's new confidence as a writer is also evident in his attitude toward his audience. In writing "Zooey," Buddy clearly followed Seymour's advice not to worry about what the critics and the public would most want to read but to write "what piece of writing in all the world Buddy Glass would most want to read if he had his heart's choice" ("Introduction," p. 161). Buddy therefore ignores Zooey's warning that his preoccupation with religious ideas can only expedite his professional undoing, and he also ignores those who are already shaking their heads over the "too vividly apparent transcendent element" in his stories.

But Buddy still wrote "Zooey" with a preconceived central idea in mind and still didn't dare to write spontaneously as Seymour had urged him to. This is apparent from the fact that he showed a rough draft to Zooey, Franny, and Bessie and asked them their opinion of it, and also from his references to the "plot line" of his "prose home movie" and to its "final, or shooting version" ("Zooey," p. 49). These references reveal that Buddy was working from a carefully thought-out plan, that he wrote from his head and not from his heart.

NOTES

[1]None of the many interpretations of the story has dealt with what it reveals about Buddy's development as a writer or his growing understanding of Seymour, but some offer keen insights into the general meaning of the story. Two essays stand out: John McIntyre, "A Preface for *Franny and Zooey*," *Critic*, 20 (1962), 25-28, and Ihab Hassan, "Almost

Voice of Silence: The Later Novelettes of J. D. Salinger," *Contemporary Literature,* 4 (1963), 5-20. Other helpful commentaries are: John Updike, "Anxious Days for the Glass Family," *New York Times Book Review,* September 17, 1961, pp. 1-52; George Panichas, "J. D. Salinger and the Russian Pilgrim," *Greek Orthodox Theological Review,* 8 (1962), 111-126, rpt. in George Panichas, *The Reverent Discipline* (Knoxville: University of Tennessee Press, 1974), pp. 372-387; Robert Detweiler, "J. D. Salinger's Quest for Sainthood," in *Four Spiritual Crises in Mid-Century American Fiction* (Gainesville: University of Florida Press, 1963), pp. 36-43; Martin Green, "Franny and Zooey," in *Re-Appraisals* (New York: Norton, 1965), pp. 197-210; and David Galloway, "The Love Ethic," in *The Absurd Hero in American Fiction* (Austin: University of Texas Press, 1966), pp. 150-169.

[2]The quotations in this chapter come from the Bantam paperback editions of *Franny and Zooey* (New York, 1964) and *Raise High the Roof Beam, Carpenters* and *Seymour—An Introduction* (New York, 1965).

CHAPTER 6

"Seymour—An Introduction"

"Seymour—An Introduction" (1959) confirms that the Glass stories form a narrative series. It clarifies the major thematic concerns of that series and it provides background information about its main character. Again, as in "Raise High the Roof Beam, Carpenters" and "Zooey," the personality of the narrator Buddy Glass is just as important to our understanding of the story as is that of Seymour, for the "Introduction" tells the story of how Buddy discovers his purpose as a writer and the form that his work should take. But the "Introduction" is even more idiosyncratic in its style and more irregular in its structure than "Zooey," and this strange shape, so Buddy explains, is due to the fact that he is finally following Seymour's advice to write spontaneously, without any pre-established plan.

Moreover, the "Introduction" is addressed to an even more limited audience than "Zooey." Buddy claims to be writing for the "general reader," but it turns out that his "very own general reader" is a very special person, a person who, like Buddy himself, is extremely interested in things spiritual and literary. The average reader would be deterred by the complexity of the story's development and the esoteric nature of its ideas.

Nevertheless, the "Introduction" can—like the earlier Glass stories—be read as a self-contained account, even if it takes considerable effort to unravel its significance. The following is a close reading of the story which pays special attention to what its peculiar structure reveals about its meaning.[1]

The most striking thing about the "Introduction" is its apparent formlessness and lack of direction. However, a close examination of the story's structure shows that it is far less rambling than it seems, since the "Introduction" is not only a description of Seymour Glass but also the story of Buddy Glass coming to "a sudden realization" concerning his motivation for writing this description. Thus the "Introduction" combines the expositore structure of a character sketch with the chronological one of a short story.

Buddy Glass himself explains what accounts for the apparent lack of direction in the "Introduction." He says that he is a narrator "with extremely pressing personal needs" and that he can't overcome his "perpetual lust to share top billing" with his brother Seymour ("Introduction," pp. 107, 212).[2] He is therefore unable "to look after the reader's most immediate want; namely to see the author get the hell on with his story." As a result, so Buddy warns us, his description of Seymour is going to be full of asides, digressions, and parenthetical comments. A symbolic representation of the form of the "Introduction" is the "bouquet of very early-blooming parentheses: (((()))))" that Buddy offers us at the beginning.

These comments notwithstanding, the "Introduction" has much more structure than Buddy lets on. Spacing and typography reveal a division into six major sections:

I	Buddy's credo
II	Seymour as God-lover
III	Seymour as artist-seer
IV	Seymour as entertainer
V	Seymour as Buddy's mentor
VI	Physical description of Seymour

The last of these sections is subdivided into eight parts which are typographically separated by dots:

1.	Seymour's hair jumping in the barber-shop
2.	Seymour's hair and teeth
3.	Seymour's height, smile, and ears
4.	Seymour's eyes, nose, and chin

5.   Seymour's hands, voice, and skin
6.   Seymour's clothes
7.   Seymour as athlete and gamesman
8.   Seymour as Buddy's Davega bicycle

Buddy's running commentary on his progress in writing the "Introduction" contains a number of time references which establish a second, chronological framework. He writes Sections I through IV in two sittings, apparently on a weekend. Then he gets sick and spends "nine weeks in bed with acute hepatitis." After re-reading some notes and an old memo from Seymour, Buddy resumes his work on the "Introduction" on a Thursday night and writes Section V in one sitting. Section VI, the eight-part physical description of Seymour, takes up seven consecutive nights of composition. Buddy writes one part each night and two parts on the last night and the next morning. He begins these last two parts of Section VI at ten o'clock on a Thursday night and arrives, sometime after midnight, at "a sudden realization" which starts him "sweating literally from head to foot." Buddy therefore decides to take a half-hour rest and stretches out on the floor. When he wakes up three hours later, he continues his work by describing the realization that turned him "into a dripping wreck." He finally finishes the "Introduction" at 7:30 on Friday morning, an hour and a half before he is due in Room 307 to teach his writing class.

The intertwined patterns of exposition and chronology reveal two different but related themes. One concerns the purpose of Seymour's life and the other the purpose of Buddy's writing about Seymour. Although these two themes are developed simultaneously and interdependently, their relationship can be better explained by examining them separately. Because we need to understand Seymour before we can understand the realization to which Buddy comes, I will begin with an examination of the expository part of the "Introduction."

Contrary to conventional expository practice, Buddy does not move from the least important aspects of Seymour's personality to the more important ones. Instead of going from appearance to essence, he goes from essence to appearance. Thus he begins his description of Seymour by stressing his essential extraordinariness. After revealing that Seymour committed suicide in 1948, Buddy says that while he lived he was "virtually all things to his brothers and sisters." He was "our blue striped unicorn, our double-lensed burning glass, our consultant genius, our portable conscience, our supercargo, and our one full poet and inevitably . . . our rather notorious 'mystic' and 'unbalanced type'."

Seymour's extraordinariness, as it is developed in the first sections of the "Introduction," has three major aspects: He is a "Sick Man," and "artist-seer," and a "God-lover." Moreover, since Seymour's suicide is mentioned several times, we are made aware, right from the start, of the central mystery of Seymour's character, the question why a God-lover would want to kill himself.

In the prefatory section of the "Introduction," Buddy suggests that Seymour's suicide was the result of a sickness shared by many artists. Like other artist-seers, he was an "unhealthy specimen" who experienced great pain because he was able to see more than ordinary mortals, and this pain eventually killed him. Buddy explains that as a "true artist-seer" and a "heavenly fool," Seymour was bound to be "dazzled to death by his own scruples, the blinding shapes and colors of his own sacred human conscience." This statement raises more questions than it answers, but it suggests that Seymour's motivation in everything he did was religious. Buddy confirms this later when he calls Seymour a "God-lover."

In the second section of the "Introduction," Buddy describes Seymour as an "advanced religious nonsectarian" who was on a life-long quest for God. References to such concepts as *karma* and reincarnation suggest that Seymour's religious philosophy consisted largely of Eastern ideas. But Seymour searched for God not only in religious philosophy but "in the queerest imaginable places—e.g. in radio announcers, in newspapers, in taxicabs with crooked meters, literally everywhere." And Buddy says that Seymour had "enormous success" in his search and became the closest thing to a "ringding enlightened man, a God-knower" that Buddy had ever encountered. Afraid that he may have overstated his point, Buddy checks himself and asks: *"Had* Seymour no grievous faults, no vices, no meannesses, that can be listed, at least in a hurry? What was he, anyway? A *saint*?" Buddy does not answer this question, but he implies that Seymour did indeed have some character defects. Because Buddy remains "graphically panegyric" throughout his description of Seymour, we tend to forget that there is something unhealthy and unsaintlike in his character.

The third section of the character sketch deals with Seymour as an artist-seer. It contains a long disquisition on the nature of Seymour's poetry which the general reader will find less interesting than some stray comments which reveal what Buddy meant earlier when he called Seymour the "consultant genius" of the family. We learn, for instance, that Seymour began to write poems when he was only six years old. At the age of eleven, he became interested in oriental poetry and began to model his own poems after those of Chinese and Japanese poets. Buddy explains that Seymour "read Chinese and Japanese poetry as it was written" and that his last poem, which he composed on the afternoon of his suicide, was written in Japanese. Seymour was attracted to oriental poetry, so Buddy explains, because much of it is created spontaneously by seers who perceive God in the simplest facts of everyday life and who translate their vision into "intelligible utterances that please or enlighten or enlarge the invited eavesdropper to within an inch of his life." Like much oriental poetry, Seymour's own poems do not refer to anything he experienced in his life, at least, so Buddy says, "not in this incarnation." And Seymour's brother Waker is sure his poems draw on experiences in previous incarnations in such places as "exurban Benares" and "feudal Japan." Thus it seems that Buddy calls Seymour an artist-seer not only because Seymour's poems reflect his ability to see God in simple, everyday objects and incidents, but also because of his ability to see into previous incarnations.

In the brief fourth section of the "Introduction," Buddy discusses Seymour's background as an entertainer. The elder Glasses, Les and Bessie, were vaudevillians who taught all their children to "sing, dance, . . . and tell Funny Jokes." And although Seymour never published any of his poems, Buddy calls them "highly literate vaudeville" since they do not "spill a single autobiographical bean." Like good vaudeville acts, Seymour's poems are performances that are intended to please the audience and not to show off the personality of the performer. That Seymour did indeed regard himself as a kind of vaude-villian comes out in his statement that throughout his life "he wasn't sure he had ever got off Joe Jackson's beautiful bicycle." He is here referring to a nickleplated trick bicycle that Joe Jackson gave him a ride on when he was five, and he suggests that ever since that time, vaudeville has been a part of his unusual character.

The fifth section describes Seymour as Buddy's teacher. We learn that at the age of twenty-three, Seymour "had just begun his fifth year of teaching English at a university in New York." This means that he must have received his Ph.D. degree at the age of eighteen, more evidence to show what an extraordinary mind he had. The core of this section, though, consists of a string of notes and a long memo from Seymour to Buddy, all of them concerning Buddy's writing. Seymour tells Buddy that writing is not merely his profession: "It's never been anything but your religion." Therefore what Buddy's readers are likely to ask when they read his stories is whether or not he really put all of his abilities into them: *"Were most of your stars out? Were you busy writing your heart out?"* Consequently, Buddy must ignore the advice of others and write what and how he feels compelled to write. "Follow your heart," Seymour tells him, "win or lose." Seymour here advocates spontaneous and intuitive composition, and, as we shall see later, Buddy follows his advice in writing the "Introduction." The memo also confirms a notion implied in the section on Seymour's poetry, namely that writing becomes a religious act if one does it when one's stars are out, that is, when one is inspired and when one follows one's heart.

The sixth section of the "Introduction" presents a physical description of Seymour. It is the longest section and consists of eight parts. Buddy remembers Seymour fondly as an "Attractively Ugly Man," and the picture that his description creates is that of a funny-looking, clownish person. In fact, Seymour's features were almost grotesque. He had hardly any chin at all; his nose was "a great, fleshy, drooping, trompe-like affair" with an "extra lopsidedness at the bridge"; his ears had "extremely long, fleshy lobes"; his hair was black and "almost kinky"; and by the age of twenty-eight, he was "getting very bald." The way he dressed emphasized the grotesqueness of his appearance. He never bought clothes that fitted him properly: "His jackets all hiked either up or down on him. His sleeves usually either extended to the middle joints of his thumbs or stopped at the wrist-bones. The seats of his trousers were always close to the worst. They were sometimes rather awe-inspiring, as if a 36-regular behind had been dropped like a pea in a basket into a 42-long pair of trousers."

In the seventh part of the last section, Buddy describes Seymour as an "athlete and gamesman." He explains that "Seymour loved sports and games, indoors and outdoors, and was himself usually spectacularly good or spectacularly bad at them, seldom anything in between." He was spectacularly bad at card games, tennis, ping-pong, soccer, and football because he was not interested in winning. But he was spectacularly good at stoopball, curb marbles, and pocket pool. In these games Seymour was unbeatable, and Buddy explains why when he re-counts some advice Seymour gave him. Once, when Buddy was playing curb marbles, Seymour told him: "Could you try not aiming so much? . . . If you hit him when you aim, it'll be just luck. . . . You'll be *glad* if you hit his marble—Ira's marble—won't you? Won't you be *glad*? And if you're *glad* when you hit somebody's marble then you sort of secretly didn't expect much to do it. So there'd have to be some luck in it, there'd have to be slightly quite a lot of accident in it." This advice is similar to the advice Seymour gave Buddy concerning his writing. He tells Buddy to shoot marbles spontaneously and instinctively without thinking of winning or losing. Buddy is to concentrate on the act itself, not on the results. This brings us back from Seymour's physical characteristics to his ideas, from his appearance to his essence.

It is while remembering Seymour's marble-shooting ad-vice that Buddy comes to his "sudden realization" about Sey-mour's influence on his life. He realizes that he feels compelled to write about Seymour because he believes that despite his suicide, Seymour was "never wrong" in spiritual matters. Buddy therefore not only follows Seymour's teaching in his own life but also wants to pass them along to others by writing story after story about Seymour.

Despite his references to Seymour as a "Sick Man" and

an "unbalanced type," the dominant impression that Buddy creates in his character sketch is that of a seer, a man of great wisdom. Grotesque in his appearance and odd in his behavior, Seymour comes across not only as a poet and genius with uncanny mental powers but also as a God-seeker whose major purpose in life was spiritual advancement. This positive picture of Seymour is reinforced by the thematic pattern that emerges when we examine the story's chronological structure.

When Buddy comes to the "sudden realization" which starts him "literally sweating from head to foot," it becomes clear that his comments about composing the "Introduction" are not mere digressions. They form a pattern which leads to an epiphany. It is at this point that we realize that the "Introduction" is just as much about Buddy as about Seymour. Buddy's movement toward his realization underscores the ideas developed in the character sketch. It clarifies the nature of Seymour's teachings and it reveals their effect on Buddy's life.

During the first two sittings, Buddy writes four sections which make up approximately half of the "Introduction." He begins with a statement of what he calls his "credo." Two epigraphs clarify his attitude toward what he is writing. They are statements by Kafka and Kierkegaard concerning "modern artistic processes," concerning the artist's problem of doing justice to his material, particularly when he is writing about a person he loves. Both Kafka and Kierkegaard comment on the phenomenon that a literary character often assumes unintended characteristics because of the author's "varying ability." Paradoxically, the more a writer loves his subject, the less he is able to do justice to it. As a result of his lack of detachment, what he writes about his character often "becomes false," and the character becomes, as it were, "a slip of the pen," with a life of his own. And Buddy is constantly aware of this problem while he writes about Seymour.

Another part of the opening section concerns the kind of reader for whom Buddy is writing. He addresses himself to the "general reader," but it soon becomes clear that what he has in mind is really an "ideal reader" who appreciates great flights of imagination and spirituality, a person quite unlike "the grounded everywhere . . . who look down their thoroughly unenlightened noses at this splendid planet. . . ." This means that Buddy does not address himself to a mass audience for he knows that what he has to say will only be understood by readers with a keen interest in spiritual matters.

But the most important part of Buddy's credo concerns his method of composition. He repeats several times that he is "an ecstatically happy man" because he is writing about the subject he loves best and because he feels "seized" by this subject. And "divine or not, a seizure's a seizure." He therefore can't be "moderate or temperate or brief," and above all, he can't be "detached." In short, Buddy has accepted Seymour's advice to follow his heart, to trust his intuition while writing. He has made up his mind to avoid any conscious plan and to let the act of writing take him wherever it may.

Because he believes in spontaneous and intuitive composition, so Buddy explains, he gave up his original plan to write a series of short stories about Seymour and call the first, "'SEYMOUR ONE,' with the big 'ONE' serving as a built-in convenience to me, Buddy Glass, even more than to the reader—a helpful, flashy reminder that other stories (a Seymour Two, Three and possibly Four) would logically have to follow. Those plans no longer exist. Or, if they do—and I suspect that this is much more likely how things stand—they've gone underground, with the understanding, perhaps, that I'll rap three times when I'm ready." Buddy says that in his present state of happiness he doesn't "dare go anywhere near the short-story form." Moreover, he believes that "the true poet has no choice of his material. The material plainly chooses him, not he it." And as he explains in a later section of the "Introduction": "The terrible and undiscountable fact has just reached me, between paragraphs, that I *yearn* to talk, to be queried, to be interrogated, about this particular dead man."

Throughout the first two sittings, Buddy keeps repeating that he is "ecstatically happy" to be writing about Seymour. But then he comes down with hepatitis, spends nine weeks in bed, and on the first day that he feels well enough to write again, he is unable to go on. He reports, "I found that I had lost my wherewithal to continue to write about Seymour. He can't understand why this has happened and says: "I panicked, and I panicked for five consecutive nights thereafter." But then he overcomes this writer's block by re-reading some notes and an old memo from Seymour. This "Nineteen-Year-Old Prescription for Writers and Brothers and Hepatitis Convalescents Who Have Lost Their Way and Can't Go On" contains advice concerning the process of literary creation, and Buddy reproduces it for us in full. Seymour tells Buddy to write only when his "stars are out" and to be concerned with nothing else but with "writing [his] heart out." The memo culminates in the admonition: "Trust your heart. You're a deserving craftsman. It would never betray you."

Seymour's memo reaffirms Buddy's belief in intuitive composition. This belief needed reaffirmation because Buddy had become too concerned where his "Introduction" was going, and as a result he had been pushing himself too hard. After he recognizes this, he limits himself to shorter sittings and writes only as long as he is sure that his "stars are out." This is illustrated at the end of the first sitting after his illness. He stops writing when he finds that he is wearing his firmament of stars "down around [his] knees."

In the following seven nights, Buddy only writes brief segments of physical description, each one about a different aspect of Seymour's appearance. But during the seventh night, he circles back to Seymour's essence. As a result of following his inspiration rather than give a full answer to the reader's question "What did your brother Look Like," Buddy reaches his moment of epiphany. This "sudden realization" which reduces him to "a dripping wreck" occurs while he is describing Seymour's uncanny success in shooting marbles.

Buddy realizes that Seymour's marble shooting advice, "Could you try not aiming so much," is the same advice that Seymour gave him in the memo concerning his writing, and that this advice represents the essence of Seymour's teachings. Buddy says: "What essentially struck me, incapacitated me, I think, was the sudden realization that Seymour is my Davega bicycle. I've been waiting most of my life for even the faintest inclination, let alone the follow-through required, to give away a Davega bicycle." Then Buddy tells the story of his brother Waker giving away the brand new bicycle that his parents had bought him at Davega's Sports Store: "An unknown boy . . . had come up to Waker and asked him for his bicycle and Waker had handed it over." His father was angry and told Waker that what he should have done is merely "give the boy a nice long ride on the bicycle." Here Waker broke in, sobbing that "the boy didn't *want* a nice long ride, he wanted the *bicycle.* He'd never had one, the boy, he'd always *wanted* one." Waker did not use his head but followed his heart in giving away his bike. Nobody but Seymour understood that. And despite everybody's exasperation with Waker, Seymour was somehow able to restore peace in the family. Buddy doesn't describe how Seymour settled the dispute except to say that he "competently blundered his way to the heart of the matter." Buddy is convinced that Seymour's "look of well-meaning but complete inaptitude for arbitrating," his spontaneous and intuitive approach to the problem, assured his success. And while telling the marble-shooting anecdote, Buddy realizes that Seymour not only preached the rightness of spontaneously following one's heart but also practiced it in everything he did, whether it was in his marble-shooting, in his settling of family disputes, or in his writing of poetry.

Having realized that at the age of forty, he is "at long last being presented with a Davega bicycle of his own to give away," Buddy now takes care to explain what he calls the "pseudometaphysical fine point" into which his sudden realization has condensed Seymour's teachings. He compares Seymour's marble-shooting advice to the principle of Zen archery: "Aiming but no aiming." He stresses, however, that Seymour developed his marble shooting technique "by sheer intuition" and that it is related "legimately and un-Easternly to the fine art of snapping a cigarette end into a small wastebasket across the room. An art, I believe, of which most male smokers are true masters only when either they don't care a hoot whether or not the butt goes into the basket or the room has been cleared of eyewitnesses, including, quite so to speak, the cigarette snapper himself." What Buddy emphasizes here is the necessity of complete detachment of the doer from the results of his act, of his enjoyment of the act for its own sake. To illustrate this point, Buddy mentions that "after Seymour himself shot the marble, he would be all smiles when he heard a responsive click of glass striking glass, but it never appeared to be clear to him *whose* winning click it was. And it's also a fact that someone almost invariably had to pick up the marble he'd won and *hand* it to him." After thirty years it has finally clicked, Glass has struck Glass, and Buddy has realized that his purpose in writing stories about Seymour is to pass on his teachings.

He tells us one more anecdote about how Seymour once beat him in a footrace and then Buddy says: "I'm finished with this. Or, rather, it is finished with me." After it has led him to his epiphany, his material has exhausted itself. Buddy therefore simply stops writing, without worrying about whether or not his "Introduction" has "a Beginning, a Middle, and an End." He does tell us, however, that he has just enough time for a half-hour nap before meeting his nine o'clock class in Room 307. Writing about Seymour has made him aware of the importance of his own teaching, for Seymour once told him that writing "has never been anything but your religion." And the teaching of writing is part of his religion, too. This is why Buddy says: "There is no single thing I do that is more important than going into that awful Room 307. . . . There's no place I'd rather go right now than into Room 307. Seymour once said that all we do all our lives is go from one little piece of Holy Ground to the next. Is he *never* wrong?" As we can see, Seymour has shaped the purpose of Buddy's life. And Buddy, in composing the "Introduction," has come to see that this purpose is to pass on Seymour's philosophy to his students and his readers.

This analysis of the dual structure of the "Introduction" shows that the piece not only describes Seymour but also explains his posthumous influence on Buddy. The essence of the expository component of the "Introduction" is that Seymour was an artist-seer and that his purpose in life was his quest for God. And the essence of the chronological component is that Buddy's purpose in life is to write about Seymour and his aesthetic and religious ideas. The core of these ideas is illustrated in several ways: In Seymour's views on poetry; in Seymour's comments on Buddy's writing; in the way in which Seymour solved the family dispute about Waker's Davega bicycle; and most clearly, in Seymour's marble shooting advice to Buddy.

A general reader, who reads the "Introduction" as an independent story might therefore see its universal message in Seymour's advice that in everything we do, we should follow our intuition and "try not aiming so much." In that way, we might learn to do things for the sake of doing them well rather than for the sake of any tangible rewards.

* * *

The "Introduction" marks the high point of Buddy's development as a writer. As we have seen, the form of the story is a direct illustration of the ideas about writing that Seymour expressed in his 1940 letter to Buddy. It took Buddy nineteen years to understand these ideas and to translate them into his very own unique form of fiction.

The characteristic style of Buddy's fiction is either highly literate vaudeville, with Buddy balancing words, emotions, or a golden cornet on his chin, or, as likely as not, a breathtaking circus act, with Buddy diving, like his great-grandfather Zozo, from immense heights into small containers of water. This style if a further development of what we encountered for the first time in "Raise High the Roof Beam, Carpenters." But Buddy has become more whimsical in his similes, metaphors, and asides, and more extravagant in his sentence patterns, stringing together clause after parenthetical clause until we worry whether he is ever going to reach the end of his statements without falling off the page. But throughout, his sentences are a joy to read because they reveal that Buddy loves playing with language. He is clearly following his heart and writing exactly the kind of story that he himself would most want to read.

By writing in this way, Buddy creates a narrative structure that has the irregularity and wholeness of a plant or tree. That this is precisely the shape that Buddy hoped to achieve comes out in his comments that in writing the "Introduction" he doesn't "dare go anywhere near the short story form" and that he has always been unhappy with his stories when "they had what that old Chekov-baiting noise Somerset Maugham calls a Beginning, a Middle, and an End." Buddy simply stops writing when the story is finished with him, for he did not choose to write this particular story, it chose him.

What is particularly impressive about the "Introduction" is the way in which its form expresses its meaning. For one thing, its simultaneous development of an expository and a chronological pattern gives the piece a dual focus which reflects Buddy's "perpetual lust to share top billing" with Seymour, a desire that is quite legitimate since Buddy has, after Seymour's death, become his surrogate and spokesman as the Glass family's spiritual guide. More importantly, though, the rambling narrative development of the "Introduction" also illustrates the way in which Buddy reaches his understanding of Seymour's teachings. This rambling development is due to Buddy's decision not to follow his head and aim for any particular form or meaning but to follow his heart and allow his intuition to guide him. Thus the very shapelessness of the story is the objective correlative of the core of Seymour's teachings, of "Aiming but no aiming."

But while the "Introduction" shows that Buddy has now finally understood the essence of Seymour's teachings, it also suggests that he has not yet fully understood why Seymour's quest for God ended in suicide. All he says is that, like a number of other great artist-seers, his brother was "dazzled to death by his own scruples, the blinding shapes and colors of his own sacred conscience." Other hints that are more revealing are Buddy's admission that Seymour was a "Sick Man," a " 'classical' neurotic," and an "unbalanced type." But Buddy does not want to deal with the negative aspects of Seymour's character. Instead Buddy decides to be "graphically panegyric" and concentrate on Seymour's positive qualities. He explains why he is going to ignore Seymour's faults, vices, and meannesses when he says that "with or without a suicide plot in his head, he was the only person I've ever habitually consorted with, banged around with, who more frequently than not tallied with the classical conception, as I saw it of a *mukta,* a ringding enlightened man, a God-knower."

Thus the "Introduction" suggests that Buddy will have to continue writing about Seymour in order to discover why a man as enlightened as Seymour suffered such a severe spiritual deterioration that he decided to kill himself. And in writing "Hapworth 16, 1924," the last installment of the Glass series, Buddy does indeed discover why Seymour's quest for God ended in suicide.

NOTES

[1]The three analyses of the "Introduction" that I find the most enlightening are John O. Lyons, "The Romantic Style of Salinger's 'Seymour—An Introduction'," *Contemporary Literature,* 4 (1963), 62-69; Ihab Hassan, "Almost the Voice of Silence: The Later Novelettes of J. D. Salinger," *Contemporary Literature,* 4 (1963), 5-20; and Bernice and Sanford Goldstein, " 'Seymour: An Introduction'—Writing as Discovery," *Studies in Short Fiction,* 7 (1970), 248-256.

Other thought-provoking commentaries are William Wiegand, "The Knighthood of J. D. Salinger," *New Republic,* October 19, 1959, 19-21; Henry Anatole Grunwald, "Introduction" to *Salinger: A Critical and Personal Portrait* (New York: Harper, 1962), pp. ix-xxviii, and Gordon Slethaugh, "Seymour: A Clarification," *Renascence,* 23 (1971), 115-128.

[2]The quotations in the chapter come from the Bantam paperback editions of *Raise High the Roof Beam, Carpenters and Seymour—An Introduction* (New York, 1965).

CHAPTER 7

"Hapworth 16, 1924"

"Hapworth 16, 1924" (1965) is a long letter from summer camp, supposedly written by Seymour Glass when he was seven years old. In a preface, Buddy Glass claims that he had not known that this letter existed until his mother, Bessie Glass, recently sent it to him. At the time, so he says, he had been working on a story "about a party, a very consequential party, that she [Bessie] and Seymour and my father and I all went to one night in 1926." But since the letter has "a marvellous relevance" to that story, Buddy decided to publish the letter instead of the story. He stresses twice in the brief preface that what he is about to present is "an exact copy" of Seymour's letter. But this repeated protestation, the positively lurid style of the letter, and its structural resemblance to "Seymour—An Introduction" suggest that we ought to interpret it not as a letter written by Seymour but as an attempt by Buddy to re-create what might have been going on in Seymour's mind at a crucial time of his life. Buddy also tells us that Seymour "died, committed suicide, opted to discontinue living, back in 1948, when he was thirty-one."[1] And the fact that Buddy mentions Seymour's self-inflicted death in the preface is a signal that "Hapworth" contains an explanation of the reasons for Seymour's suicide, an explanation that Buddy had so far been unable to give because it was not until he wrote "Hapworth" that he understood why Seymour's quest for God ended in despair.[2]

* * *

The first unusual thing that we notice about the form of "Hapworth" is its extravagant and emotional style. Since the letter writer chiefly talks about himself, the style in which he writes tells us just as much about his character as what he actually says. Right from the start, the sentence construction and the word choice show that he is a very precocious and a very emotional seven-year-old:

DEAR BESSIE, LES, BEATRICE, WALTER, AND WAKER:

> I will write for us both, I believe, as Buddy is engaged else-where for an indefinite period of time. Surely sixty to eighty per cent of the time, to my eternal amusement and sorrow, that magnificent, elusive, comical lad is engaged elsewhere! As you must know in you hearts and bowels, we miss you all like sheer hell. Unfortunately, I am far from above hoping the case is vice versa. This a matter of quite a little humorous despair to me, though not so humorous. It is entirely disgusting to be forever achieving little actions of the heart or body and then taking re-course to reaction.

The most noticeable peculiarity of the language in this passage is its unnaturalness and stiltedness. But Seymour is fully aware of this shortcoming of his style. This is illustrated in the second paragraph of the letter:

> While bearing in mind that my loss of you is very acute to-day, hardly bearable in the last analysis, I am also snatching this stunning opportunity to use my new and entirely trivial mastery of written construction and decent sentence formation as ex-plained and slightly enriched upon in that small book, alternately priceless and sheer crap, which you saw me poring over to excess during the difficult days prior to our departure for this place. Though this is quite a terrible bore for you, dear Bessie and Les, superb or suitable construction of sentences holds some passing, amusing importance for a young fool like myself! It would be quite a relief to rid my system of fustian this year. It is in dan-ger of destroying my possible future as a young poet, private scholar, and unaffected person.

The "fustian" to which Seymour refers, his use of recondite words and his unnecessarily complex sentence construction, contrasts ludicrously with his often colloquial and even slangy diction. Seymour likes to show off by using such rare words as "dégringolade," "feculent," "nemophilous," and "pauciloquent," and he often gets himself entangled in such unnatural construction as, "I am far from above hoping the case is vice versa," or, "I was born without any great support in the event of continued absence of loved ones." Yet a moment later, he will slip back into the more natural speech patterns of a precocious seven-year-old, for instance when he writes, "We miss you all like sheer hell," or, "Here is the entire crappy incident in a nutshell," or, "As God is my judge, Mr. Happy is no prize package."

Another peculiarity of Seymour's style has to do with his use of adjectives. Most of his adjectives carry connotations that reveal his strong emotional responses to the persons, objects, or ideas he describes. His favorites are "moving," "touching," "stirring," "thrilling," and "heartrending." In addition, he often uses superlatives such as "superb," "magnificent," and "excellent." Adjectives of this kind are partly responsible for the emotional tone of the letter.

What further contributes to the emotionality of Seymour's style is his frequent use of exclamations such as "Jesus," "Oh, my God," and "God Almighty," and of such emphatic vulgarities as "damn," "Hell," and "crap." These elements of his style suggest that Seymour is in a very agitated state of mind when he writes his letter.

Whenever Seymour becomes aware of his emotional attitude toward what he describes, he tries to be more objective and detached. This accounts for his piling up of adjectives. For instance, he calls another camper "this excellent, droll, touching, intelligent lad"; he refers to the boy's mother as a "young, attractive, bitter, lonely woman"; he calls his own homesickness "a simple, nagging, humorous fact"; he talks about giving some "good, sensible, merciless advice"; and he describes a discussion as "helpful, quite spooky, or openly distasteful." Seymour's piling up of adjectives suggests that he tries to look at the things he describes from more than one angle. This is particularly apparent when he modifies the same noun with several adjectives whose connotations are contradictory, and when he chooses adjectives that express amused detachment, words such as "comical," "humorous," "droll," and "ridiculous." Seymour's attempts at achieving detachment are particularly obvious when he discusses his own state of mind and refers to his *"humorous* despair" and to the "constant turmoil in [his] *ridiculous* breast" (my emphasis). But as the emotional intensity of style shows, Seymour does not manage to achieve the desired distance from the events, people, and ideas that he is writing about.

Thus the style of the letter tells us two things about Seymour's character which are of great importance to an understanding of his inner turmoil: The verbal sophistication and complex sentence construction show that he is an extremely precocious seven-year-old, and the contrasting elements of his style reveal the nature of his conflict. The contrast between pretentiousness and slanginess and the contrast between adjectives suggesting enthusiasm and detachment both reveal that Seymour is torn between two desires. On the one hand he wants to be "a regular boy" who responds uncritically to the world, and on the other hand he wants to be a "poet and private scholar" who maintains a detached attitude toward everything around him. This conflict is one of several manifestations of the crisis which Seymour is trying to resolve. And this crisis determines the structure of the letter.

At first glance, "Hapworth" seems to have a very arbitrary expository structure. This structure consists of an introduction, an account of camp life, some advice for the family, a request for a long list of books, and a conclusion. Moreover, the letter appears to contain much redundant material, and it seems much longer than necessary. But there is a good reason why the letter is so long, and close examination reveals that its structure is anything but arbitrary. In fact, every segment of the letter serves an important function in developing its overall meaning.

The great length of the letter is explained by two circumstances. One is that Seymour is separated from his family for the first time in his life, and the other is that he has a lot of time on his hands because he is laid up with a serious leg injury. He begins writing the letter "shortly after dawn," on Thursday, July 17, 1924, his and Buddy's sixteenth day at Camp Hapworth, and he does not finish it until some time after supper on that same day. Since Seymour is alone during most of that time, he has ample opportunity to reflect on his experiences at camp. These experiences, particularly those of the last three days, have been very upsetting to Seymour. In writing about them, he realizes that he has come to a turning point in his life and that he must make a decision about the direction in which he wants to go. Thus his writing the letter is really not so much an act of communication as an act of self-analysis. Once we understand this, we will see that "Hapworth" is much more logically structured than it seems.

The plot of "Hapworth" develops largely in terms of interior action. Seymour moves slowly toward a realization and then begins to act upon it. This development depends on two conflicts, an exterior and an interior one. The exterior conflict pits Seymour against the other boys and the staff at Camp Hapworth, and it is resolved near the end of the first and longest section of the body, approximately two-thirds into the letter. The parallel inner conflict concerns Seymour's relationship with God, and it is resolved near the end of the letter.

To understand the nature of these two conflicts we must first examine Seymour's character as it is revealed by the content. The style suggests, as we have seen, that Seymour is an extremely precocious boy, but the content shows that he is more than merely precocious. The seven-year-old Seymour refers to himself not only as "a young poet and private scholar" but on occasion also as a "genius." And we find that Seymour is not exaggerating, for he mentions that he "masters" three foreign languages, French, Italian, and Spanish, and he shows himself to be thoroughly familiar with the works of authors such as Montaigne, Cervantes, Bunyan, Goethe, Blake, Tolstoy, and Proust. Moreover, Seymour also demonstrates his acquaintance with Eastern philosophy when he comments on the ideas of Buddha, Lao-Tse, and Vivekananda.

Just as remarkable as Seymour's academic precociousness is his "consuming admiration for God, straightforward and shapeless," which permeates, as he confesses, all of his other interests. This obsession with God began when Seymour was six and started his systematic reading in a neighborhood branch of the New York Public Library. He mentions in his letter that he has "exhausted" all of that library's "unbigoted or bigoted books on God or merely religion, as written by persons whose last names begin with any letter [before] H." However, Seymour's consuming admiration for God is not, as we might expect, an emotional infatuation with a divine father figure. Such an anthropomorphic conception of God, so Seymour says, "stinks to high heaven." Instead, his interest in God is a very intellectual and abstract preoccupation, for he prefers to see his "beloved, shapeless God" without "a human head" and without an "impressive, charming beard." This abstract God, so Seymour believes, is inherent in all human beings, and Seymour's "own dubious methods" of studying and worshipping God have therefore led him to an "industrious absorption with the human heart and brain."

Seymour's advanced religious thinking is also apparent in the ethical standards he imposes on himself. At the beginning of the letter, he expresses his disappointment with himself for not being able to "achieve missing my beloved family without yearning that they quite miss me in return!" Seymour would like to achieve unselfishness and complete detachment from his "actions of the heart and body," and he illustrates this idea with the following example: "I am utterly convinced that if A's hat blows off while he is sauntering down the street, it is the charming duty of B to pick it up and hand it to A without examining A's face or combing it for gratitude." In other words, Seymour wants to be able to perform all of his physical and mental actions without thinking of their results. Selflessness and desirelessness thus seem to be the chief goals of his religious striving.

In addition to being a young genius and an advanced religious person, the seven-year-old Seymour also has some uncanny psychic powers. One of these is his clairvoyance. He mentions a number of "glimpses" he has of incidents in his own and other people's previous incarnations. He says, for instance, that the camp director, Mr. Happy, "made ropes in his previous appearance, but not very well, somewhere in Turkey or Greece," and that he was "executed for making a defective rope, resulting in the death of some influential climbers." Some of Seymour's "glimpses" also concern the future. He predicts that sometime during the following two years, his parents will give a party to celebrate their retirement from vaudeville, and he says that during this party, he and Buddy will be made a "business and career offer" which will "involve our prowess as singers and dancers," and that "at a later date by unnumerable years," Buddy will be writing a short story about this very party. As we know from Buddy's introductory note, he had indeed been "working for several months on a long short story about a particular party, a very consequential party" when his mother sent him Seymour's old letter from Camp Hapworth which he "had never read before in [his] life." Another one of Seymour's extraordinary powers is his ability to control his nervous system. This is illustrated after he has injured his leg and takes eleven stitches without anesthesia. As he explains, he simply "snapped the communication of pain between the leg and the brain."

These unusual mental powers, which Buddy shares to some extent, set the two Glass boys apart from average, normal people and create difficulties for them at Camp Hapworth. Seymour admits that his clairvoyance threatens his own "normalness," and he agrees with Buddy "on the desirability of keeping our mouths firmly shut on the subject of some of our endowments and peculiarities." Nevertheless, Seymour insists that he and Buddy are "exceedingly regular boys from the word go" and that they are "every bit as decent, foolish, and human as every single boy or counsellor in this camp, quite tenderly and humorously equipped with the same likeable, popular, heartbreaking blindnesses." However, Seymour's account of their first sixteen days at camp shows that he and Buddy are not considered "regular boys" by the other campers and the staff. In fact, their extraordinariness has alienated them from all but three people.

But most important for an understanding of the way in which Seymour resolves his conflicts is his emotional instability. Seymour is fully aware of this problem and says that this "vein of instability runs through me like some turbulent river; this cannot be overlooked; I have left this troublesome instability incorrected in my previous two appearances, to my folly and disgust; it will not be corrected by friendly, cheerful prayer. It can only be corrected by dogged effort on my part. . . ." And then Seymour explains that this problem manifests itself particularly in his inability to control his malice when talking to people whom he despises. He therefore says that "the human tongue could all too easily be the case of my utter dégringolade in this appearance, unless I get a move on."

The section about Seymour's and Buddy's conflicts with the people at Camp Hapworth forms the first and longest part in the body of the letter and takes up approximately two-thirds of its total length. These conflicts result in two major confrontations between Seymour and members of the staff. The second of these confrontations resolves the external conflict, but it also deepens the inner conflict that lies at the heart of the story.

Seymour's account of camp life shows that he and Buddy are very unhappy at Camp Hapworth. This is in part due to the fact that neither of them wanted to be sent to the camp in the first place. Several times in the letter, Seymour complains about that. He refers to "the difficult days prior to our departure for this place"; he says that he "cannot stand useless separations from [his] family"; and he wishes that he and Buddy could be with their parents "and two other, quite unknown boys had this opportunity to stay off the streets."

Because they only went to Hapworth under protest, Seymour and Buddy are very critical of the way the camp is run. Both boys immediately take a dislike to the food because the cooks, Mr. and Mrs. Nelson, don't care enough about the campers "to prepare affectionate food or even to keep the bent silverware on the tables spotless and clean as a whistle." "The sight of forks alone," so Seymour reports, "often whips Buddy into a raw fury." And Seymour cannot accept the camp's policy of assigning siblings to separate bungalows. He thinks that there is no one in his bungalow with whom he can have an intelligent conversation and he therefore enlists the help of Mrs. Happy, the camp director's wife, in getting permission for Buddy to move in with him. Seymour also finds it exasperating that the camp's lights are turned off at nine o'clock every night. This forces him and Buddy to do their studying with their flashlights under their covers. Seymour says that he has "apporached Mr. Happy in this matter several times, but to no avail." And Seymour also finds the daily inspections of the beds and bungalows "an inexcusable and insulting imposition on every boy in this place. . . ."

Seymour's attitude toward the other boys and the counsellors at the camp is not very positive, either. Although he
protests several times that he and Buddy are "regular boys,"
he can't help feeling contemptuous of most of the other campers,
and especially of the counsellors, because they do not share
his and Buddy's values. Seymour explains:

> Few of these magnificent, healthy, sometimes remarkably hand-
> some boys will mature. The majority, I give you my heartbreak-
> ing opinion, will merely senesce . . . . The counsellors themselves
> are counsellors in name only. Most of them appear slated to go
> through their entire lives from birth to dusty death, with pica-
> yune, stunted attitudes toward everything in the universe and
> beyond . . . . No single day passes that I do not listen to the
> heartless indifferences and stupidities passing from the coun-
> sellors' lips without secretly wishing I could improve matters
> quite substantially by bashing a few culprits over the head with
> an excellent shovel or stout club! ("Hapworth," p. 34)

Seymour's and Buddy's contemptuous attitude toward
the people at Camp Hapworth and toward camp life in general
soon results in open conflict. Because they are not willing to
submit to the camp's routine, they have received quite a few
demerits during their first sixteen days, most of them for such
reasons as "continually sloppy bungalows . . . , not singing at
pow wow, and leaving pow wow without permission." Rather
than taking an interest in the camp's scheduled activities, Seymour and Buddy use every chance they get to study, write,
and meditate. Since their arrival, Seymour has composed fifty-
one poems and Buddy has written six short stories. Moreover,
they are, as Seymour says, "continuing to master Italian and
reviewing Spanish after taps." Because their interests are so
different from those of everyone else at camp, Seymour and
Buddy "are not too popular with the other campers." In fact,
the only people they are getting along with are the lisping and
bed-wetting Griffith Hammersmith, who is even more despised
than Seymour and Buddy; the intrepid John Kolb, who is secure
enough so that he doesn't have to shun the unpopular Glass
boys; and the lonely and unloved Mrs. Happy, who is a big fan
of Seymour's and Buddy's parents, the Gallagher-Glass vaude-

ville team.   Otherwise, so Seymour admits, "we are currently
being ostracized."

These tensions eventually lead to confrontations with
members of the staff, and during these confrontations Seymour's
instability causes him to lose his temper. Seymour says that
he has been "trying like hell since our arrival to leave a wide
margin for human ill will, fear, jealousy, and gnawing dislike
of the uncommonplace." But his hostility toward those who
don't respect his values eventually spills out. The first incident
occurs on Tuesday, after Buddy has won a bet with Mr. Nelson, the cook. In order to be allowed to use the empty mess
hall for study and meditation during off-hours, Buddy memor-
izes a sizeable book, *The Hardwoods of North America,* in less
than half an hour. News of Buddy's amazing feat quickly spreads
all over the camp, and later that day, the head counsellor makes
a sarcastic remark about Buddy's intelligence. Seymour is
enraged and reports: "Quite afterwards, I embraced an opportunity to tell Roger Pittman, the full name his hapless parents
gave him, that I would kill myself, possibly before nightfall,
if he ever spoke to that chap again in that manner."

The second confrontation occurs on Wednesday during a
strawberrying expedition. While helping to push the camp's
horsedrawn wagon out of a mudhole, Seymour severely injures
his leg on a piece of iron sticking out of the vehicle. He blames
Mr. Happy for this injury, and his instability again gets the better of him. This is how Seymour describes the incident for his
parents:

> It had several fleeting, humorous moments. Quite in the first
> place, it is very hard for me, I regret to say, to be less than con-
> temptuous and scathing around Mr. Happy personally. I am
> working on it, but that man brings to the fore supplies of hid-
> den malice I thought I had worked out of my system years ago.
> In my own, flimsy defense, let me suggest that a man thirty years
> of age has no earthly business forcing small, useless boys to push
> a damnable, fake cart out of the mud where a veritable team of
> four or six young, stalwart horses was really required. My malice
> shot forward like a snake. I told him . . . that you would prob-
> ably sue him, Les, for every dime he had in the event that I lost
> my ridiculous leg from infection, loss of blood, or gangrene ("Hap-
> worth, p. 66).

In both confrontations, that with Roger Pittman and
that with Mr. Happy, Seymour's instability makes him unable
to control the contempt he feels for people whose attitudes
he considers to be picayune and devoid of spirituality. But
Seymour's major problem is not that he cannot suppress his
contempt for people like Roger Pittman and Mr. Happy but
that he feels this contempt in the first place. After all, he claims
to be a "regular boy" and to feel sympathetic toward "all forms
of human folly and bestiality." It seems, however, that his experiences at Camp Hapworth make him realize that he is *not* a
"regular boy" and that he does not really want to be one, either.

Seymour resolves his external conflict with the people at
Camp Hapworth by showing them that he is a very special person and must be treated differently than the other campers.
He does this by refusing to accept any anesthesia while the
doctor is preparing to sew up his leg. He writes: "When I polite-
ly declined the anesthesia, the doctor assumed I was showing
off, Mr. Happy, at his side, sharing this maddening opinion.
Like a born fool, which I can assure you I am, I foolishly demon-
strated that I had snapped the communication of pain utterly."
By taking eleven stitches without anesthesia, Seymour proves
that he does indeed have some very special abilities which regular boys do not have. He thus violates his agreement with Buddy
not to reveal their extraordinary endowments and peculiarities. Buddy, as we have seen, also violated this agreement when
he proved to Mr. Nelson that he has a photographic memory.
As these two incidents show, Seymour and Buddy have given
up trying to convince themselves and others that they are average, regular boys.

But although Seymour's demonstration of his special
powers resolves his external conflict, it intensifies his even more
severe internal one. This is apparent from his continued agitation, and this agitation is reflected in his style. It is also con-
firmed in a number of explicit statements. At the end of the
section about camp life, for instance, Seymour comments on the
"constant turmoil in [his] ridiculous breast" and near the conclusion, he again admits that his "nerves are too raw today."
Moreover, on five separate occasions, he confesses that he can't
help weeping while writing the letter. All this indicates that
Seymour is experiencing an inner crisis, a crisis that is brought

on by his inability to get along with the people at Camp Hapworth.

Seymour's crisis is a struggle to reconcile the opposite demands of the spiritual and the physical worlds. This, he explains, is "the crux" of his crisis. Although he recognizes the essential unreality of physical phenomena, he says: "I am also, in my heart, exceedingly fond of them all." He calls this fondness for the physical and his commitment to the spiritual world a "vicious cycle," and he says: "What I am seeking, with the very ample but in some ways scrawny amount of time left in this appearance, is a solution to the problem that is both honorable and unheartless." Seymour's head, his moral perfectionism, wants him to pursue his spiritual quest without regard to the demands of the physical world, while his heart draws him toward the physical world, toward average, everyday life. Seymour realizes that the abstractness of his quest might lead to "heartlessness," that it might estrange him not only from people he dislikes but also from those he is fond of. This comes out when he says: "One is never more separated from one's loved ones than when one ponders this delicate matter." And it is his violent confrontations with the counsellor and the camp director which have forced him to ponder these problems.

The structure of the letter suggests that the difficulties Seymour has in getting along with normal people eventually make him withdraw from the physical world. In this withdrawal, the world of the Glass family serves as a transitional stage. For after Seymour has spent two-thirds of his letter on his account of his relationships with the other campers and the staff at Camp Hapworth, he devotes the remainder to advice for his family and to comments on some thirty authors whose works he wants to have sent him. This shift in focus reveals the outcome of Seymour's inner struggle, his decision to withdraw from the world of ordinary people and to devote himself to the spiritual guidance of his family and to intellectual pursuits. And the ideas in the last two sections of the letter bear out what its structure suggests.

Although the advice that Seymour gives to his family is in part very practical, this section does represent a withdrawal from everyday reality, for the Glasses are certainly not average people.　Some of Seymour's advice concerns his family's activities as professional entertainers.　He knows, for instance, that his father has "a deep, torturous desire for a smash hit," and he therefore gives him and his mother some tips on how to improve their singing when they record their next song, "Bambalina."　He also advises his brothers Walter and Waker, who plan to become entertainers like their parents, to practice their tap-dancing and juggling "fairly constantly" and to wear their tap shoes and carry with them their juggling objects "for at least 2 hours a day."　For his sister Boo Boo, however, Seymour provides chiefly spiritual advice.　He imposes on her his own advanced ethical standards when he tells her to mind her notoriously bad manners in public, and, more importantly, not to be "quite a dirty pig when alone in a room."　He also gives her a new bedtime prayer.　Her old one has become offensive to her because she no longer believes in a personal God and even has come to hate the word "God" itself.　She is to begin her prayer with these words: "I address the nameless hallmark, preferably without shape or ridiculous attributes, who has always guided my destiny both between and during the splendid, touching use of human bodies."　Seymour's advice to his mother combines the practical and the spiritual. He reminds her of a breathing exercise which will calm her nerves, and he warns her not to be in too great a rush to give up show business, because his "glimpses" into the future have told him that the best time for her to quit is after October of 1924.　In that context, he discusses the notion of "tampering with fate out of season." In season, so he says, "fate can be dealt stunning blows, but out of season, regrettably, mistakes are quite usual and costly."

In the third part of the letter, Seymour retreats even further from average, everyday life and from the problems at Camp Hapworth.　He spends almost six pages discussing some fifty books which he would like to have sent him to camp so he can continue his and Buddy's education.　He comments, for example, on Goethe's stature as a writer, on a book of raja yoga meditation exercises by Vivekananda, on John Bunyan's objectionable conception of God's perfection, and on the relative merits of several biographies of Guy de Maupassant. Because Les and Bessie would have to be quite well-read in literature and religious philosophy in order to understand his ideas, it appears that in this section Seymour is really no longer communicating with his parents. His comments about the books confirm that he is trying to work out his conflict between the demands of the physical and those of the spiritual world.

Near the end of the booklist, Seymour resolves this conflict by deciding what his "everlasting duty" is and how to discharge it. Right after he requests some books of "religious writings in China after those two, towering, incomparable geniuses of Lao-Tse and Chuang-Tse," Seymour concedes that his "consuming admiration for God" might be having some negative effects on him. A librarian who read his poems told him that he has "the makings of a splendid American poet" but that his religious preoccupation might "upset the delightful apple cart of [his] poetry" and turn him into "a crashing failure." Seymour acknowledges that possibility but explains that he feels obliged to continue his quest for God and "to remain absorbed in [his] own dubious methods, such as industrious absorption with the human heart and brain." And these "dubious methods" of achieving enlightenment involve the study of literature and religion, the best records of the workings of the human heart and brain. In short, Seymour decides to withdraw even more into the spiritual world, to concentrate even more on his studies.

Thus the structure of the main part of the letter supports its meaning. Its three sections reveal a progressive narrowing down of the letter's focus from the physical to the spiritual world:

Events at Camp Simon Hapworth

Advice to the Family

Booklist

The first section of the letter deals with the physical world as represented by the people and events at Camp Hapworth. The second deals with the world of the Glass family where Seymour's spiritual quest finds sympathy, if not approval. And the last section consists of the booklist which represents the world of the spirit.

In the conclusion of the letter, Seymour expresses his

awareness that his stay at Camp Hapworth marks a significant
change, a turning point in his life. Earlier in the letter, he referred to his sixteenth day at camp as "this sultry *memorable*
day of my life" (my emphasis), and in the conclusion he once
more implies that some extraordinary change has occurred.
This becomes clear when he tells his parents: ". . . in more
ways than one, dear Bessie and Les, you are paying an exorbitant price for our frivolous summer's enjoyments and recrea-
tions." What this means becomes clear when we consider how
Seymour's changed notion of his duty in life is going to affect
his family. His father Les, so Seymour told us earlier, takes
it very hard as it is that his two eldest sons "don't remind [him]
freely and movingly of other regular boys." And now Seymour
is not even going to try any longer to be a "regular boy." Instead he is going to withdraw even more deeply into his studies
and he is going to pull Buddy along with him. This is indeed
an "exorbitant price" to pay for sending Seymour and Buddy
to summer camp against their wishes.

Just as Seymour's parents must have reacted negatively to
his decision to withdraw even more from normal, average life,
so we as readers must consider his withdrawal as a turn in the
wrong direction. Although we may admire the energy and
determination with which Seymour pursues his quest for God,
we can't help suspecting that by intensifying his studies and by
limiting himself to the spiritual guidance of his siblings, Seymour is taking the path of least resistance. He has found out at
Camp Hapworth that his instability makes it very difficult for
him to control his malice when dealing with those who are less
spiritual than he is. He admits that he already left this instability uncorrected in his last two incarnations and knows that
"it can only be corrected by dogged effort on my part." But
as the letter shows, he is unwilling to make that effort. For
such an effort would require that he seek out the company of
unspiritual people in order to learn how to control his malice.
His decision to avoid such people as much as possible suggests
that he will not be able to correct his instability, at least not
in his current incarnation.

The meaning of "Hapworth" therefore lies in Seymour's
decision to withdraw from average humanity. Even though
the letter explains that this decision is motivated by Seymour's

earnest desire to serve God and to do what he considers his "everlasting duty," we nevertheless get the impression that his withdrawal is going to have grave consequences. After all, Buddy mentions in his preface that Seymour eventually committed suicide, and we are reminded of that fact when Seymour blows up at a counsellor and threatens to kill himself. Also, Seymour himself says that he is afraid that his instability might turn out to become the cause of his "dégringolade in this appearance." The letter thus suggests that, because of his withdrawal from others, Seymour never did correct his instability and that it eventually became so severe that it made him commit suicide.

Even though Seymour's problems are certainly not common ones, "Hapworth" still implies a universal statement. It can be said to make the point that those who share Seymour's consuming admiration for God should be careful not to let their spiritual quests estrange them from others because this estrangement would ultimately defeat their purpose. Instead of withdrawing from others, they should make every effort to share their ideas and insights even with those who don't feel sympathetic toward them. In short, "Hapworth" suggests that those who see more should not withdraw but share their vision—for their own good—with those who see less.

* * *

If we see "Hapworth" in the context of the other parts of the Glass series and assume that it was written by Buddy rather than Seymour, then the letter reveals that Buddy has finally understood why Seymour's spiritual quest failed. In pondering this question over the years, Buddy may have realized that Seymour's problems began in the summer of 1924, at Camp Hapworth, but Buddy apparently wasn't sure what the exact nature of these problems was. Therefore he decided to find out by impersonating Seymour and by writing the kind of letter that Seymour might have written at the age of seven. By following Seymour's advice and allowing the process of composition to become a process of discovery, Buddy comes to understand that Seymour doomed his quest for God to failure when he decided to avoid interaction with unspiritual people because such people bring out his instability and his malice. And we see this instability and malice in "A Perfect Day for Bananafish" when Seymour decides to shoot himself in his hotel room while sitting on a bed near the sleeping Muriel. By mentioning Seymour's suicide in the preface to "Hapworth," Buddy suggests that "Hapworth" and "Bananafish" are companion stories, much like "Franny" and "Zooey," and that in writing "Hapworth" he has now completed the Glass series. After seventeen years of writing about Seymour, Buddy has finally understood the reasons for his suicide.

But "Hapworth" not only shows that Buddy has come to understand Seymour's religious ideas, both in their positive and negative effects, the letter also marks the final stage in Buddy's movement toward a full understanding of Seymour's aesthetic ideas. When he wrote the "Introduction," Buddy began to write spontaneously but lost his nerve because he had the feeling that he wasn't reaching any particular insight. He therefore had to stop and re-read Seymour's letter which told him to trust his heart, win or lose. Only after being reassured by Seymour's advice was he able to continue without worrying if his spontaneous, intuitive way of writing would produce a successful piece of fiction. But when he wrote "Hapworth," Buddy was confident from the start that spontaneous composition would lead him to new insights.

Also, "Hapworth" is written for an even smaller audience than the "Introduction." The letter is ostensibly addressed to Bessie, Les, Beatrice, Walter, and Waker, but its enormous length and its learned disquisitions on literary and religious topics show that the writer is not keeping his audience in mind at all. He is really talking to himself, trying to solve a pressing personal problem by writing about it. And that problem is his inability to understand the failure of Seymour's spiritual quest. By impersonating Seymour and writing the kind of letter that Seymour might have written home from Camp Hapworth, Buddy is doing exactly what Seymour once told him to do when he said Buddy shouldn't write rattling good stories but ask himself "what piece of writing in all the world would Buddy Glass most want to read if he had his heart's choice." And then, so Seymour told Buddy, he should "just sit down shamelessly and write the thing himself ("Introduction," p. 161).

And a letter from Seymour that would explain the reasons for the failure of his spiritual quest is what Buddy would most want to read. Thus Buddy wrote "Hapworth" for an audience of one, for himself.

But Buddy decided to publish the letter, and this raises the question what kind of reader he really had in mind. Certainly, "Hapworth" does not appeal to the general reader who is unfamiliar with other Glass stories. Also, most readers do not have the interest in langage and in literary experimentation, let alone the sheer stamina, that are necessary to enjoy the letter. Thus the kind of reader for whom Buddy published "Hapworth" is once again his ideal reader, the person who is as interested in Seymour and his ideas about writing as is Buddy himself.

In addition, the reader of "Hapworth" also has to be interested in Seymour's religious ideas, as Buddy knew the general reader is not when he mentioned in "Zooey" that he has already been criticized for the religious emphasis in his work. Even though "Hapworth" can be interpreted without the help of outside information about Eastern religion, nevertheless its frequent references to such ideas as *karma* and reincarnation suggest that we will only reach a superficial understanding of the letter unless we inform ourselves at least about the most basic concepts of Eastern philosophy. Moreover, "Hapworth" goes deeper into the reasons for the failure of Seymour's spiritual quest than does any other part of the Glass series, and these reasons cannot be fully understood in Western terms.

With his last installment of the series, Buddy serves notice that we can reach a better understanding of the Glass stories if we familiarize ourselves with Eastern thought. And as I will show in the next chapter, familiarity with Eastern ideas will not only allow us a better understanding of the meaning of Seymour's life and death, but also of the philosophy of composition according to which Buddy wrote the later parts of the series.

NOTES

[1]The quotations in this chapter come from "Hapworth 16, 1924," *New Yorker,* June 19, 1965, pp. 32-113, and from the Bantam paperback edition of *Raise High the Roof Beam, Carpenters and Seymour—An Introduction* (New York, 1965).

[2]For previous interpretations of "Hapworth," see: Samuel Bellman, "New Light on Seymour's Suicide: Salinger's *Hapworth 16, 1924*," *Studies in Short Fiction,* 3 (1966), 348-351; Max F. Schultz, "Epilogue to *Seymour: An Introduction:* Salinger and the Crisis of Consciousness," *Studies in Short Fiction,* 5 (1968), 128-138; Gordon Slethaugh, "Seymour: A Clarification," *Renascence,* 23 (1971), 115-128; Anthony Quagliano, "Hapworth 16, 1924: A Problem in Hagiography," *University of Dayton Review,* 8 (1971), 35-43; Frank Metcalf, "The Suicide of Salinger's Seymour Glass," *Studies in Short Fiction,* 9 (1972), 243-246; and Bernice and Sanford Goldstein, "Ego and 'Hapworth 16, 1924'," *Renascence,* 24 (1972), 159-167.

CHAPTER 8

Buddy's Philosophy of Composition

In the seventeen years between the publication of "A Perfect Day for Bananafish" (1948) and "Hapworth 16, 1924" (1965), Buddy's storytelling changed radically.[1] "Bananafish" is a very compact short story which combines brevity of detail and compression of incident. Moreover, it is told from a totally objective point of view which forces the reader to draw his own conclusions about what is going on in the minds of the characters. The style of the story adds to its compactness, for it has a Flaubertian polish that reveals painstaking craftsmanship and innumerable revisions. Every word is *le mot juste,* and there is virtually not a word in the whole story that can be omitted without changing the overall meaning. The form of "Hapworth" is in every respect the opposite. The piece is more than seven times as long as "Bananafish" and it is full of detail whose relevance is not at all clear. Told in the first person, it is extremely subjective because the writer spends considerable time analyzing his own thoughts and emotions. And the style is so unbalanced, so involuted and so full of verbal *faux pas* that serious ideas often appear ridiculous. Moreover, the structure of "Hapworth" shows that Buddy has deliberately gone beyond the tradition of the short story and created a type of fiction which combines expository with narrative elements. These changes in the form of Buddy's fiction are due to his growing understanding of Seymour's aesthetic ideas, and by applying these ideas to his writing, Buddy has succeeded in developing a form that is right for him.

In "Raise High the Roof Beam, Carpenters" (1965), Buddy makes his first comments on the way he writes his stories. But it is not until "Zooey" (1957) and "Seymour—An Introduction" (1959) that his statements reveal a deliberate search for his own form of fiction. In "Carpenters," he comments on the shape of the story when he says: "It is, in my opinion, a self-contained account, with a beginning and end, and a mortality all its own." This description suggests that the story is conventional in structure and that Buddy is making no attempt to break away from the short story form. However, in his introduction to "Zooey," Buddy tells us that what he is about to offer "isn't really a short story at all but a sort of prose home movie" and he admits that he is no longer striving for "brevity of detail and compression of incident." Similarly, in "Seymour—An Introduction," Buddy says that he no longer dares "go anywhere near the short story form" and he explains that he has come to loathe stories that have "a Beginning, a Middle, and an End."

In "Seymour—An Introduction," Buddy also says that his movement away from the conventional short story is a result of Seymour's influence. He spells out Seymour's aesthetic ideas when he describes his brother's attitude toward poetry and quotes some advice that Seymour gave him concerning his writing. And Buddy's running commentary on the manner in which he is composing the "Introduction" reveals that Buddy is actually following Seymour's advice. The content and form of the "Introduction" thus allow us to piece together the aesthetic ideas that explain the strange shape of the later Glass stories.

A string of memos from Seymour clarifies why Buddy moved away from the Flaubertian aesthetics of the well-made story. These memos concern short stories that Buddy asked Seymour to comment on. Buddy was taking a writing course from a Professor B. and trusted the professor's judgment of his stories more than his own. Seymour therefore asked him not to be content with what Professor B. called a "rattling good story." He tells Buddy: "I mind getting a rattling good story from you. I want your *loot*." Seymour believed that Buddy was too worried about mechanical perfection and that his quest for form hampered his inspiration. This comes out when Seymour comments on how Louis Bouilhet and Max Du Champ prodded Flaubert into making *Madame Bovary* the marvel of craftsmanship that it is:

> "All right, so between the two of them, with their exquisite taste, they got him to write a masterpiece. They killed his chances of ever writing his heart out. He died like a celebrity, which was the

one thing he wasn't. His letters are unbearable to read. They're so much better than they should be. They read waste, waste, waste. They break my heart" ("Introduction," pp. 159-160).[2]

As we can see, Seymour believed that Flaubert's genius is better reflected in his letters than in his fiction. Too concerned with mechanical perfection, Flaubert produced his novels and stories only with his head, while his letters came straight from his heart. Seymour therefore tells Buddy: "Please follow your heart, win or lose. . . . Oh, dare to do it Buddy! Trust your heart. You're a deserving craftsman. It would never betray you." And Buddy's later stories clearly show that he eventually gave up conscious and deliberate composition and wrote spontaneously from the heart.

This belief in spontaneous creation is part of a well-defined system of aesthetics which is expressed chiefly in the "Introduction" but also in "Zooey" and "Hapworth." Seymour's aesthetic ideas are similar to those developed by Plato in the "Ion" and other dialogues, and Buddy also compares them to the views of art expressed by Blake, the American Transcendentalists, Kierkegaard, Kafka, and Van Gogh.[3] But the essential traits of Seymour's aesthetics are derived from Eastern philosophy.

The foundation of Seymour's theory of art, and of the aesthetics underlying the later Glass stories, is the belief that true art is not created by the artist but comes directly from God: The artist merely serves as an instrument. Kierkegaard, to whom Buddy defers when it comes to "modern artistic processes," shared this belief. Kierkegaard explains that his work as a writer is the result of "the prompting of an irresistible inward impulse" which comes from God. God is giving him "His assistance" in writing. Kierkegaard labels his divine inspiration "Governance" and says: ". . . it seems to me as if, had I a winged pen, yes, ten of them, I still could not follow fast enough to keep pace with the wealth which presents itself."[4] Plato expresses a similar notion in the "Ion," when he says that "beautiful poems are not human, or the work of man, but divine and the work of God" and that "the poets are only the interpreters of the Gods . . . ."[5] This means that the work of art already exists in its ideal form before the artist gives physical shape to it. As Emerson expresses the idea, "poetry was all written before time was."[6]

Hindu aesthetics similarly assert that "the work of art is completed before the work of transcription or representation is begun."[7] But while Plato, Emerson, and Kierkegaard, in their dualistic view of man and God, assume that ideal forms exist in the mind of God, that is, outside of the artist, Hindu aestheticians, following the monistic philosophy of Advaita Vedanta, see God immanent in all things. And since they perceive God as absolute Truth and Beauty, they see the essence of all true art inherent in man's heart, or as Franny Glass puts it, "in some absolutely non-physical part of the heart—where the Hindus say that *Atman* resides." The work of art therefore originates inside the artist, not somewhere outside. This view of the origin of divine form is explained by Ananda Coomaraswamy when he summarizes ideas from several Sanskrit texts:

> The mind "pro-duces" or "draws" (*akarsati*) this form to itself, as though from a great distance. Ultimately, that is, from Heaven, where the types of art exist in formal operation; immediately, from "the immanent space in the heart" (*antar-hrdaya-akasa*), the common focus (*samstava*, "concord") of seer and seen, at which place the only possible experience of reality takes place . . . .
>
> The *antar-hrdaya-akasa*, "space in the heart" is the totality of this ideal space at the inmost core of our being, where only the full content of life can be experienced; that content, from the point of view of epistemology is "Truth," . . . and from the standpoint of ethics "Perfection." Thus while Beauty may be equated with Perfection and Truth absolutely (*rasa . . . brahmasvada-sahodara, Sahitya Darpana*, II, pp. 1-2), loveliness is merely a good, ugliness merely an evil. Beauty is invisible and indivisible, only to be known as the Deity is known, in the heart . . . .[8]

It is because Seymour believed that all true works of art come from God and that God resides in the "immanent space in the heart" that he told Buddy: "Please follow your heart, win or lose."

But not everyone can produce works of art simply by following his heart. According to Seymour's aesthetics, the true artist must have three important qualifications. He must have been born a poet as the result of his *karma;* he must be a "seer";

and he must be a "deserving craftsman."

Seymour believed that poetic genius cannot be acquired but must be innate. This notion is shared by Platonic and Hindu aesthetics. Plato says that poetic genius is a "gift" of God, and Hindu texts such as the *Sahitya Darpana* assert that true artists are individuals "in whom the knowledge of ideal beauty is innate."[9] But while Plato assumes that God dispenses poetic genius arbitrarily, the Hindus believe in the divine law of cause and effect and see poetic genius as the result of *karma*. As one Indian author explains: "The karma (good and bad deeds) of every man . . . as well as the background of his experience determines his genius."[10] According to the law of *karma*, every one of our physical or mental actions results in a similar reaction either in this life or in a future incarnation. Hence, what we are in this lifetime is determined by our actions and desires in previous lives. This notion is expressed by Zooey when he tells Franny: "Somewhere along the line—in one damn incarnation or another, if you like—you not only had a hankering to be an actor or an actress but to be a *good* one. You're stuck with it now. You can't just *walk* out on the results of your own hankerings. Cause and effect, buddy, cause and effect" ("Zooey," p. 198). Seymour himself knew at a very early age that his *karma* had destined him to write poetry. This comes out in the letter from Camp Hapworth, when the seven-year-old Seymour talks about his "karmic responsibility" and says: "There is monumental work to be done in this appearance, of partly undisclosed nature . . ." ("Hapworth," p. 36). The part of his "karmic responsibility" that has been disclosed to him is his vocation as a poet, and during the first sixteen days at Camp Hapworth, Seymour writes fifty-one poems. Significantly, he admits that ten of them "have turned out to be in unconscious, disastrous imitation of William Blake" ("Hapworth," p. 50). And Seymour was probably familiar with Blake's views on innate genius as expressed in his statements: "Knowledge of Ideal Beauty is Not to be Acquired. It is Born with us," and "One power alone makes a Poet: Imagination, the Divine Vision."[11]

According to the aesthetics of the later Glass stories, the most important quality of the born artist is his divinely inspired vision, his ability to see more than others. This is most clearly expressed in the "Introduction" when Buddy Glass says that the "true artist-seer" is the person who is able to "produce beauty" out of "the blinding shapes and colors of his own sacred human conscience" ("Introduction," p. 105). He is an individual who comes as close to being "pure spirit" as is humanly possible,[12] and he is therefore able to see divine beauty and truth "in the queerest imaginable places," that is, in the most commonplace objects and incidents ("Introduction," p. 108). Similarly, Plato believed that true poets have a divine vision akin to that of "the producers of oracles and holy prophets." They are able to see the divine truth "with the eyes of the soul" and their works therefore "interpret to us the voice of God."[13] Hindu poetics express the same view concerning the nature of the true poet. As one Hindu aesthetician explains: "The Poet is one who is a seer, a prophet, who sees visions and possesses the additional gift of conveying to others less fortunate through the medium of language his visions . . . ."[14]

But while Plato does not explain how poets come by their visions except to assert that they are "inspired and possessed,"[15] there is a large body of literature in Hindu aesthetics dealing with the workings of divine inspiration. According to Hindu belief, spiritually advanced individuals, true artist-seers, can call forth their vision of the divine at will during Yoga meditation. A famous example is the story of how Valmiki received his inspiration to write the great epic, the *Ramayana*:

> . . . seating himself with his face toward the East, and sipping water according to the rule (of Hindu religious ritual), he set himself to *Yoga*-contemplation of his theme. By virtue of his *Yoga*-power, he clearly saw before himself Rama, Laksahamana and Sita, and Dasaratha, together with his wives, in his kingdom, laughing, talking, acting and moving as if in real life, . . . by *Yoga*-power that righteous one beheld all that had come to pass and all that was to come to pass in the future, like a nelli fruit (*phyllantus emblica*, denoting clear insight) on the palm of his hand. And having truly seen all by virtue of his concentration, the generous sage began setting forth the history of Rama.[16]

The inspiration that the artist-seer receives comes to him when he reaches the state of *samadhi*, pure consciousness and ecstasy. The exact nature of this state is a much discussed topic in Hindu aesthetics.   A key concept associated with it is that of *rasa*, the flavor or the divine essence of the poet's subject which he grasps during meditation.   An important work on that subject is Vishvanatha's *Sahitya Darpana* (ca. 1450) to which even contemporary aestheticians still defer.[17]   Ananda Coomaraswamy translates a key passage from that work as follows:

> Pure aesthetic experience (*rasa*) is theirs in whom the knowledge of ideal beauty is innate; it is known intuitively, in intellectual ecstacy without accompaniement of ideation, at the highest level of conscious being; born of one mother with the vision of God, its life is as it were a flash of blinding light of transmundane origin, impossible to analyze, and yet in the image of our very being.[18]

Seymour Glass was familiar with the "flash of blinding light" that Vishvanatha speaks of.   He mentions such flashes of light in his letter from Camp Hapworth where he spent much time meditating and writing poetry (See Hapworth," pp. 42, 50). The notion that poetic inspiration comes in the form of flashes of light also explains Seymour's comment to Buddy that the best advice one can give to an artist is to "beg him to let his stars come out" ("Introduction," p. 159).   These "stars" represent the divine light by which the true artist is able to see more than others.

But in order to express his vision of divine beauty and truth adequately, the artist-seer must also be a skilled craftsman.   Seymour explains this notion in his memo to Buddy when he tells his brother: "Trust your heart. You're a deserving craftsman. It would never betray you." This idea is more reflective of Hindu aesthetics than of the views of Plato and the Romantics.   Plato assumes that the poet creates his work only "when he is inspired and is out of his senses," and that, as soon as he consciously shapes his work, he will fall prey to his desire to please his audience.[19]   Similarly, in Romantic aesthetics, particularly in the writings of Emerson, we find a de-emphasis of craftsmanship and a belief that the form will take care of itself if the artist listens closely enough to his inspiration.[20]   Hindu aesthetics, however, stress that years of practice are required before an artist can begin to produce works which reflect the ideal beauty of his vision.   According to one of the oldest texts in Hindu aesthetics, Bharata's *Natya Shastra*, "The one thing most necessary to the human workman is *abhyasa*, 'practice,' otherwise thought of as *anusila*, 'devoted application' or 'obedience,' the fruit of which is *slistatva*, 'habitus,' or second nature, skill, lit. 'clingingness,' 'adherence'; and this finds expression in the performance as *madhurya*, 'grace' or 'facility'."[21] Like Bharata, Seymour believed that it is only after the artist has come to master the skills of his craft that he can begin to "follow his heart" and to express his divine inspiration.

But according to Seymour's aesthetics, the artist should not be conscious of the established rules of his craft but abandon himself entirely to his inspiration, or, as Plato put it, to his "heaven-sent madness."[22] In commenting on Shelley's poetry, for instance, Buddy Glass says that what is wrong with it is that "Mad Shelley wasn't quite mad enough. Assuredly, in any case, his madness wasn't a madness of the heart" ("Introduction," p. 150). In Buddy's view, Shelley's poetry is too contrived because his vision was not strong enough to make him forget conventional rules.

Buddy's and Seymour's notion of the relationship between craftsmanship and spontaneous creation is very similar to that expressed in Hindu aesthetics. According to Coomaraswamy: "The ultimate liberty of spontaneity is indeed conceivable only as a workless manifestation in which art and artist are perfected. . . . Ascertained rules should be thought of as the vehicle assumed by spontaneity, in so far as spontaneity is possible for us, rather than as a kind of bondage . . . . In tending toward an ultimate coincidence of discipline and will, the artist does indeed become ever less and less conscious of rules, and for the virtuoso intuition and performance are apparently simultaneous . . . ."[23] Spontaneous creation is also the essence of Chinese and Japanese Zen poetry which Seymour dearly loved.[24] In the West, spontaneous creation is advocated by Kierkegaard, Kafka, and Van Gogh; and Buddy Glass tells us that he frequently turns to their journals, diaries, and letters, "when I want any perfectly credible information about modern artistic processes" ("Introduction," p. 101).

The belief in spontaneous creation implies a belief in organic form. If the artist allows his intuition free rein and does not consciously impose any form on it, then the work will grow its own shape. This idea is only implied in Platonic and Hindu aesthetics, but it has been explicitly stated by various Romantic and modern artists. Thoreau, for instance, said that true poetry "is a natural fruit. As naturally as the oak bears an acorn, and the vine a gourd, man bears a poem, either spoken or done."[25] Kafka and Van Gogh have expressed similar notions of organic growth. Van Gogh, for example, said that when he created a painting he felt like "a woman in childbirth,"[26] and Kafka once said that one of his stories came out of him "like a real birth."[27] Kafka extended this simile when he wrote in his diary:

> The beginning of every story is ridiculous at first. There seems to be no hope that this newborn thing, still incomplete and tender in every joint, will be able to keep alive in the completed organization of the world, which like every completed organization, strives to close itself off. However, one should not forget that the story, if it has any justification to exist, bears its complete organization within itself even before it has been fully formed; for this reason, despair over the beginning of a story is unwarranted; in a like case parents should have to despair of their suckling infant, for they had no intention of bringing this pathetic and ridiculous thing into the world.[28]

Although the form of the work of art, according to these views, is inherent in its essence and should therefore not be consciously shaped by the artist, it stands to reason that the artist's inborn sense of form gives the work its unmistakable character just as a parent passes on to his offspring certain of his own physical characteristics and character traits.

Buddy's belief in organic form is apparent in the later experimental stories, and it is made explicit in a number of his comments. He expresses his disdain for restrictive conventional patterns when he says that he burned some thirty-five or fifty early stories because they had what "Somerest Maugham calls a Beginning, a Middle, and and End." It is particularly contrived endings which Buddy doesn't like, for he believes that a writer should never impose a conclusion on a story. Instead, he should simply stop writing when the story is finished with him. Thus, at the end of the "Introduction," he says: "I'm finished with this. Or, rather, it's finished with me."

The way in which a work grows its organic shape is illustrated in Buddy's commentary on how he is composing the "Introduction." Buddy begins the composition of the "Introduction" very confidently because he feels "seized" by his subject, the character and life of his brother Seymour. And he says: "divine or not, a seizure's a seizure." Because he feels that way about writing, so Buddy tells us repeatedly, he is "an ecstatically happy man." This happiness makes it impossible for him to be "moderate or temperate or brief." Worst of all, so Buddy says, he is "no longer in a position to look after the reader's most immediate want; namely, to see the author get the hell on with his story." And he warns us: "I'm here to advise that not only will my asides run rampant from this point on (I'm not sure, in fact, that there won't be footnote or two) but I fully intend, from time to time, to jump up personally on the reader's back when I see something off the beaten plot line that looks exciting or interesting and worth steering toward." Buddy then serves notice that he doesn't want to "go anywhere near the short story form." Instead, so he says, "I want to follow my nose."

For a while, Buddy is happy enough to follow his nose, that is, to write spontaneously. But halfway through the "Introduction," his happiness disappears, and he can't go on. He therefore decides to re-read and quote for us some old memos containing Seymour's advice on how to write spontaneously. In this connection, Buddy recalls some advice Seymour once gave him on how to shoot marbles. And while he tells us about it, Buddy suddenly understands that the principle of spontaneous action, which Seymour advocated in marble shooting, also applies to writing.

Seymour's marble shooting technique is expressed in his advice to Buddy, "Could you try not aiming so much?" Buddy compares this idea to the principle of Zen archery: "I believe he was instinctively getting at something very close in spirit to the sort of instructions a master archer in Japan will give when he forbids a willful new student to aim his arrows at the target; that is, when the archery master permits, as it were, Aiming but no aiming." What Buddy means by this becomes clear when he explains that "after Seymour himself shot a marble, he would be all smiles when he heard a responsive click of glass striking glass, but it never appeared to be clear to him *whose* winning click it was.　And it's also a fact that someone almost invariably had to pick up the marble he'd won and *hand* it to him."

The secret of Seymour's success in marble shooting does not lie as much in his technique as in his attitude, and his attitude is that taught by the *Bhagavad Gita:* "You have the right to work, but for the work's sake only.　You have no right to the fruits of work.　Desire for the fruits of work must never be your motive in working. . . . Perform every action with your heart fixed on the Supreme Lord.　Renounce attachment to the fruits" ("Zooey," p. 177).　That Seymour was following these teachings is suggested by the fact that he was not interested in winning marbles but in making perfect shots.　His aim was not some physical object but a spiritual principle, that of perfection.[29]　This is what is meant by "Aiming but no aiming."　And this principle also applies to Seymour's views of artistic creation, for as Zooey tells Franny: "An artist's only concern in to shoot for some kind of perfection."　Moreover in terms of Seymour's abstract religious philosophy, Perfection is one of the names of God.　Hence marble shooting or writing becomes an act of worship when it is done with detachment from tangible results and with only absolute perfection in mind.

Worship of God is indeed one of the two major purposes of art, according to the aesthetics of the later Glass stories. This view of art as worship comes out when Seymour tells Buddy: "Writing . . . [has] never been anything but your religion.　Never" ("Introduction," p. 160), and when Zooey tells Franny: ". . . the only religious thing you can do is *act.* Act for God, if you want to—be *God's* actress . . ." ("Zooey," p. 198).　And this religious view of art is also implicit in Buddy's description of Seymour in the "Introduction" when he keeps referring to him as an "artist-seer" and a "God-knower."

Seymour's identification of art and religion can be explained in terms of his eclectic religious philosophy.　The basis of this philosophy is Vedanta Hinduism and its core the teachings of the *Bhagavad Gita.*　But as Ananda Coomaraswamy says about the notion of art as worship: "This is not, of course, exclusively a Hindu view: it has been expounded by many others, such as the Neoplatonists, Hsieh Ho, Goethe, Blake, Schopenhauer and Schiller."[30] And we might add to this list Seymour's and Buddy's favorites, Kierkegaard, Kafka, and Van Gogh. Van Gogh, for example, labelled one of his later self-portraits "Worshipper of the Eternal Buddha";[31] Kafka referred to "writing as a form of prayer";[32] and Kierkegaard similarly said that writing to him was "a divine worship."[33]

The second major purpose of art, according to Seymour, is service to man. This is a prevalent notion in Western aesthetics ever since Plato demanded that art should be "pleasant but also useful to States and to human life." According to Plato, it was the function of the artist to interpret the will of God and thereby "educate and improve mankind."[34] But unlike the Platonic tradition, which is based on a dualistic conception of God and man and sees the artist as an intermediary between the two, Seymour's aesthetics are based on a monistic notion of God's immanence in man. He therefore saw the two aims of worship of God and service to man as essentially identical. Seymour felt that the artist must not only strive for perfection for its own sake, but that he must also communicate this sense of perfection to others. In Seymour's view, classical Chinese and Japanese poetry does that. Buddy explains why Seymour was so attracted to it when he says: "Chinese and Japanese classical verses are intelligible utterances that please or enlighten or enlarge the invited eavesdropper to within an inch of his life" ("Introduction," p. 118). Seymour believed that his own poems did not quite accomplish this because they were "too un-Western, too lotusy" and therefore "faintly affronting" to most readers. Buddy tells us that "after he'd finished a poem he thought of Miss Overman [a spinster librarian he knew]. He said he felt he owed Miss Overman a painstaking sustained search for a form of poetry that was in accord with his own peculiar standards and yet not wholly incompatible, even at first sight, with Miss Overman's tastes." He had not yet found this form of poetry, and this is why he refused to publish his poems. Buddy tried to convince Seymour to publish them anyway but was unable to. Buddy explains: "You can't argue with someone who believes, or just passionately suspects, that the poet's function is not to write what he must write but, rather, to write what he would write if his life depended on his taking responsibility for writing what he must in a style designed to shut out as few of his old librarians as possible" ("Introduction," pp. 125-126).

This idea may explain why we haven't heard from Buddy Glass since he published "Hapworth" in 1965. By taking Seymour's advice "Please follow your heart, win or lose," Buddy eventually found himself writing stories that are so difficult that they definitely shut out all of his old librarians. It might be argued that in writing "Zooey" and the "Introduction," Buddy followed his heart and won, because most readers respond favorably to these stories. But in writing "Hapworth," Buddy followed his heart and lost because only very few readers can enjoy and understand that story, and Miss Overman would probably only read it because it was written by an old acquaintance of hers. Thus it may well be that Buddy did not publish any more stories after "Hapworth" because he realized that his work no longer pleased and enlightened many readers.

Seymour's and Buddy's concern about not shutting out readers like Miss Overman underlines their belief that in order to serve God, the artist must serve man. This also becomes apparent when Seymour tells his brother Zooey to shine his shoes for the Fat Lady. As Zooey explains to Franny, shining one's shoes for the Fat Lady means performing for one's audience as though one were performing for God. And since God, according to the Glass philosophy, is inherent in man, Seymour and Buddy believed that the artist must strive for perfection for the sake of his audience, for the Fat Lady.

Thus the Glass series illustrates the idea that true art is religious, for its central theme is Seymour's, Buddy's, Franny's, and Zooey's quest for God. And since the four Glasses are all artists—Seymour a poet, Buddy a writer of fiction, and Franny and Zooey actors—they pursue their spiritual quests chiefly through their art. This is why the overall meaning of the Glass series is simultaneously aesthetic and religious. And the religious meaning of the series becomes clear when we read the stories in the chronological order of their events. Read that way, they form a composite novel about Seymour's life and his teachings, the subject of the second part of this book.

NOTES

[1] Most critics have either ignored the irregular form of the later Glass stories or have roundly condemned it. Among the few commentators who have offered useful insights are: Ihab Hassan, "Almost the Voice of Silence: The Later Novelettes of J. D. Salinger," *Contemporary Literature*, 4 (1963), 5-20; Bernice and Sanford Goldstein, " 'Seymour: An Introduction': Writing as Discovery," *Studies in Short Fiction*, 7 (1970), 243-256; and Gordon Slethaugh, "Form in Salinger's Later Fiction," *Canadian Review of American Studies*, 3 (1972), 50-59.

[2] The quotations from the Glass Stories in this chapter come from the Bantam paperback edition of *Raise High the Roof Beam, Carpenters* and *Seymour—An Introduction* (New York, 1965).

[3] Although the ideas of these artists may be dissimilar in many ways, their views concerning the nature of art show striking similarities. Like Plato and the Hindus, they all see art as originating in divine inspiration, and they all consider the artist a seer and prophet. Moreover, they all believe that spontaneous creation results in organic form. These ideas are expressed in Blake's comments on the *Discourses* of Sir Joshua Reynolds and on the poetry of Homer, Virgil, and Wordsworth; in Emerson's "The Poet"; in Thoreau's *A Week on the Concord and Merrimack Rivers*; in Whitman's "Song of Myself"; in Kierkegaard's *Fear and Trembling* and *The Point of View For My Work as an Author*; in Kafka's *Diaries*; and in Van Gogh's letters.

[4] Soren Kierkegaard, *The Point of View for My Work as an Author*, trans. Walter Lowrie (New York: Harper, 1962), pp. 6, 67.

[5] Plato, "Ion," in *The Dialogues of Plato*, trans. Benjamin Jowett (Chicago: Encyclopedia Britannica, 1952), p. 144.

[6] Ralph Waldo Emerson, "The Poet," in *The Selected Writings of Ralph Waldo Emerson*, ed. Brooks Atkinson (New York: Modern Library, 1950), p. 332.

[7] Ananda Coomaraswamy, *The Dance of Shiva* (New York: Noonday Press, 1957), p. 28.

[8] Ananda Coomaraswamy, "The Theory of Art in Asia," in *The Transformation of Nature in Art* (New York: Dover Publications, 1956), pp. 5-6, 174.

[9] Plato, "Ion," in *The Dialogues*, p. 144; Coomaraswamy, "The Theory of Art in Asia," p. 49.

[10] Mulk Raj Anand, *The Hindu View of Art* (Bombay: Asia Publishing House, 1957), p. 59.

[11] William Blake, "Annotations to Sir Joshua Reynold's *Discourses,*" and "Annotations to 'Poems' by William Wordsworth," in *The Complete Writings of William Blake,* ed. Geoffrey Keynes (London: Oxford University Press, 1966), pp. 459, 782.

[12] Buddy Glass compares true poets to birds "who seem of all created beings the nearest to pure spirit" ("Introduction," pp. 96-97; 113-114). This recalls Plato's statement that the true poet is "a light and winged thing," in the "Ion," *Dialogues*, p. 144.

[13] Plato, "Ion," in *The Dialogues*, p. 144.

[14] P. V. Kane, *History of Sanskrit Poetics* (Delhi: Motilal Banarsidass, 1971), p. 348.

[15] Plato, "Ion," in *The Dialogues*, p. 144.

[16] Anand, pp. 74-75.

[17] See the last chapter in Krishna Chaitanya, *Sanskrit Poetics* (Bombay: Asia Publishing House, 1971), esp. pp. 397-416.

[18] Coomaraswamy, "The Theory of Art in Asia," p. 49.

[19] Plato, "The Republic," Book X, and "Laws," Book II, in *The Dialogues*, pp. 432, 656.

[20] In "The Poet," Emerson writes: "For it is not metres, but a metre-making argument that makes a poem—a thought so passionate and alive that

like the spirit of a plant or an animal it has an architecture of its own. . . ." *Selected Writings*, p. 323.

[21] Coomaraswamy, "The Theory of Art in Asia," p. 19.

[22] Plato, "Phaedrus," in *The Dialogues*, p. 124.

[23] Coomaraswamy, "The Theory of Art in Asia," pp. 23-24.

[24] See Alan Watts, "Zen in the Arts," in *The Way of Zen* (New York: Random House, 1957), pp. 174-201.

[25] Henry David Thoreau, "A Week on the Concord and Merrimack Rivers," in *Walden and Other Writings*, ed. Brooks Atkinson (New York: Modern Library, 1950), p. 345.

[26] Vincent Van Gogh, Letter #181 in *The Complete Letters of Vincent Van Gogh* (Greenwich, Conn.: New York Graphic Society, 1959), I, 324.

[27] Frank Kafka, *Diaries*, ed. Max Brod (New York: Schocken Books, 1948), I, 278.

[28] Kafka, *Diaries*, II, 104.

[29] In "Raise High The Roof Beam, Carpenters," Seymour reports that a psychiatrist once told him that he has "a perfection complex of some kind," and Seymour asks, "Can I deny that?" ("Carpenters," p. 74).

[30] Coomaraswamy, *The Dance of Shiva*, p. 41.

[31] See H. R. Graetz, *The Symbolic Language of Vincent Van Gogh* (New York: McGraw-Hill, 1963), p. 286.

[32] Franz Kafka, *Dearest Father: Stories and Other Writings*, trans. Ernst Kaiser and Eithne Wilkins (New York: Schocken Books, 1954), p. 32.

[33] Kierkegaard, *The Point of View For My Work as an Author*, p. 68.

[34] Plato, "The Republic," Book X, in *The Dialogues*, pp. 430, 434.

PART II

THE STORY OF SEYMOUR

CHAPTER 9

Seymour—A Chronology

When we read the Glass stories in the order in which they were published, we get a clearer understanding of Buddy and his development as a writer than of Seymour and his quest for God. To understand the religious meaning of the Glass series better, we therefore need to re-read the stories in the chronological order of their events. Read this way, the series becomes a composite novel about the meaning of Seymour's life and death.

The central problem in the Glass series is Seymour's decision to kill himself. His suicide is difficult to understand because it seems incongruous with his quest for God and because the Glass stories present only a fragmentary account of his life. It is therefore not surprising that his death has been explained in a number of different ways. Most explanations agree, however, that Seymour's death is that of a saint or martyr. According to one typical view, he killed himself out of despair about the materialism and superficiality of his wife Muriel; according to another, he was spiritually so far advanced that he only needed to shed his body in order to pass into *nirvana*. [1]

In order to understand Seymour's suicide, it is necessary to get a clear picture of the events of his life and to develop a basic conception of the religious ideas that guided him in his quest for God. Before I analyze the Glass stories in terms of what they say about Seymour's life and teachings, I will therefore present a chronology of his life and an outline of his religious ideas.

CHRONOLOGY

1917   February, Seymour Glass is born, the first child of the vaudeville performers Les Glass and Bessie Gallagher ("Zooey," pp. 181-182).[2]

1919   "Buddy," Webb Gallagher (?) Glass, is born ("Hapworth," p. 32).

1920   "Boo Boo," Beatrice Glass, is born ("Introduction," p. 115).

1921   The twins, Walter F. and Waker Glass, are born ("Hapworth," p. 80).

1921-1923 The Glasses tour Australia ("Introduction," p. 145).

1922   Seymour, 5, is taken for a ride all over a Brisbane stage on Joe Jackson's nickel-plated trick bicycle ("Introduction," p. 148).

1923   Early spring, Seymour, 6, begins to frequent a branch of the New York Public Library and systematically reads everything he can find on God and religion ("Introduction," p. 125; "Hapworth," p. 88).

1923   May, Seymour begins to see the "magnificent light" mentioned in Vivekananda's *Raja Yoga* and tries to teach Bessie one of the breathing exercises from that manual ("Hapworth," pp. 58, 77, 92).

1924   January, Seymour, 6, begins to acquire limited clairvoyance; he mentions "an abominable glimpse [he] had at recess period right after Christmas" during which he was able to see that in a previous incarnation his and Buddy's relationship with Les was "fraught with discordancy" ("Hapworth," p. 50).

1924   July 2, Seymour 7, and Buddy 5, arrive at Camp

Simon Hapworth in Maine (This date is suggested by comments in "Hapworth" on pp. 34, 35, 40, 42, 44, 68, 86, 112).

1924   July 16, Seymour injures his leg and snaps the communication of pain between his leg and his brain so he can take eleven stitches without anesthesia ("Hapworth," p. 73).

1924   July 17, on his sixteenth day at camp (hence the title of the story), Seymour spends seven and a half hours writing an enormous letter to his parents. In his letter, he mentions over a dozen "glimpses" into previous "appearances" or into the future. He predicts, for example, that he will not live much beyond the age of thirty ("Hapworth," pp. 60-61).

1925   Spring, Les and Bessie Glass retire from vaudeville ("Introduction," p. 145).

1926   January, during their parents' retirement party, Seymour and Buddy meet a man who later signs them up for the radio program "It's a Wise Child" ("Hapworth," p. 61).

1926   Seymour, 9, outraces Buddy, 7, to the drugstore at Broadway and 113th Street ("Introduction," p. 211).

1927   Seymour, 10, advises Buddy, 8, to try "not aiming so much" when playing curb marbles ("Introduction," p. 202).

1927   Seymour and Buddy become regulars on the radio quiz show "It's a Wise Child" ("Carpenters," p. 7).

1927   Seymour helps Charlotte Mayhew get on "It's a Wise Child" ("Carpenters," p. 80).

1928   Seymour, 11, writes the John Keats poem ("Introduction," p. 124).

1928   Seymour discovers Chinese poetry and begins to imitate poets such as P'ang, Tang-li and Ko-huang ("Introduction," p. 122).

1929   On "It's a Wise Child," Seymour says that his favorite word in the Bible is "Watch!" ("Introduction," p. 152).

1929   Summer, Seymour, 12, injures Charlotte by hitting her in the face with a rock ("Carpenters," p. 89).

1929   Charlotte Mayhew leaves "It's a Wise Child" ("Carpenters," p. 80).

1929   The Glasses move to an apartment in the East Seventies ("Zooey," p. 74).

1930   "Zooey," Zachary Martin Glass, is born ("Introduction," p. 146).

1932   Seymour, 15, enters Columbia University as a freshman ("Carpenters," p. 26).

1932   Seymour settles a family dispute created by Waker's giving away his brand new Davega bicycle ("Introduction," p. 204).

1933   Seymour, 16, is "bounced off" the "It's a Wise Child" program because of his comment about President Lincoln. Buddy also leaves "It's a Wise Child" ("Carpenters," pp. 44, 77).

1935   "Franny," Frances Glass, is born ("Introduction," p. 146).[3]

1935   Seymour, 18, reads a Taoist tale to ten month old Franny ("Carpenters," p. 3).

1936   Seymour, 19, receives his Ph.D. from Columbia and starts teaching at a university in New York ("Introduction," p. 156).

1937   Zooey, 7, gets on "It's a Wise Child" ("Zooey," p. 153).

1937   Seymour, 20, tells Zooey to polish his shoes for the Fat Lady before going to the radio station ("Zooey," p. 200).

1938   Seymour, 21, is now "a nearly full professor of English" ("Introduction," p. 186).

1938   Summer, Seymour is able to trace, apparently during meditation, that he and Buddy and Zooey "have been brothers for no fewer than four incarnations, maybe more" ("Introduction," p. 158).

1939   Buddy, 20, urges Seymour, 22, to publish some of his poetry, but Seymour refuses ("Introduction," p. 124).

1940   Seymour, 23, and Buddy, 21, move to their own apartment on 79th Street, near Madison Avenue ("Zooey," p. 181; "Introduction," p. 160).

1940   Seymour and Buddy register for the draft ("Introduction," p. 160).

1940   Seymour writes a long comment about one of Buddy's stories and tells him not to be too clever but to trust his heart when writing short stories ("Introduction," p. 161).

1941   Seymour, 24, is drafted and begins basic training at Fort Monmouth, New Jersey ("Carpenters," pp. 9, 26).

1941   Seymour attempts to commit suicide by slashing his wrists ("Carpenters," p. 70).

1941   Winter, Seymour meets Muriel Fedder and comes into New York almost every night to be with her ("Carpenters," pp. 9, 72-73).

1941   Seymour now drinks quite a bit; he says, for instance, that he can't discuss an unpleasant topic, his injuring Charlotte Mayhew, "over just one drink" ("Carpenters," pp. 66-67, 74, 77).

1942   Seymour, 25, is transferred to a B-17 base in California ("Carpenters," p. 7).

1942   June 4, Seymour fails to show up for his own wedding but later that day "elopes" with Muriel ("Carpenters," pp. 9, 13, 86).

1944   Seymour, 27, is transferred to the "European Theater of Operations" and participates in the occupation of Germany ("Introduction," p. 113).

1945   Seymour, 28, has a nervous breakdown and is treated in an Army hospital ("Bananafish," p. 6).

1945-48   Seymour remains in psychiatric wards of Army hospitals for most of the last three years of his life ("Introduction," p. 114).

1948   Around March 12, Seymour returns to New York on a commercial flight ("Introduction," pp. 113, 134).

1948   Between March 12 and 15, Seymour spends a few days with Muriel's family. During that time he is rude to Muriel's grandmother; he rips up some of his in-laws' family photographs; he calls Muriel names; he wrecks his in-laws' car in an apparent suicide attempt; and he reads to Buddy a poem he wrote about a widower and a white cat ("Bananafish," pp. 5-6; "Introduction," p. 132).

1948   March 17, Wednesday morning, Seymour and Muriel arrive in Florida ("Bananafish," p. 5).

1948   March 19, Friday, early afternoon, Seymour writes a poem (in Japanese) on the desk blotter in his in his hotel room. It is about a little girl and her doll ("Zooey," p. 64; "Introduction," p. 134).

1948   March 19, Friday, around 3:30 p.m., Seymour 31, sits down on his hotel bed, looks at the sleeping Muriel, and fires a bullet through his right temple ("Bananafish," p. 18).[4]

   This chronology shows that it doesn't make much sense to blame Seymour's suicide on Muriel. He married her during the war when he was in the Army, and he could not have seen much of her between the time of his wedding in 1942 and the time he was released from an Army hospital in 1948. Although he had been married to her for six years when he died, he may not even have spent six weeks with her in all that time. Another reason why his marriage to Muriel cannot be considered the major cause of his suicide is that he made an unsuccessful attemp to kill himself in 1941, before he ever met Muriel. This first suicide attempt has so far been overlooked by Salinger scholarship and it suggests that the failure of Seymour's relationship with Muriel is not the cause of his suicide but the symptom of something else that went wrong.

   The facts of Seymour's life suggest that his suicide was the result of a gradual process of emotional and spiritual deterioration. This deterioration begins to be apparent when Seymour is only seven years old and threatens to kill himself because he has an argument with a counsellor at summer camp. We see more of it when Seymour is twelve and deliberately injures a girl by hitting her in the face with a rock, when he slashed his wrists in a suicide attempt at the age of twenty-four, and again a year later when he fails to show up for his own wedding because he feels too happy. The extent of his deterioration is illustrated by his decision to blow his brains out while sitting near his sleeping wife, a decision that seems motivated by his desire to make his death as upsetting to her as possible.

   Thus it becomes clear that Seymour is by no means a saint or martyr when he kills himself but a God-seeker whose quest failed. The central question in the Glass series is therefore not really why Seymour killed himself but what went wrong with his quest. In order to understand the reasons for Seymour's failure, we need to examine in detail what each of the six stories reveals about the way in which he pursued his quest for God. But before we can do that, we need to understand the nature of the religious ideas that guided Seymour in his quest.

NOTES

[1] See for instance, Ihab Hassan, *Radical Innocence* (Princeton: Princeton University Press, 1961), pp. 267-268; Charles Genthe, "Six, Sex, Sick: Seymour, Some Comments" *Twentieth Century Literature*, 10 (1965), 171; Gordon Slethaugh, "Seymour: A Clarification," *Renascence*, 23 (1972), 127-128; and Gary Lane, "Seymour's Suicide Again: A New Reading of J. D. Salinger's 'A Perfect Day for Bananafish'," *Studies in Short Fiction*, 10 (1973), 32-33.

[2] All quotations from the Glass stories come from the Bantam paperback editions of *Nine Stories, Raise High the Roof Beam, Carpenters, and Seymour—An Introduction; Franny and Zooey*; and from "Hapworth 16, 1924" as printed in the *New Yorker*, June 16, 1965, pp. 32-113.

[3] There is a discrepancy between the dates of Franny's birth as given by Buddy Glass in the "Introduction" and in "Carpenters." In the "Introduction," he clearly says that Franny was born in 1935 ("Introduction," p. 146), but according to information in "Carpenters," she was born in 1934. In that story, Buddy says that she was ten months old and that Seymour was seventeen when he read her the Taoist tale ("Carpenters," p. 4-5). Since Seymour turned eighteen in February of 1935, Franny couldn't have been ten months old when he read her the tale.

[4] Another discrepancy concerns the day of Seymour's suicide. According to Buddy's comment in his letter to Zooey, Seymour killed himself on March 18, 1948 ("Zooey," p. 62), but the story was published in the *New Yorker* more than a month earlier, on January 31, 1948. Also, March 18, 1948 was a Thursday, but according to the information in "A

Perfect Day for Bananafish," Seymour shot himself on a Friday, March 19, 1948, and not on Thursday, March 18, 1948, as Buddy writes in his letter to Zooey.

CHAPTER 10

The Eastern Roots of the Glass Philosophy

The first reference to Eastern philosophy in Salinger's fiction occurs in *The Catcher in the Rye* (1951).[1] Carl Luce, an old acquaintance of Holden Caulfield's, tells Holden that he finds "Eastern philosophy more satisfactory than Western." As it turns out, this preference stems from a sexual relationship that Luce has with a Chinese woman. He says that he likes Oriental girls because they "regard sex as both a physical and a spiritual experience" (*Catcher*, p. 146).[2] When Holden asks him to explain what he means, Luce exposes himself as a phony intellectual who is pre-occupied with sex. This characterization of Luce is not an attack on Eastern philosophy but on those who are attracted to it because they think it allows them to have their spiritual cake and eat it, too. And although Luce is clearly a negative character, his comment that he finds Eastern philosophy more satisfactory than Western foreshadows the direction in which Salinger's later fiction developed.

The first short story which mentions Eastern philosophy and pursues a religious theme is "DeDaumier-Smith's Blue Period" (1952). Its protagonist makes a comment that suggests where Salinger's interest in Eastern philosophy may have begun. Daumier-Smith calls himself "a student of Buddhism" and mentions that he has been "studying various religions as a hobby" ever since he "read volumes 36, 44, 45 of the *Harvard Classics*." These volumes contain selections from Christian, Hebrew, Buddhist, Hindu and Islamic scriptures. The story does not make it clear how much Smith actually knows about Eastern philosophy since it does not refer to any specific texts or concepts. But Smith quotes St. Francis of Assisi, and he is quite familiar with the New Testament, as we can see when he is able to recollect the name of Joseph of Arimathea, in whose garden Christ's tomb was located. And although Smith claims to be "an agnostic," he is looking to religion for guidance in his disjointed life. This is apparent when he is standing in front of an orthopedic appliance store and can't help thinking of himself as at best "a visitor in a garden of enamel urinals and bed-pans, with a sightless dummy-deity standing by in a marked-down rupture truss." Smith's epiphany is described as a "trans-cendent" experience and it occurs as he is once again looking into the display window of the orthopedic appliance store. He says that suddenly "the sun came up and sped toward the bridge of my nose at the rate of ninety-three million miles a second. Blinded and very frightened—I had to put my hand on the glass to keep my balance. The thing lasted no more than a few seconds." When he regains his sight, the display window is trans-formed into "a shimmering field of exquisite, twice-blessed, enamel flowers" ("DeDaumier-Smith," p. 164). Smith's trans-cendent experience has been described in Zen terms as a mom-ent of *satori*, or temporary illumination.[3] But since the context of the story is predominantly Christian, Smith's epiphany ought to be compared, instead, to the experience of St. Paul on the road to Damascus.[4] Like Paul, Smith experiences an over-whelming flash of light which blinds him and makes him lose his balance. But most importantly, this mystical experience is a turning point in his life, a moment of conversion. Just as such an experience turns Saul into Paul, so it turns the pre-tentious would-be artist Jean DeDaumier-Smith into the simple John Smith who is going to devote the summer to studying "that most interesting of all summer-active animals, the Ameri-can Girl in Shorts." Thus, despite a direct reference to Buddhism and indirect references to other Eastern religions, the story's ideological framework is essentially Christian.

Salinger's involvement with Eastern philosophy became more apparent the following year, in 1953, when he published "Teddy." In that story, Salinger provides an exposition of the key concepts of Vedanta Hinduism. The story consists largely of a conversation between the ten-year-old child prodigy Ted-dy McArdle and the education professor Bob Nicholson. In this conversation, Teddy explains to the skeptical Nicholson the nature of his mystical vision of life. We learn that Teddy had his first mystical experience when he was six years old. At that time he recognized that God is an impersonal force, inherent in all things: " 'I was six when I saw that everything was God and my hair stood up, and all that,' Teddy said. 'It was on a Sunday, I remember. My sister was only a very tiny child then, and she was drinking her milk, and all of a sudden I saw that *she* was God and the *milk* was God. I mean, all she was doing was pouring God into God, if you know what I mean'." When Nicholson asks him about the "Vedantic theory of reincarnation," Teddy protests that it is not a theory, since he is able to remember that in his previous incarnation he was living in India and "making very nice spiritual advancement." But in that previous incarnation he eventually "met a lady" and "sort of stopped meditating." And because he gave in to sensuality, this caused him to "get incarnated in an *American* body." He does not like living in America because "it's very hard to meditate and live a spiritual life in America. People think you're a freak if you try to" ("Teddy," p. 188). Despite his lapse in his previous life, Teddy is spiritually so far advanced that he can see into past incarnations and into the future. In one of his glimpses, he foresees his own death and predicts that he will die in an accident. He does nothing to avoid this accident because he knows that he will move to another incarnation when he dies, probably to a life in which he will be able to make better spiritual progress toward "stopping and staying with God" than in his present life.

Nine Stories, also published in 1953, illustrates both the mystical and the eclectic nature of Salinger's religious philosophy. The collection opens with a Zen Buddhist epigraph, the famous *koan*: "We know the sound of two hands clapping. But what is the sound of one hand clapping?" and it contains two stories, "DeDaumier-Smith" and "Teddy," that present a mystical view of life, one based on Christian and the other on Hindu ideas.

The stories that Salinger published up to 1957, "Franny" (1955), "Raise High the Roof Beam, Carpenters" (1955) and "Zooey" (1957), further widen the religious eclecticism of his religious philosophy. "Franny" points out similarities among Christian, Hindu, and Buddhist mysticism; "Carpenters" introduces Taosim as an additional Eastern system of thought; and "Zooey" contains quotes from Christian, Hindu, Taoist, and Buddhist sources.

Salinger's early critics singled out Zen Buddhism as the dominant religious philosophy in his work and all but ignored the many references to other Eastern religions and to Christianity.[5] In "Seymour—An Introduction" (1959), Salinger responded to these misinterpretations of his religious outlook by disclaiming Zen as a pervasive influence in his fiction and by stressing the essential eclecticism of the religious ideas in the Glass stories. He was clearly irritated that the critics had lumped him together with Beat writers such as Jack Kerouac (*The Dharma Bums,* 1959) who were popularizing and perverting Zen Buddhism. This is apparent when his narrator and alter ego, Buddy Glass, attacks the "Dharma Bums" and "Zen Killers" who do not understand his work (Buddy claims authorship of "Teddy," *The Catcher in the Rye,* and the Seymour stories). Because of these people, so Buddy says, "Zen is rapidly becoming a rather smutty, cultish word . . ." ("Introduction," pp. 97, 207). And although Buddy shows that he and Seymour are well acquainted with Zen Buddhist literature, he insists on his and Seymour's "extreme Zenlessness." To clarify his brother's and his own religious ideology, he writes:

> . . . Seymour's and my roots in Eastern philosophy—if I may
> hesitantly call them "roots"—were, are planted in the New and
> Old Testaments, Advaita Vedanta, and Classical Taoism . . . ("In-
> troduction," p. 208).

But despite Buddy's insistence on his and Seymour's Zenlessness, Zen references occur more frequently in the Glass stories than references to Taoism and almost as frequently as Christian and Vedanta ideas. Hence the role of Zen in the Glass stories needs to be clarified.

Zen Buddhism

Buddhism originated in India as a reaction against decadent Hinduism, and Zen is a later Chinese-Japanese development. The word Zen has its origin in the Sanskrit *dhyana,* which means meditation. *Dhyana* became *ch'ana* in Chinese and *zenna* in Japanese, and was ultimately abbreviated to Zen. The term is appropriate since it is through meditation and intuitive perception, and not through the study of scriptures of performance of rituals, that Zen wants its followers to reach enlightenment. This essential quality of Zen is illustrated in the story of its origin. Zen begins with Gautma Buddha's flower sermon. According to the legend, the Buddha was about to preach a sermon to a large congregation when one of his disciples handed him a boquet of lotus flowers.   Instead of giving the sermon, the Buddha simply lifted up the flowers for the congregations to see. As Dr. Suzuki explains the incident: "Not a word came out of his mouth. Nobody understood the meaning of this except the old venerable Mahakasyapa, who quietly smiled at the master, as if he fully comprehended the purport of this silent but eloquent teaching on the part of the Enlightened One. The latter perceiving this opened his gold-tongued mouth and proclaimed solemnly, 'I have the most precious treasure, spiritual and transcendental, which this moment I hand over to you, O venerable Mahakasyapa'!"[6] Thus Mahakasyapa became the founder and first patriarch of the Dhyana School of Buddhism. He was succeeded by twenty-seven patriarchs, and in the year 520 A.D., the twenty-eighth, Bhodidharma, transplanted this school of Buddhism from India to China. Zen flourished in China for over eight hundred years. In the twelfth century A.D. it spread to Japan where it still is a major religion. The most prolific and respected exponent of Zen Buddhism in the twentieth century was Dr. Daisetz Teitaro Suzuki to whom Salinger refers in several places in the Glass stories.

The essence of Zen Buddhism, according to a traditional definition, is that it consists of:

> A special transmission outside the Scriptures,
> Not depending upon the letter,
> But pointing directly to the Mind,
> And leading us to see into the Nature itself, thereby
> making us attain Buddhahood.[7]

To attain Buddhahood means to attain full enlightenment or *nirvana*, a state of absolute peace and non-being. This is the long-range goal of Zen Buddhism, a goal most individuals can reach only after passing through innumerable incarnations.

The exceptional individuals who reach Buddhahood or full enlightenment are called *arhats* and *bodhisattvas* (See "Zooey,"

p. 65). The difference between the two is that *arhats* are chiefly concerned with their own enlightenment while *bodhisattvas* choose to forego *nirvana* for themselves so they can be reborn and lead others to enlightenment. A number of interpretations of the Glass stories have treated Seymour as a *bodhisattva*,[8] but I believe this is an erroneous notion.

One of the most authoritative texts dealing with the concept of the *bodhisattva* is a text called the *Prajnaparamita*. In his discussion of this text, Dr. Suzuki explains that "the motive which prompts the Bodhisattva to realize within himself the supreme enlightenment is not for his own benefit but for all beings. . . . The Bodhisattva's desire is to benefit the world. . . . Thus the Bodhisattva is no retiring, negative soul always wishing to flee from the world for his own perfection and enlightenment; but he is a most aggressive rescuer of the world; he positively works upon it to yield the result he wishes from his active contact with it."[9] Therefore, a true *bodhisattva* "feels compassionate toward his fellow-beings who are not fully enlightened" and he "entertains no sense of superiority; he is not at all inclined to think slightingly of others; he maintains his attitude of reverence toward all beings as possible Buddhas. . . ."[10] The compassion and humility of the true *bodhisattva* stands in sharp contrast to the contempt for unspiritual people that Seymour expresses in "Hapworth" and "Bananafish." I believe therefore, that Seymour is neither a *bodhisattva* nor even an *arhat*, but merely a person who has dedicated his whole life to a singleminded pursuit of enlightenment and God-consciousness.

Even if Seymour is no Zen saint, Zen Buddhism can nevertheless help us understand his quest for God. For one of the things that Zen has in common with Hinduism, Taoism, and Christian mysticism is its concept of God as an impersonal essence inherent in all things, something that cannot be known by the mind, only by the heart. As Dr. Suzuki says: "Zen experience, one may say, is a kind of intuition which is the basis of mysticism."[11] Because the Godhead can only be perceived intuitively, Zen avoids giving names to it. Whenever the concept comes up, it is referred to with such abstract phrases as "mind of no-mind," "the ultimate reality," or "the unconscious conscious." Dr. Suzuki attempts to explain the Zen concept of God when he says: "The highest being is to be comprehended or intuited even prior to time. It is the Godhead who *is*, even before it became God and created the world."[12] This Godhead is beyond logic and words. Attempts to describe it usually result in paradoxes, as for instance when Dr. Suzuki says: "When the Godhead asserted himself he became God, which was the negation of himself. The Godhead ceased to be the Godhead in order to be himself. . . . The Godhead cannot help being a creator. But as soon as he creates, he is no more himself. There is the creator and the created."[13] Because this Godhead is beyond rationality, it can and must be intuited in the phenomena of everyday existence. Dr. Suzuki compares this notion of God to that of the Christian mystic Meister Eckart who also saw God as "the Wordless Godhead," and "the Nameless Nothing."[14] Moreover, there are also similarities between the Zen conception of God and that of the British romantics and of the American transcendentalists, as has been pointed out by R. H. Blyth, an orientalist whom Buddy Glass calls a "sublime" translator of Zen poetry ("Introduction," p. 118).[15]

While the long-range goal of Zen Buddhism is to lead its followers toward the attainment of Buddhahood, toward full illumination and liberation from the cycle of death and rebirth; the short-range goal is to lead them to *satori*, or temporary illumination. Referring to a statement by Dr. Suzuki, Buddy Glass explains that to achieve *satori* is "to be in a state of pure consciousness . . . to be with God before he said, Let there be light" ("Zooey," p. 65). In less religious and more philosophical terms, Dr. Suzuki defines *satori* as "an intuitive looking into the nature of things in contradistinction to the analytical or logical understanding of it. Practically, it means the unfolding of a new world hitherto unperceived in the confusion of a dualistically trained mind."[16] This unfolding occurs in the form of sudden flashes of insight. The more advanced a person is in his spiritual development, the more often will he be able to achieve such insights. And the rare person who achieves Buddhahood may be said to be living in a constant state of *satori*.

In order to help its followers to attain *satori*, and eventually Buddhahood, Zen Buddhism developed specific rules of conduct and methods of instruction. Salinger's Zooey, for instance mentions that the religious training he received from Seymour and Buddy as a child contained some Zen instruction. As a result, he claims, he still cannot sit down to a meal without first saying the Four Great Vows under his breath. And then he quotes them from Dr. Suzuki's *Manual of Zen Buddhism:* " 'However in*num*merable the beings are, I vow to save them; however inex*haust*ible the passions are, I vow to extinguish them; however immeasurable the Dharmas are, I vow to master them; however incomparable the Buddha-truth is, I vow to *attain* it' " ("Zooey," pp. 104-105).[17] While these vows are intended to help the Zen Buddhist keep his long-term goal, the attainment of Buddhahood, in view, the specific instructional methods of Zen Buddhism are directed toward the short-term goal, *satori*.

The most notable means of instruction in Zen is the *koan*, a puzzling statement or action. As Dr. Suzuki explains: "Zen teachers train their pupils in two ways—intellectual and conative or affective. To develop the speculative power of the pupil, a *ko-an* or 'judicial case,' which was discussed or constructed by the old masters, is given to him as the object of reflection. . . . When one case is settled, another and perhaps more complicated one will be given. . . ." In the conative or affective phase, the student "is required to sit quietly for a certain length of time, during which he will think of the *ko-an* given to him."[18] During *za-zen*, or meditation, the student is supposed to solve the *koan* not rationally but intuitively. Zen Buddhist literature contains some 1700 *koans*, and a Zen master will select from them a series of examples which will put the intuitive perception of his student to increasingly more difficult tests until the master is convinced that the student has advanced to the point where he is able to achieve *satori* on his own.[19] A famous Zen *koan* is the following one: "A monk asked Tozen (Tung-shan, 806-869): 'Who is Buddha?' And the master replied: 'Three pounds of flax'."[20] Another famous *koan* is the epigraph of Salinger's *Nine Stories*: "We know the sound of two hands clapping. But what is the sound of one hand clapping?"[21] And in "Raise High the Roof Beam, Carpenters," Salinger quotes yet another *koan*. It occurs in Seymour's diary when he mentions that the mother of his bride, Mrs. Fedder, asked him what he planned to do after the war was over. Did he intend to resume teaching or did he consider becoming a radio commentator? Seymour reports telling her that "if peace ever came again I would like to be a dead cat."[22] This comment troubled Mrs. Fedder a great deal until Seymour explained to his bride Muriel, several days later, that "in Zen Buddhism a master was once asked what was the most valuable thing in the world, and the master answered that a dead cat was, because no one could put a price on it."

In addition to verbal *koans*, Zen masters often also use non-verbal ones in the so-called "direct method" of Zen instruction. The most famous example is the incident in which Gautama Buddha silently held up a bouquet of flowers in lieu of giving a sermon. Such a *koan* also occurs at the end of "Carpenters." After Buddy has made his peace with Seymour's choice of Muriel as a marriage partner, he considers sending the couple as a wedding present a cigar end, left in an ashtray by a wedding guest: "Just the cigar, in a small, nice box. Possibly with a blank sheet of paper enclosed, by way of explanation."

The direct method of Zen instruction occasionally involves physical violence. When the monk Jō asked the master Rinzai what the fundamental principle of Buddhism was, so Dr. Suzuki reports, "Rinzai came down from his straw chair, and taking hold of the monk slapped him with the palm of his hand, and let him go. Jō stood still without knowing what to make of the whole procedure, when Jō all of a sudden awoke to the truth of Zen."[23] Zen masters will occasionally go to extremes to bring about their disciples' enlightenment. As Dr. Suzuki explains:

> When the thing is at stake, the masters do not hesitate to sacrifice anything. In the case of Nansen, a kitten was done away with; Kyozan broke a mirror in pieces; a woman follower of Zen burned up a whole house; and another woman threw her baby into a river. This latter was an extreme case and perhaps the only one of its kind ever recorded in the history of Zen. As to minor cases such as mentioned above, they are plentiful and considered almost matters of course with Zen masters.[24]

This use of violence as a means of Zen instruction may well explain one of the most puzzling incidents in Seymour's life, his deliberate injuring of Charlotte Mayhew. As Buddy reports the incident, Charlotte "sat down in the middle of our driveway one morning to pet Boo Boo's cat, and Seymour threw a stone at her. He was twelve. That's all there was to it. He threw it at her because she looked so beautiful sitting there in the middle of the driveway with Boo Boo's cat." The stone hit Charlotte in the face and she needed nine stitches. As Buddy says, "Charlotte never did understand why Seymour threw that stone at her." And it is not surprising that Charlotte did not understand it. After all, how can a none-too-bright twelve-year-old from Upper Manhattan be expected to understand a Zen *koan* that leaves her with a big cut in her face? If Seymour's injuring Charlotte is indeed to be understood as his attempt to bring her to a spiritual insight, then it shows that he lacked the understanding and compassion which characterize the true *bodhisattva*. Even if Seymour's hitting Charlotte with a stone was not intended as Zen instruction, other passages in the Glass stories leave no doubt about his fondness for *koans*.

What probably attracted Salinger to koans was that they are intended to bring about an intuitive perception of the divine in the facts and objects of everyday life. This perception is, so Buddy Glass explains in the "Introduction," what distinguishes not only Zen *koans* but also all good poetry and literature. Seymour's and Buddy's attraction to Zen was, I believe, chiefly a matter of this interest in the aesthetics rather than the philosophy of Zen. This comes out when Buddy comments on his own and Seymour's "extreme Zenlessness" but admits that they were both "profoundly attracted to classical Zen *literature* [my emphasis]" ("Introduction," p. 208).

Buddy explains what attracted him and Seymour to Zen literature when he says that, at their best, "Chinese and Japanese classical verses are intelligible utterances that please or enlighten or enlarge the invited eavesdropper to within an inch of his life" ("Introduction," p. 118). Buddy lists as Seymour's favorites the Chinese poets P'ang, Lao Ti-kao, Tang-li, and Ko-Huang, and the Japanese poets Saygio, Issa, Buson, and Shiki. Their poems do not illustrate any specific philosophical ideas but they reflect the same view of the divine in everyday life as the Zen *koans*. Moreover the purpose of these poems is, like that of the *koans,* to bring the reader to moments of spiritual insight.

   Another aesthetic idea that is illustrated by Zen poetry is the belief that poetry should be created spontaneously and that it should be shaped more by the poet's intuition than by established poetic conventions. In poems of this kind, so R. H. Blyth explains, "the words and ideas are undivided and indivisible" so that "you can't explain why it's poetry (but you do)."[25]   Buddy illustrates that point when he quotes a line from Kafka's diaries which was not meant to be a poem but which sounds very much like a haiku by one of the Japanese poets whom Seymour admired: "The young girl who only because she was walking arm in arm with her sweetheart looked quietly around" ("Introduction," p. 112).[26] Compare this to the poem that Seymour wrote a few hours before his death: "The little girl on the plane/ Who turned her doll's head around/ To look at me" ("Zooey," p. 64). Then compare Seymour's haiku to these Japanese poems: "I turned my back to see/ But the man I passed was veiled/ in mist already" (Shiki); "The young girl/ blew her nose/ in the evening glory" (Issa); "The old temple:/ a baking pan/ Thrown away among the parsley" (Buson). Poetry of this kind looks so very much like no-poetry that it appears extremely easy to write. It is not, of course; at least not for everybody. A true poet, however, can write such poems without effort, intuitively and spontaneously; for the essence of the best poetry is not something the poet struggles to create but something he can't help creating.   To explain this notion of the organic and spontaneous process of artistic creation, R. H. Blyth quotes Thoreau: "As naturally as the oak bears an acorn, the vine a gourd, a man bears a poem, spoken or done."[27]

   Since it was primarily aesthetic and not religious ideas that attracted Seymour and Buddy to Zen literature, it seems to me that the two most important Zen concepts in the Glass stories are the notion that composition should be intuitive and spontaneous, that it should parallel the "Aiming but no aiming" principle of Zen Archery, and that literature should "Enlighten or enlarge" the reader "to within an inch of his life." Like a *koan* it should bring him to a spiritual insight.   These ideas are more important in the Glass stories than the religious ideas of Zen Buddhism, some of which are very similar to ideas in other systems of Eastern philosophy. The notion of an impersonal, abstract God, for example, is essentially the same in Zen as in Taoism, Christian mysticism, and Vedanta Hinduism; the concept of *satori* also has parallels in the other three religious philosophies; and so does the concept of spiritual evolution toward union with the Ultimate Reality.

Thus the function of the Zen references in the Glass stories is not so much to clarify the Glass philosophy as to explain Seymour's and Buddy's notions of the nature and purpose of literature. Buddy's comments in the "Introduction" leave no doubt about it that his and Seymour's roots in Eastern philosophy are not planted in Zen Buddhism but in the New and Old Testaments, Advaita Vedanta, and classical Taoism. And as I will show, these three systems of religious philosophy indeed explain the meaning of Seymour's life and of his influence on his siblings better than does Zen Buddhism.

Classical Taoism

There are fewer references to Taoism in Salinger's fiction than to the other three systems of Eastern philosophy that Buddy Glass mentions in "Seymour—An Introduction." Nevertheless I believe that Taoism is more important in Salinger's work than Zen Buddhism.[28] Although it is much older than Zen Buddhism and has been a great influence on Zen, Taoism is even less dependent on tradition and institutions. In fact, it is completely free of dogma and ritual. This is probably why Seymour and Buddy prefer Taoism to Zen. Nevertheless, Taoism has much in common with Buddhism, and also with Hinduism and Christian mysticism. As Witter Bynner, Salinger's favorite translator of the *Tao Teh Ching*, points out, "neither the great Indian nor the great Jew would have found anything unacceptable in Laotzu's mystical uses . . . ."[29] And another one of the authorities on Eastern philosophy to whom Salinger defers, Dr. Suzuki, has also described important parallels between Taoism, Zen Buddhism, and the Christian mysticism of Meister Eckart.[30]

Classical Taoism has produced only a small body of writings. The founder of Taoism is the legendary Lao-tse (Lao-Tzu). A contemporary of Confucius, he was born around 605 B.C. But unlike the more popular Confucius, Lao-tse did not establish a school of his own, and·he did not write down any of his teachings until the very end of his life when he composed a slim volume of poems, the *Tao Teh Ching*. Chuang-tse (Chuang Tzu), whom Salinger quotes on two occasions, was a follower of Lao-tse and lived approximately two centuries later, around 370-319 B.C. According to Lionel Giles, a translator of Taoist texts, Chuang-tse "was to the Founder of Taoism what St. Paul was to the Founder of Christianity."[31] He wrote more than Lao-tse and modified in some ways the philosophy of his master. The third major figure of Taoism is Lieh-tse (Lieh-Tzu). Not a theoretician but a teller of tales, he is not as well known as Lao-tse and Chuang-tse.

The essence of Taoism lies in its conception of the Tao. The Tao is an abstraction similar to the "ultimate reality" of Zen Buddhism. Lionel Giles explains:

> Lao Tzu, interpreting the plain facts of Nature before his eyes, concludes that behind her manifold workings there exists an ultimate Reality which in its essence is unfathomable and unknowable, yet manifests itself in laws of unfailing regularity. To this Essential Principle, this Power underlying the sensible phenomena of Nature, he gives, tentatively and with hesitation, the name of Tao, "the Way". . . .[32]

This conception of the Godhead is expressed in the opening poem of the *Tao Teh Ching*. But in the following translation Witter Bynner has chosen to translate the Tao not as "the Way," but as "Existence":

> Existence [the Tao] is beyond the power of words
> To define:
> Terms may be used
> But are none of them absolute.
> In the beginning of heaven and earth there were no words,
> Words came out of the womb matter;
> And whether a man dispassionately
> Sees to the core of life
> Or passionately

Sees the surface,
The core and the surface
Are essentially the same,
Words making them seem different
Only to express appearance.
If name be needed, wonder names them both:
From wonder into wonder
Existence [the Tao] opens.[33]

Because the Tao is beyond words, we can only perceive it intuitively. To do this, we must, as Chuang-tse explains, enter "into subjective relation with all things" and "reject all distinctions of this and that."[34]

The ability to perceive the Tao, the essence of all things, is what identifies the wise man in Taoism. This is well illustrated in Lieh-tse's story about Chiu-fang Kao, which Salinger quotes in "Carpenters." In this tale, Kao is sent to select a horse for Duke Mu, and when he has finally found one, he tells the Duke that it is "a dun-colored mare." But when the horse arrives, it turns out to be "a coal-black stallion." The Duke wonders what Kao can possibly know about horses since he isn't even able to distinguish an animal's color and sex. But a friend who had recommended Kao, says: "What Kao keeps in view is the spiritual mechanism. In making sure of the essential, he forgets the homely details; intent on the inward qualities, he loses sight of the external." This assessment of Kao's wisdom is proven correct when the horse "turned out indeed to be a superlative animal."[35]

The highest form of wisdom, which ignores superficial distinctions and sees the essential identity of all things, appears, according to Taoism, very much like indiscrimination. As Lionel Giles says: "Contraries no longer stand in sharp antagonism, but are in some sense actually identical with each other, because there is an all-embracing Unity beyond them."[36] This idea is illustrated in "Carpenters" when Seymour comments in his diary on the advice a psychiatrist gave him concerning "the virtues of living the imperfect life, of accepting one's own and others' weaknesses." Seymour writes:

I'll champion indiscrimination till doomsday, on the gound that it leads to health and a kind of very real, enviable happiness. *Followed purely*, it's the way of the Tao, and undoubtedly the highest way. But for a discriminating man to achieve this, it would mean that he would have to dispossess himself of poetry, go *beyond* poetry. That is, he couldn't possibly learn or drive himself to *like* bad poetry in the abstract, let alone equate it with good poetry. He would have to drop poetry altogether ("Carpenters," p. 74).

Although Buddy explicitly compares Seymour to the Taoist sage Chiu-fang Kao and suggests that Seymour's perceptiveness equals that of Kao, Seymour himself, as we can see from his diary, does not believe he has reached that stage of spiritual development. He realizes that he is a "discriminating man" and that this makes him aware of his own and others' weaknesses. While he is in tune with the Tao, or what he elsewhere calls "the main current of poetry that flows through things, all things," he is unable to follow *purely* the way of the Tao. For as Lao-tse says, the way of the Tao requires giving up discrimination, going beyond discrimination and becoming a child again, a heavenly fool: "Leave off fine learning! End the nuisance/ Of saying yes to this and perhaps to that,/ Distinctions with how little difference!"[37] Taoism thus helps us understand one of the problems of Seymour's personality. He is an extremely erudite man and he finds that his erudition prevents him from achieving true spiritual health and real happiness.

The connection that Seymour makes in his diary between the concept of the Tao and poetry suggests that Taoism may also have been an influence on Salinger's notions of artistic creation. In the "Introduction," Buddy Glass reveals his belief that true poetry is not a matter of form but of perception. Hence, the true poet has to be primarily a "Seer," a man who sees the essence of all things. Such a man does not even have to write anything in order to be a true poet, because his life itself is poetry. As Buddy says about Seymour in "Carpenters": "If he never wrote a line of poetry, he could still flash what he had at you with the back of his ear if he wanted to." But Seymour *did* write poetry, because a true poet cannot help writing poetry, just as a flower cannot help producing blossoms. And this notion, too, has its parallel in Taoism, in the concept of *wu-wei*, which designates the attitude of the true artist. This idea is usually

translated as "inaction." But as Burton Watson, one of the foremost translators of Chuang-tse, explains, this term does not mean
"forced quietude, but a course of action that is not founded upon any purposeful motives of gain or striving."[38] This idea, that
the true artist should create his work in a detached fashion
without thinking of applause or reward, comes out in Chuang-
tse admonition: "Resolve your mental energy into abstraction,
your physical energy into inaction. Allow yourself to fall in
with the natural order of phenomena, without admitting the
element of self."[39]

Thus, the most important Taoist ideas in the Glass stories
are the conception of an abstract Godhead inherent in all things,
the emphasis on intuitive perception of this ultimate essence,
and the insistence on detachment from one's actions in order
to achieve harmony with the natural order of all things. These
are all ideas that Taoism shares with Christian mysticism and
with Vedanta Hinduism.

Christian Ideas

There are more direct references to Christian ideas in the
Glass stories than to Taoist and to Zen Buddhist ideas. But
this does not mean that the composite novel is predominantly
Christian in its religious philosophy. In fact, the Glasses interpret the Bible and the personality of Jesus Christ not in terms
of Christian theology but in terms of Eastern mysticism.[40]

Although Buddy Glass says that his and Seymour's roots
extend into both Testaments, all direct Bible quotations in
the Glass stories come from the New Testament. The Old
Testament is only represented by a few references to figures
such as Moses, Solomon, and David. The Glasses' favorite
gospel is that of St. Matthew; more than half of their Bible
quotations come from it.

The Glass story that contains more Bible quotations than
any other is "Zooey." When trying to help Franny overcome
her religious crisis, Zooey quotes I Thessalonians, v, 17: "Pray
without ceasing." Then he adds: "There's another, similar line
in Timothy—'I will therefore that men pray everywhere.' And

Christ, as a matter of fact, says, 'Men ought always to pray and not to faint'." The passages that Zooey quotes from memory are I Timothy, ii, 8, and Luke xviii,1. And when he tells Franny that she has a mistaken view of the personality of Christ, Zooey remembers that Franny was once reading the Bible and suddenly decided that she "didn't like Jesus any more." He reminds Franny, "you didn't approve of his going into the synagogue and throwing all the tables and idols all over the place." The passage is Matthew xxi, 12: "And Jesus went into the temple of God and cast out all of them that sold and bought in the temple, and overthrew the tables of the moneychangers, and the seats of them that sold doves." And then Zooey pinpoints the crux of Franny's disenchantment with Christ, a passage in Matthew vi, 26: " 'Behold the fowls of the air: for they sow not, neither do they reap, nor gather into barns: yet your heavenly Father feedeth them.' *That* was alright. That was lovely. That you approved of. *But*, when Jesus says in the same breath, 'Are ye not much better than they?'—*ah*, that's where little Franny gets off. That's where little Franny quits the Bible cold and goes straight to Buddha, who doesn't discriminate against all those nice fowls of the air." According to Zooey, Franny does not understand that Christ is the only man in the Bible who "*knew—* that we're carrying the Kingdom of Heaven around with us, *inside*, where we're all too goddam stupid and sentimental and unimaginative to look . . . ." Here Zooey is referring to the passage in Luke vii, 21, in which Christ says: ". . . behold the kingdom of God is within you." These Bible quotations show that both Franny and Zooey studied the New Testament intensively and that Christian ideas form a major component of the religious philosophy that Seymour and Buddy passed on to them.

In "Seymour—An Introduction" and in "Hapworth" there are three Bible quotations which illustrate Seymour's relationship to the New Testament. In the "Introduction," Buddy says about Seymour that "the thing he loved best in the Bible was the word WATCH!" As Buddy explains it, Seymour meant that "we're required only to keep looking" and we are bound to see the essence of all things unfolding to us "like a flower." The Bible passage to which Buddy alludes is Matthew xxiv, 42: "Watch therefore: for ye know not what hour the Lord doth come" (This idea is repeated in Matthew, xxv, 13). To Seymour, the coming of the Lord represents the hour of one's enlightenment, for he regards the Bible as part of Eastern philosophy.   Another Bible passage illustrating Seymour's unorthodox way of reading the New Testament is mentioned by Buddy in the "Introduction" when he reports a childhood incident.   Buddy reports that Seymour once woke him up from a sound sleep because "he wanted to tell me that he thought he finally knew why Christ said call no man Fool. (It was a problem that had been baffling him all week, because it sounded to him like a piece of advice, I believe, more typical of Emily Post than of someone busily about his Father's Business.) Christ had said it, Seymour thought I'd want to know, because there are no fools. Dopes, yes—fools, no." The passage apparently bothered Seymour because it contains a very strong injunction against calling anyone a fool. In Matthew v, 22, Christ says: ". . . whoever shall say, Thou fool, shall be in danger of hell fire." Seymour interprets His remark to mean that we should never be angry with anyone because no man is in his essence a fool. When he acts foolishly he is merely a "dope," that is, someone who is not able to see things the way they really are, someone who has not yet achieved the enlightenment we are all destined to achieve.

Seymour's unorthodox conception of Christ is best illustrated in "Hapworth." In that letter from summer camp, Seymour quotes Matthew v, 48, "Be ye therefore perfect, even as your Father which is in heaven is perfect." Seymour finds this admonition of "the incomparable Jesus Christ" thoroughly sensible and takes John Bunyan, the author of *Pilgrim's Progress*, to task for suggesting that what Christ really said was: "Be ye therefore flawless, even as your Father which is in heaven is flawless." What attracts Seymour to Jesus Christ is His wisdom in making the distinction between perfection and flawlessness. To Seymour, Christ's puzzling comment suggests that "even our magnificent God's perfection allows for a touching amount of maddening leeway, such as famines, untimely deaths, on the surface, of young children, lovely women and ladies, valiant, stubborn men, and countless other, quite shocking discrepancies . . . ."

Seymour's view of Christ comes out even more clearly in a passage in which he addresses himself directly to God:

> If You have the stomach to read this letter, dear God, be assured that I am meaning what I say! Do not sprinkle any dubious sugar on my destiny! . . . Do not ask me to join any élite organization of mortals that is not widely open to all and sundry! Recall quite fervently that I have felt equipped to love Your astonishing, noble Son, Jesus Christ, on the acceptable basis that you did not play favorties with Him or gave Him carte blanche throughout his appearance! Give me one, single inkling that You gave Him carte blanche and I will regretfully wipe His name from the slim list of those human beings I respect without countless reservations, despite His many and diverse miracles, which were perhaps necessary in the general circumstances but remain a dubious feature, in my forward opinion . . . ("Hapworth," pp. 105-106).

Seymour here not only insists on the essential humanity of Christ, but he also rejects the notion that Christ is part of a triune God. To Seymour, Christ is not the only son of God but merely an individual who has achieved God-consciousness, a true enlightened man, one name on his "list of human beings" whom he "respect[s] without countless reservations." This list also includes, as we learn in a letter from Buddy, several fully enlightened individuals from other religions. In this letter, Buddy explains to Zooey what he and Seymour had in mind when they began to give religious instruction to their younger siblings before they even entered grade school: ". . . we wanted you both to know who and what Jesus and Gautama and Lao-tse and Shankaracharya and Hui-neng and Sri Ramakrisha etc., were before you knew too much or anything about Homer or Shakespeare or even Blake or Whitman, let alone George Washington and his cherry tree or the definition of a peninsula or how to parse a sentence." As a result of this religious training, Zooey sees Christ in the same way as Seymour does. This is apparent when he explains to Franny that Christ is "only the most intelligent man in the Bible that's all! Who isn't he head and shoulders over. Who? Both Testaments are full of pundits, prophets, disciples, favorite *sons*, Solomons, Isaiahs, Davids, Pauls—but, my God, who besides Jesus really knew which end was up? *Nobody*." And to Zooey, as to Seymour, the essential thing about the historical Christ was that "Jesus realized there *is* no separation from God."

Aside from seeing Christ as one of the few truly enlightened men that ever lived, Seymour and his siblings also see Him
as a symbol of God's omnipresence both in man and in matter.
This is illustrated when Buddy reports in the "Introduction"
that Seymour was one of those "persons who look for God in
the queerest imaginable places—e.g., in radio announcers, in
newspapers, in taxicabs with crooked meters, literally everywhere." And then Buddy gives us an example: "My bother,
for the record, had a distracting habit, most of his adult life,
of investigating loaded ashtrays with his index finger, clearing
all the cigarette ends to the sides—smiling from ear to ear as he
did it—as if he expected to see Christ Himself cherubically curled
up in the middle, and he never looked disappointed." But the
most famous illustration of the Glasses' notion of the omnipresence of God is the famous story of the Fat Lady in "Zooey."
Zooey recalls that he once was on his way to the broadcast
studio to perform on the radio quiz show "It's A Wise Child,"
when Seymour stopped him at the door and told him to shine
his shoes. Zooey argued with him, but Seymour won the argument by telling him to shine his shoes for the Fat Lady. Franny
had once been given similar advice, and Zooey tells her: *"There
isn't anyone out there who isn't Seymour's Fat Lady. . . . don't
you know who the Fat Lady really is? . . .* Ah, buddy. Ah,
buddy. It's Christ Himself. Christ Himself, buddy."

As we can see, the Christian component of the Glass philosophy does not reflect the mainstream of Christian thought
but the mysticism of such sources as the writings of Meister
Eckart, *The Cloud of Unknowing, The Philokalia,* and *The
Way of a Pilgrim* (See "Franny," pp. 36-39). Like the writings
of the Christian mystics, the Glass stories stress the notions
that God is immanent in all things, that Christ is merely a fully
enlightened human being, and that the goal of man's striving
should be to become like Christ and to reach full enlightenment.
Although these ideas are supported with New Testament passages, they are not, in essence, Christian but oriental. The
theologian Kenneth Hamilton, therefore, comments that the
Glass stories use the Bible "largely to reflect light derived from
other sources."[41] And these sources are Eastern texts in general and Vedanta ones in particular. That the Glass stories do
indeed interpret the Bible in the light of Vedanta is illustrated
when Buddy Glass quotes the Hindu philosopher Vivekananda

in order to define what a good Christian is: "See Christ, then you are a Christian. All else is talk" ("Introduction," p. 109).[42]

Vedanta Hinduism

There are more direct and indirect references to Advaita Vedanta in the Glass stories than to any other religious philosophy, and these references are more helpful in explaining Seymour's motivation and the overall meaning of the composite novel than the Christian, Taoist, and Zen Buddhist ideas. I believe, therefore, that Hinduism forms the basis of Salinger's eclectic ideology. This notion is supported by biographical information. In a 1972 doctoral dissertation, Sumitra Paniker mentions a letter from Swami Nikhilananda, the founder of the Ramakrishna Vivekananda Center in New York. The letter reveals that Salinger studied Advaita Vedanta at the Center sometime in the early fifties and that he became a good friend of the Swami's.[43] In the course of my own studies with Nikhilananda's successor, Swami Adiswarananda, I learned that Salinger has remained associated with the Center to this day. He corresponds with the Swami and occasionally orders Vedanta texts; he attends lectures when he is in New York; and he has, in recent years, attended a summer seminar at the Center's retreat at Thousand Island Park.

Because Vedanta is the basis of the Glass philosophy, I will discuss its ideas at somewhat greater length than those of the other religious philosophies. I will illustrate the basic concepts of modern Advaita Vedanta with passages from the Glass stories and from the Vedanta texts they mention. All of the texts that I shall be quoting were available to Salinger in the library of the Ramakrishna-Vivekananda Center.[44]

Vedanta is a system of Hindu philosophy that is based on the oldest Sanskrit scriptures, the Vedas (ca. 1500 B.C.) and particularly on the Upanishads which cyrstallize the philosophical concepts of the Vedas.[45] Literally, Vedanta means "the end of the Vedas." This can be taken to refer to the fact that the Upanishads form the end portions of the Vedas, or to the fact that *veda* also means "knowledge" since the word comes from the Sanskrit verb *vid*, to know. Hence Vedanta can also mean "the ultimate knowledge." As this emphasis on scriptures and knowledge suggests, Vedanta is the most intellectual of the various branches of Hinduism.

Advaita, or non-dualistic Vedanta, is a system of thought whose first great expositor was Shankaracharya (ca. 700 A.D.). Shankara expresses the monism of Advaita Vedanta in these basic statements: "Brahman—the absolute existence, knowledge, and bliss—is real. The universe is not real. Brahman and Atman (man's inner self) are one."[4] [6] Salinger's teacher, Swami Nikhilananda, says about this ultimate reality: "Brahman becomes real to us to the extent that the universe, with its time, space, and causal principle, is realized as unreal. That is to say, Brahman becomes real to the extent that we can shake off from our minds the world of appearance."[4] [7] This world of appearance is called *maya*, but it is not different from *Brahman,* it is part of *Brahman*, a veil that *Brahman* wears. Thus, unlike the dualistic philosophy of Platonism, which sees essential differences between appearances and essences, Advaita Vedanta is non-dualistic because it considers appearances and essences as merely two aspects of the ultimate reality, *Brahman*.

The Vedanta ideas to which the Glass stories refer are those of the Ramakrishna-Vivekananda school. Sri Ramakrishna was a nineteenth-century Hindu saint (1836-1886) whom his followers consider a divine incarnation. Ramakrishna never wrote down any of his teachings, but his disciples recorded and systematized his wisdom. Conversations between the master and his disciples are collected in *The Gospel of Sri Ramakrishna* and in *Sri Ramakrishna: The Great Master*, and his philosophy is presented in systematic form in the works of his chief disciple Swami Vivekananda (1870-1902).[4] [8] The writings of successive generations of Ramakrishna's followers further clarify and extend the teachings of their master and his chief apostle.

The Ramakrishna-Vivekananda school of Advaita Vedanta differs from other schools of Hindu thought in that it is at once more eclectic and more esoteric. Its major authors accept Gautama Buddha and Jesus Christ as divine incarnations and happily quote from the scriptures of other religions to illustrate their own ideas. This eclecticism is strikingly illustrated in the following declaration by Vivekananda:

> I accept all the religions that were in the past and worship with them all; I worship God with every one of them, in whatever form they worship Him. I shall go to the mosque of the Mohammedan; I shall enter the Christian church and kneel before the Crucifix; I shall enter the Buddhist temple, where I shall take refuge in Buddha and his Law. I shall go into the forest and sit down in meditation with the Hindu, who is trying to see the Light which enlightens the hearts of everyone.[49]

Similarly, Ramakrishna studied under Mohammedan, Christian, and Buddhist preceptors. He immersed himself in each religion in turn, and he expressed great reverence for each one throughout his life. It is in this spirit that the Ramakrishna-Vivekananda Center in New York annually celebrates the birth of Buddha with an elaborate program and the birth of Christ with a Christmas service and the singing of traditional Western Christmas carols.

But despite its fondness for other religions, modern Vedanta is also more esoteric in its teachings than most other branches of Hinduism. Vedanta places great emphasis on knowledge as a path toward enlightenment, and it also advocates the practice of a system of very demanding meditation exercises derived from the Yoga school of Hinduism. These two paths toward God-consciousness are called *jnana yoga* and *raja yoga*. Since they are very important in modern Advaita Vedanta and in the Glass stories, I will discuss them in detail later on. Both are paths toward enlightenment that most other schools of Hinduism consider to be unsuitable for the average individual.

Although modern Vedanta is the most non-sectarian and the most intellectual branch of Hinduism, it offers a view of life that is firmly grounded in basic Hindu teachings. Six major concepts form the core of this philosophy. They are the traditional ideas of *Brahman;* of *mukti* and reincarnation; of the law of *karma;* of the four *asramas*; and of the three *yogas*. The only non-traditional part of the Vedanta view of life is a fourth path toward God, *raja yoga*, which the Ramakrishna-Vivekananda school added to the traditional three.

B r a h m a n

The notion of God that informs all of the Glass stories is the abstract and polymorphous one of *Brahman*. Seymour's God is unlike the personal God of orthodox Christianity or Judaism. His God is abstract and omnipresent, and Seymour looks for Him, as Buddy tells us, "in the queerest imaginable places—e.g., in radio announcers, in newspapers, in taxicabs with crooked meters, literally everywhere." As Seymour explains in "Hapworth," his "beloved shapeless God" is a "nameless hallmark, preferably without attributes." Seymour here refers to what Vedanta calls *Nirguna Brahman*, the Godhead without attributes. Swami Nikhilananda describes this concept in this way: "The Supreme Brahman cannot be identified by any characteristic sign or attribute . . . . It is a negation of all attributes and relations. It is beyond time, space and causality."[50] But Vedanta also recognizes a concrete form of this abstract divine principle, and Nikhilananda explains: "Nirguna Brahman is the basis of Saguna Brahman, or the Personal God. . . . Without compulsion from outside, Brahman imposes upon Itself, as it were, a limit and thus becomes manifest as God, soul, and world."[51] As God with attributes, *Saguna Brahman* takes on the form of the Hindu trinity Brahma, Vishnu, and Shiva (Creator, Preserver, and Destroyer), and of such divine incarnations as Krishna, Buddha, and Christ. Moreover, as *Atman, Brahman* dwells in man's soul, and as *maya, Brahman* appears as the phenomenal world, as the universe of appearances. This view of *Brahman*, as God with and without attributes, reconciles the anthropomorphic conception of God in the hymns of the Vedas with the more philosophical notion of God in the Upanishads. And it is this sophisticated conception of God as both *Nirguna* and *Saguna Brahman* which Seymour adopted at a very young age.

M u k t i *and Reincarnation*

The Hindus distinguish four goals after which individuals in different stages of spiritual advancement strive: *Kama* (pleasure); *artha* (wealth); *dharma* (righteousness); and *moksha* or *mukti* (oneness with God and liberation from the cycle of reincarnation). Nikhilananda describes the highest of these goals when he writes:

> The goal of spiritual life is *mukti*, or liberation—liberation from imperfection, bondage, separateness, misery, and death. It is the ultimate blessedness, the outcome of the realization of man's unity with the universal Consciousness . . . . The man who realizes the state of God-consciousness in this life is called a jivanmukta. . . . Realizing all souls in himself and himself in all souls, he loves all beings . . . .[52]

The attainment of this state of God-consciousness became young Seymour's goal shortly after he began his systematic studies in religious literature at a branch of the New York Public Library. In his letter from Camp Hapworth, the seven-year-old Seymour comments on his "consuming admiration for God" and mentions that he has exhausted all "books on God or merely religion" written by authors whose names begin with the letters A through H. This admiration for God never abated but became a life-long quest for *mukti*.

However, *mukti* cannot be reached in one lifetime. It requires spiritual progress through many incarnations. But as an individual approaches oneness with *Brahman* and liberation from the cycle of death and rebirth, so Vedanta teaches, he acquires extraordinary mental powers. This happens because *Brahman* is not only absolute existence and bliss, but also absolute knowledge.[53]

In his last few incarnations, Seymour had come closer to *mukti* than most people. This explains his superhuman intelligence and his supernatural ability to see into past incarnations and into the future. Buddy Glass refers to Seymour's advanced state of spiritual development when he says about him that "he was the only person I've ever habitually consorted with . . . who more frequently than not tallied with the classical conception, as I saw it, of a *mukta*, a ringding enlightened man, a God-knower." Buddy does not claim that Seymour *was* actually a *mukta*. He knew that Seymour did not reach oneness with *Brahman* and liberation from the cycle of reincarnation when he died because of the negative *karma* he had accumulated.

The Law of Karma

Vivekenanda defines *karma* in this way: "The word *karma* is derived from the Sanskrit *kri*, 'to do.' All action is karma. Technically this word also means the effects of actions. In connexion with metaphysics it sometimes means the effects of which our past actions were the causes."[54]   The law of *karma* is the spiritual equivalent of the physical law of cause and effect.   As Swami Abhedananda explains: "The law of causation or of *Karma* includes the law that the like produces the like, or that every action must be followed by a reaction of a similar nature . . . . Motives, desires, thoughts and other mental functions being subject to the same law, produce . . . results according to the nature of these mental activities."[55] But the effects of physical or mental actions extend beyond a single lifetime: "A man may reap the result of . . . his works either in this life or after death in another incarnation, just as now we are reaping the results of the works of our previous lives."[56]   Thus, "what we call rewards or punishments of God are nothing but the reactions of our own mental and physical actions.   The doctrine of *Karma* denies the arbitrary Ruler and teaches that God never rewards the virtuous nor punishes the wicked."   Instead, "the virtuous reward themselves and the sinners punish themselves by their own thoughts and deeds." Therefore, so Abhedananda warns us, it is necessary "for every one of us to be extremely cautious in performing the duties of daily life, so that we will not sow the seeds which bear unpleasant and disagreeable fruit and which will make us unhappy and miserable either in this life or hereafter."[57]

Seymour knew that the effects of the actions in his previous appearances and in his current incarnation would prevent him from reaching union with God at the end of his life.   In "Hapworth," the seven-year-old Seymour reveals that his last two incarnations were particularly "tough ones" because he was plagued by sensuality and instability.   Due to the law of *karma*, both problems persist in his present life.   This is why he calls his sensuality a special "karmic responsibility."   But he thinks that he will be able to overcome this obstacle by the end of the summer of 1924.   His instability presents a more serious problem.   He says about it: "I have left this troublesome instability uncorrected in my previous appearances . . . it will not be corrected by friendly, cheerful prayer. It can only be corrected by dogged effort on my part." An incident which illustrates this instability occurs when a counsellor at Camp Hapworth insults Buddy. Seymour gets extremely upset and later reports that he told the counsellor "that I would kill him or myself . . . if he spoke to this chap again in that manner . . . ." Despite his awareness of the problem, Seymour is unable to control it. He therefore says about his chances of correcting this instability in his present incarnation: "I do not honestly see thrilling results in the general picture." And in a letter written sixteen years later, he also comments on his "private and longstanding karma" and says: "It can't be nullified." Thus it appears that Seymour knew throughout his life that his *karma* would prevent him from reaching *mukti* at the end of his current appearance.

The Four Asramas

According to the traditional Hindu view, a God-seeker's life proceeds through four *asramas*, or stages of life, each with sharply different responsibilities. As Vivekenanda explains:

> The Hindu begins his life as a student [*brahmacharya* stage]; then he marries and becomes a householder [*garhasthya* stage]; in old age he retires [*vanaprasthya* stage]; and lastly he gives up the world and becomes a sannyasin [*sannyasa*, monk and teacher stage].[58]

The chief responsibilities of the student are to not injure any living thing, to be celibate, to honor his parents and teachers, and to study the scriptures. The responsibilities of the householder are to support his family and to contribute to the welfare of his community. In the defense of his family and community, the householder may even be required to take up arms and to kill or be killed. And while material values are to be ignored in other stages, Vivekananda stresses that "a householder who does not struggle to get wealth is immoral."[59] But the householder must not get attached to his wealth. He must remember that by serving his wife and children and his community, he is serving God. After his children have left home and he is too old to be of much practical use to his community, the householder will retire into the forest where his responsibility will be to continue the religious studies he began as a student. After years of study and meditation, he will enter the final stage, renounce the world altogether, and embrace the monastic life. Now his responsibility will be to serve as spiritual guide to others.

Seymour's diary in "Carpenters" shows that he saw his life in terms of the Hindu *asramas* and that he considered the step from the life of the student to that of the householder a profound change in the direction of his spiritual development. On the day before his wedding, he mentions that he has "been reading a miscellany of Vedanta all day" and says: "I feel as though I'm about to be born. Sacred, sacred day." And he ends the diary entry with the exclamation: "The joy of responsibility for the first time in my life." As these comments show, Seymour knew that in the householder stage he would have to pursue his quest for God along a different path than before, along the path of service.

The Four Yogas

Traditional Hinduism distinguishes three *yogas*, or paths of spiritual advancement, *bhakti yoga*, *karma yoga*, and *jnana yoga*. But the Ramakirshna-Vivekenanda school of Advaita Vedanta recognizes a fourth, *raja yoga*. The word *yoga* means literally "union with the soul of God." Swami Nikhilananda explains:

> . . . yoga is the goal of all religions and the basis of all religious practices. It implies much more than religion in its usual sense. Instead of laying down creeds and doctrines for acceptance by religious aspirants, it emphasizes the psychological approach to self-unfoldment. Thus yoga takes into consideration the different types of human minds—the active, the philosophical, the emotional, and the psychic—and expounds for them, respectively, the path of work (karma yoga), the path of knowledge (jnana yoga), the path of love and devotion (bhakti yoga), and the path of concentration and self-control (raja yoga).[60]

Each individual will pick his path or paths of spiritual advancement according to his inborn personal tendencies and also according to the stage of life he is in. In the student stage, he will priamrily follow *jnana yoga*, the path of study and knowledge; in the householder stage it will be chiefly *karma yoga*, the path of work and service; and in the remaining two stages it will be a combination of *jnana* and *raja yoga*, the paths of study and meditation.

Shankara, one of the founders of Advaita Vedanta, is of the opinion that the paths of work and study, *karma* and *jnana yoga*, are essentially incompatible and are intended for two different classes of God-seekers. [61]   This is disputed by some later authorities, but Ramakrishna agreed with Shankara and told his disciples: "It is not good for the householder to read Vedanta or the Yogavasishta [a major Vedanta text]. It is very harmful for them to read these books." [62]   Shankara and Ramakrishna take the position that the path of study is unsuitable for the householder because in this stage of life, man's major responsibility is to serve his family and community and not to pursue a self-directed path of spiritual advancement. Hence, when one marries and becomes a householder, one has to give up the path of study, *jnana yoga*, in favor of the path of work and service, *karma yoga*.

The "Introduction" and "Hapworth" show that Seymour Glass followed *jnana yoga*, the path of study and knowledge, for most of his life. Because of the mental and spiritual accomplishments he inherited from previous incarnations, his intellectual development was spectacular. By the age of seven, he had read most of the classics of world literature and begun to study Eastern philosophy; by the age of eighteen, he had received his Ph.D. degree; and by the age of twenty-three, he was almost a full professor of English and—in the opinion of his brother, Buddy—one of the three or four most important American poets.

When he was twenty-four, Seymour decided to give up *jnana-yoga*, the path of study, in favor of *karma yoga*, the path of service. At that time of his life, he saw himself as entering into the householder stage, and according to Hindu belief, a householder should pursue his quest for spiritual advancement by serving his family and his community. Seymour therefore decided to get married and to allow himself to be drafted into the military service.

Unlike his brother Waker, who spent the war years in a conscientious objector's camp in Maryland, Seymour saw service in the Army as service to the community and hence as service to God. While Waker's opposition to military service was apparently motivated by his Christian beliefs—Waker later became a Roman Catholic priest—Seymour's acceptance of it reflects the teachings of the *Bhagavad Gita*, a major Hindu scripture that advocates the *karma yoga* ideal. In the *Gita*, the Lord Krishna tells the warrior Arjuna that it is basically wrong to injure or kill any living thing; but for a warrior who fights in a righteous war, the killing of enemies is not a sin but a holy duty (*Bhagavad Gita*, II, pp. 31-33). Seymour was not only familiar with the *Gita*, he also accepted its teachings. This is suggested by the fact that he inscribed a key passage from the *Gita* at the head of many other quotations on the door of his and Buddy's room. The essence of that *Gita* passage is the idea that the most religious thing we can do is perform all our duties with our hearts "fixed upon the Supreme Lord."

Seymour's acceptance of the *karma yoga* ideal is also reflected in the reasons he gives in his diary for getting married. On the day before his wedding, Seymour mentions that he has been studying Vedanta all day; then he explains the Vedanta view of marriage as a means of serving God by serving one's partner: "Marriage partners are to serve each other. Elevate, help, teach, strengthen each other, but above all *serve*."

But *karma yoga* and *jnana yoga* are not the only paths of spiritual advancement that Seymour followed. During the student phase of his life, he also pursued *raja yoga*, a complicated system of meditation exercises that he began to practice when he was only six years old. Like *jnana yoga*, it is a self-directed path which Seymour had to give up when he married Muriel because it would have prevented him from performing to the best of his abilities his duties as a householder and *karma yogin*.

R a j a   Y o g a

Raja yoga, the "royal" or most difficult path of spiritual advancement, was developed out of the teachings of the Upanishads and codified by Patanjali in his *Yoga Sutra* (ca. 400 B.C.). Its aim is to speed up spiritual progress and to lead God-seekers to moments of illumination by making them concentrate all their physical, mental, and spiritual powers. The basis of *raja yoga* is the idea that *prana*, the primal energy of the universe, is inherent in man as the *kundalini* force, and that this force can be released into man's brain to bring about illumination with perfect knowledge. One of the best translations of Pantanjali's *Yoga Sutra*, and one of the best introductions for Western readers, is Vivekananda's *Raja Yoga* which Seymour mentions in his letter from Camp Hapworth.

The practice of *raja yoga* requires acceptance of a metaphysical conception of human anatomy. According to Patanjali, man has a "gross" and a "subtle" body. The core of the subtle body is the *sushumna*, the spiritual equivalent of the spine. The *sushumna* has located on it seven "subtle centers" or *chakras* (Explained in the story "Zooey," p. 113). To achieve illumination, the person who practices *raja yoga* must liberate the *kundalini* force which is stored in the lowest *chakra*, at the bottom of the spine, and make it travel through the five intermediary *chakras* until it reaches the seventh, the "thousand-petalled lotus of the brain." Vivekananda explains:

> According to the yogis there are two nerve currents in the spinal column called the Pingala and the Ida, and a hollow canal called the Sushumna running through the spinal cord. At the lower end of the canal is what the yogis called the "lotus of the Kundalini." They describe it as triangular in form. In it, in the symbolical language of the yogis, there is coiled up a power called the Kundalini. When the Kundalini awakes, it tries to force a passage through this hollow canal, and as it rises step by step, as it were, layer after layer of the mind opens up and many different visions and wonderful powers come to the yogi. When it reaches the brain, the yogi becomes perfectly detached from the body and mind; the soul realizes its freedom.[63]

As described by Vivekananda, the practice of *raja yoga*

involves eight stages or disciplines. The two preparatory ones alone are too demanding for all but the most determined God-seekers. The first of these is called *yama* and requires non-injury to any living thing, complete truthfulness, non-covetousness, absolute chastity, and non-acceptance of gifts. The second discipline is called *ni-yama* and requires austerity, study, contentment, cleanliness, and constant worship of God. Only when one fulfills the requirement of *yama* and *ni-yama* can one go on to the actual practice of *raja yoga*.

The physical part of *raja yoga* consists of *asana*, posture exercises, and *pranayama*, breath control. Upright posture will permit the *kundalini* force to travel freely along the *sushumna* and it will facilitate free breathing. *Pranayama*, the breathing exercises, are based on the notion that by controlling our breath we can control our vital force. The following is the basic breathing exercise that Vivekananda recommends:

> Slowly fill the lungs with breath through the left nostril, and at the same time concentrate the mind on the Ida, the left nerve current. You are, as it were, sending the nerve current down the spinal column and striking violently at the last plexus, the basic lotus, which is triangular in form, the seat of the Kundalini. Then hold the current there for some time. Next imagine that you are slowly drawing that nerve current, with the breath, through the other side, the Pingala; then slowly exhale it through the right nostril. This you will find a little difficult. The easiest way is to stop the right nostril with the thumb and then slowly draw in the breath through the left; then close both nostrils with thumb and forefinger, and imagine that you are sending that current down and striking the base of the Sushumna; then take the thumb off and let the breath out through the right nostril. Next inhale slowly through that nostril, keeping the other closed with the forefinger; then close both as before . . . begin with four seconds and slowly increase. Draw in for four seconds, hold in for sixteen seconds, then exhale in eight seconds. This makes one pranayama.[64]

The remaining four stages of *raja yoga* all concern progressively intensive meditation and must be combined with the breathing exercises.

The first two stages of meditation are preparatory ones for the more difficult last two. In the first stage, *prathayahara*, or unrestrained meditation, one lets the mind run freely. Then, in the next stage, *dharana*, one controls the mind by fixing it on a physical object or spot. Once the mind is steady, one can go on to the next higher stage of meditation, *dhyana*. In *dhyana*, the mind is concentrated on an abstraction, usually on a *mantra*, a holy word or prayer. The most famous *mantra*, and the one that Vivekananda recommends, is the Gayatri Prayer (See "Hapworth," p. 90) from the Rig *Veda*: "We meditate on the glory of that Being who has produced this universe; may He enlighten our minds." [65] This *mantra*, preceded and followed by the holy word "Om," must be repeated incessantly during meditation, three times during each *pranayama*.

When the basic conditions of *yama* and *ni-yama* are met; when the proper upright posture is maintained; when the breathing exercises are executed perfectly; and when the mind is steady in the repetition of the *mantra*, then one can reach the highest stage of *raja yoga*, the trance-like state of *samadhi*. And it is during *samadhi* that the *raja yogin* achieves temporary illumination and oneness with God.

One of the side effects of the practice of *raja yoga* is that the person who practices it experiences visions and acquires extraordinary powers. Those who practice hard will get many signs of their progress. For example, they may see "little specks of light floating and becoming bigger and bigger." And Vivekananda tells us, "when these things appear, know that you are progressing fast." [66] Eventually, when one achieves *samadhi*, one will experience "the full blaze of illumination" and one's mind will be bathed in "effulgent light." [67] The mind will then be capable of unlimited supersensory knowledge. "Then the whole of nature will begin to change," so Vivekananda says, "and the door of knowledge will be open. No more will you need to go to books for knowledge; your mind will be your book, containing infinite knowledge." [68] This knowledge can take the form of the ability to read other people's thoughts or to have "glimpses" of "something happening at a long distance.[69] The advanced *raja yogin* who meditates on his *karma* is able to discern events in previous incarnations, and he can also see into the future and see "when his body will fall. He knows when he will die—at what hour, even at what minute."[70] Vivekananda stresses however that the *raja yogin* must "reject these miraculous powers" in order to advance spiritually, for the aim of *raja yoga* is not the acquisition of such powers but God-consciousness.

Raja yoga is called the "royal path" because it is more difficult than the other three. It is based on the idea that "that which naturally takes a long time to accomplish can be shortened by the intensity of the action . . . ."[71] For while only a very advanced person who travels the path of devotion, service, or knowledge, can hope to achieve God-consciousness in less than a lifetime, a determined *raja yogin* can, in Vivekananda's opinion, achieve *samadhi* within six months. This, however, requires intense application and does not allow for normal interaction with others.

Raja yoga is therefore a path that is unsuitable for most people and should only be pursued by *sannyasins* who have given up the world. Average individuals who expect to lead normal lives had better pursue one of the other three paths, *bhakti, karma,* or *jnana yoga.* For if these paths are followed earnestly, the individual will eventually reach the same goal as the *raja yogin.* Vivekananda illustrates this point with a story from the *Mahabharata,* India's great epic:

> A young sannyasin went to the forest. There he meditated, worshipped, and practiced yoga for a long time. After much hard work and practice, he was one day sitting under a tree, when some dry leaves fell upon his head. He looked up and saw a crow and a crane fighting on the top of the tree, which made him very angry. He said: "What! How dare you throw these dry leaves upon my head?" As with these words he angrily looked at them, a flash of fire went out—such was the yogi's power—and burnt the birds to ashes. He was very glad, almost overjoyed, at this development of power: he could burn the crow and the crane by a look! After a time he had to go to the town to beg his bread. He stood at a door and called out: "Mother, give me food." A voice came from inside the house: "Wait a little, my son." The young man thought: "You wretched woman, how dare you make me wait? You do not yet know my power." While he was thinking thus, the voice said again: "Boy, don't be

thinking too much of yourself. Here is neither crow nor crane."
He was astonished. Still he had to wait. At last the woman came,
and he humbly said to her: "Mother, how did you know that?"
She said: "My boy, I do not know your yoga or your other practices. I am a simple, ordinary woman. I made you wait because
my husband is ill and I was nursing him. All my life I have strug-
gled to do my duty. When I was unmarried, I did my duty to my
parents; now that I am married, I do my duty to my husband.
That is all the yoga I practice. But by doing my duty I have become illuminated; thus I could read your thoughts and know what
you had done in the forest.[72]

This story illustrates the point that each of the four *yogas*
leads to the same goal, and that *raja yoga*, the path of meditation, is ultimately not superior to *karma yoga*, the path of
service.

Seymour Glass discovered Vivekananda's *raja yoga* manual as a six-year-old when he began his studies in religious philosophy. A year later, in his letter from Camp Hapworth, Seymour
calls Vivekananda "one of the giants of this century" and mentions that he was "fully acquainted" with "the lights" that
he had begun to see as a result of his practice of *raja yoga* ("Hapworth," p. 92). In this letter, Seymour also reviews a breathing
exercise from Vivekananda's book which he had tried to teach
his mother the previous year. Vivekananda says about this
breathing exercise that "for those who practice it once or twice
a day . . . calmness of body and mind will ensue."[73] Seymour
apparently recommended it to the notoriously nervous Bessie
because he hoped it would have a calming effect on her. But
Seymour himself was interested in more than "calmness of
body and mind." He practiced *raja yoga* because he wanted
to achieve God-consciousness as quickly as possible.

"Hapworth" and the "Introduction" reveal that Seymour
practiced *raja yoga* for most of his life and that he attained some
of the special powers that Vivekananda describes. As early as
May of 1923, when he was only six years old, Seymour was able
to achieve the state of *samadhi* and experienced illumination
of his mind with "magnificent light." A few months later,
he had the first of many "glimpses" into previous incarnations
and into the future. However, at this stage of life, his glimp-

ses were still somewhat indistinct and unreliable. For instance, he was not able to predict with any accuracy the time of his death. All he could say is that he would live "a generous matter of thirty (30) years or more," and he incorrectly predicted that Buddy would be present when he died. However, with continued practice of *raja yoga*, Seymour was able to extend the length of his periods of illumination and also the scope of his glimpses. And in 1940, he wrote to Buddy: "That time two summers ago when I was out so long, I was able to trace that you and Z. [Zooey] and I have been brothers for no fewer than four incarnations, maybe more."

As this brief exposition of Advaita Vedanta shows, Hindu ideas explain much about Seymour that is otherwise difficult to understand. They explain Seymour's superhuman erudition as a result of his advanced spiritual state and of his ability to draw on knowledge acquired in previous incarnations, and they explain his ability to see into past incarnations and into the future as a result of his practice of *raja yoga* meditation. Vedanta ideas also clarify the nature of Seymour's life long quest. These ideas explain that he saw *mukti*, full enlightenment and union with God, as the goal of his life, and they help us understand the paths of spiritual advancement he chose.

But most importantly, Vedanta ideas also shed light on the two central questions in the Glass novel: Why Seymour's quest for God failed and why his siblings consider him a near-saint despite his suicide. But in order to answer these questions, we need to examine in detail the texts of the individual stories and the role that Vedanta ideas play in each one of them.

NOTES

[1] In a biographical essay entitled "Sonny: An Introduction," John Skow asserts that Salinger "eagerly studied Zen" as early as 1946 and "gave reading lists on the subject to his dates." *Time*, September 15, 1961,

pp. 84-90.

If that were true, then there would surely be some references to Zen or Eastern philosophy in the stories he wrote at that time. However, there are no such references in any of the twenty-seven stories he published before 1951.

[2] The quotations from Salinger's work that appear in this chapter come from the Bantam paperback editions of *The Catcher in the Rye* (New York, 1964); *Nine Stories* (New York, 1964); *Raise High the Roof Beam, Carpenters and Seymour—An Introduction* (New York, 1965); and *Franny and Zooey* (New York, 1964); and from "Hapworth 16, 1924," as printed in the *New Yorker,* June 19, 1965, pp. 32-113.

[3] See John Russell, "Salinger: from Daumier to Smith," *Contemporary Literature,* 4 (Winter, 1963), 70-87.

[4] See Acts, ix, pp. 3-4.

[5] See Donald Barr, "Saints, Pilgrims, and Artists," *Commonweal,* 67 (October, 1957), 90; William Wiegand, "J. D. Salinger: Seventy-Eight Bananas," *Chicago Review,* 11 (Winter, 1958), 16-19; and Frederick Gwynn and Joseph Blotner, "Zen Buddhism and the Glass Menagerie," in *The Fiction of J. D. Salinger* (Pittsburgh: University of Pittsburgh Press, 1958), pp. 42-45.

[6] Daisetz Teitaro Suzuki, "History of Zen Buddhism from Bodhidharma to Huineng (Yeno)," in *Essays in Zen Buddhism, First Series* (London: Rider, 1949), p. 167.

[7] D. T. Suzuki, "Zen Buddhism," in *Studies in Zen* (New York: Philosophical Library, 1955), p. 48.

[8] Donald Barr (see above) was the first critic to label Seymour a *bodhisattva.* This notion has also been advanced by Sam Baskett in "The Splendid/Squalid World of J. D. Salinger," *Contemporary Literature,* 4 (Winter, 1963), 56; by John Russell in "Salinger's Feat," *Modern Fiction Studies,* 12 (1966), 310; by Anthony Quagliano, in "Hapworth 16, 1924: A Problem in Hagiography," *University of Dayton Review,* 8 (1971), 37; and by Bernice and Sanford Goldstein in "Some Zen References in Salinger," *Literature East and West,* 15 (1971), 87.

[9]D. T. Suzuki, "The Philosophy and Religion of the *Prajnaparamita*," in *Essays in Zen Buddhism, Second Series* (London: Rider, 1950), p. 277.

[10]Suzuki, "Prajnaparamita," p. 278.

[11]D. T. Suzuki, "An Interpretation of Zen Experience," in *Studies in Zen*, p. 82.

[12]D. T. Suzuki, "The Role of Nature in Zen Buddhism," in *Studies in Zen*, pp. 192-193.

[13]D. T. Suzuki, "Mondo," in *Studies in Zen*, pp. 170-171.

[14]Suzuki, "An Interpretation of Zen Experience," p. 75.

[15]R. H. Blyth is the author of *Zen and Zen Classics*, 5 vols. (Tokyo: Hokuseido Press, 1962).

[16]D. T. Suzuki, "On Satori—The Revelation of a New Truth in Zen Buddhism," in *Essays in Zen Buddhism, First Series*, p. 230.

[17]Quoted from D. T. Suzuki, *Manual of Zen Buddhism* (London: Rider, 1950), p. 14.

[18]D. T. Suzuki, "The Zen Sect of Buddhism," in *Studies in Zen*, p. 36.

[19]D. T. Suzuki, "Practical Methods of Zen Instruction," in *Essays in Zen Buddhism, First Series*, pp. 257-313.

[20]Suzuki, "The Zen Sect of Buddhism," p. 27.

[21]Salinger probably quoted this *koan* from Nyogen Senzaki and Paul Reps, *101 Zen Stories* (London and Philadelphia: Rider, 1939), rpt. in Paul Reps, *Zen Flesh, Zen Bones* (Garden City: Doubleday, 1961), pp. 24-26.

[22]Also from *101 Zen Stories*; in Reps, p. 61.

[23]Suzuki, "Practical Methods of Zen Instruction," p. 306.

[24] Suzuki, "Practical Methods of Zen Instruction," pp. 307-308.

[25] R. H. Blyth, *Zen and Zen Classics*, V, 81.

[26] Franz Kafka, *The Diaries,* ed. Max Brod (New York: Schocken Books, 1948), I, 140.

[27] R. H. Blyth, *Zen and Zen Classics*, V, 65.

[28] The only detailed study of Taoist ideas in any of Salinger's stories that I have come across so far is an analysis of "Raise High the Roof Beam, Carpenters" entitled "Seymour's Way" which Dennis O'Connor, Georgetown University, presented at the Salinger Session of the 1977 MLA Convention in Chicago. A revised version of this excellent essay is scheduled for publication in the *Southern Review* in 1983.

[29] Witter Bynner, "Laotzu," in *The Way of Life According to Laotzu* (New York: Capricorn Books, 1944), p. 21.

[30] D. T. Suzuki, "Meister Eckart and Buddhism," in *Mysticism: Christian and Buddhist* (London: Allen & Unwim, 1957), pp. 3-35.

[31] Lionel Giles, "Introduction" to *Musings of a Chinese Mystic: Selections from the Philosophy of Chuang Tzu* (New York: Dutton, 1909), p. 14.

[32] Lionel Giles, "Introduction" to *Taoist Teachings: Translated from the Book of Lieh-Tzu* (London: Murray, 1947), p. 10.

[33] Bynner, p. 25

[34] Giles, *Musings of a Chinese Mystic*, p. 18.

[35] Giles, *Taoist Teachings*, pp. 105-107.

[36] Giles, *Musings of a Chinese Mystic*, p. 18.

[37] Bynner, pp. 36-37.

[38] Burton Watson, "Introduction" to *The Complete Works of Chuang Tzu* (New York: Columbia University Press, 1968), p. 6.

[39] Giles, *Musings of a Chinese Mystic*, p. 19.

[40] Kenneth Hamilton has published a number of essays and a mono-graph on the Christian ideas in Salinger's work. See for example, "One Way to Use the Bible: The Example of J. D. Salinger," *Christian Scholar*, 47 (Fall, 1964), 243-251 and *J. D. Salinger: A Critical Essay* (Grand Rapids: Eerdmans, 1967). He observes that "Buddy Glass classifies the Bible as a sub-type of Eastern philosophy . . . and assumes that the Bible is one source, among others, of 'mystical' wisdom." Hamilton concludes, "When such a view is adopted, it follows that much of biblical teaching must be excluded" (*J. D. Salinger*, pp. 40-41). Another author who recog-nized that the Christian ideas in Salinger's fiction have little to do with orthodox Christianity is Robert Detweiler in *Four Spiritual Crises in Mid-Century American Fiction* (Gainsville: University of Florida Press, 1963), pp. 36-53.

[41] Hamilton, "One Way to Use the Bible," p. 251.

[42] Swami Vivekananda, *Inspired Talks* (New York: Ramakrishna-Vivekananda Center, 1958), p. 197. This miscellany also contains an essay entitled "Christ, the Messenger" which reveals an attitude toward Christ that is identical to that of Seymour, Buddy, and Zooey.

[43] Sumitra Paniker, "The Influence of Eastern Thought on 'Teddy' and the Seymour Glass Stories of J. D. Salinger," Unpublished Disserta-tion, University of Texas at Austin, 1971, p. 2.

[44] See the section on "Salinger's Sources" in the bibliography at the end of this book.

[45] The four Vedas are the *Rig Veda*, the *Sama Veda*, the *Yajur Ve-da*, and the *Atharva Veda*. Each one of them is several times the length of the Old and New Testaments combined, and each consists of four sec-tions. The first three sections of each Veda are the *Sambitas*, *Brahmanas*, and *Aranyakas*, and they contain hymns, religious ceremonies, and rules of conduct. The fourth section of each Veda consists of the *Upanishads* and contains the religious philosophy underlying the other sections.

[46] Swami Prabhavananda and Christopher Isherwood, trans., *Shan-kara's Crest-Jewel of Discrimination (Viveka Chudamani)* (Hollywood: Vedanta Press, 1947 [rpt. New York: New American Library, 1970]), p. 9.

[47] Swami Nikhilananda, trans., *The Upanishads* (New York: Harper

Brothers, 1949), I, 53.

[48]Swami Vivekananda, *The Complete Works* (Calcutta: Advaita Ashram, 1958 [first edition 1922]). The core of Vivekananda's teachings is contained in four small volumes, all published by the Ramakrishna-Vivekananda Center in New York: *Karma Yoga and Bhakti Yoga* (1955); *Jnana Yoga* (1955); *Raja Yoga* (1955); and *Inspired Talks* (1958).

[49]Vivekananda, *Jnana Yoga*, pp. 307-308.

[50]Nikhilananda, *Upanishads*, I, 33, 48.

[51]Nikhilananda, *Upanishads*, I, 49.

[52]Swami Nikhilananda, *The Essence of Hinduism* (New York: Ramakrishna-Vivekananda Center, 1946), pp. 70-72.

[53]Unlike the Buddhist concept of *nirvana* which describes a negative state, a state of absolute non-being, the Hindu concept of *mukti* or *moksha* refers to a positive state, a state of absolute being (*Sat*), absolute knowledge or consciousness (*Chit*), and absolute bliss or happiness (*Ananda*). See Nikhilananda's discussion of *Brahman* as *Sat, Chit, Ananda*, in *Upanishads*, I, 35-48.

[54]Vivekananda, *Karma Yoga and Bhakti Yoga*, p. 3.

[55]Swami Abhedananda, *Doctrine of Karma* (Calcutta: Ramakrishna Vedanta Math, 1944), p. 15.

[56]Abhedananda, p. 27.

[57]Abhedananda, pp. 20, 34, 40.

[58]Vivekananda, *Karma Yoga and Bhakti Yoga*, p. 20.

[59]Vivekananda, *Karma Yoga and Bhakti Yoga*, p. 24.

[60]Swami Nikhilananda, trans., *The Bhagavad Gita* (New York: Ramakrishna-Vivekenanda Center, 1952), pp. 6-7.

[61]Nikhilananda, *Upanishads*, I, 195.

[62]M. [Mahendranath Gupta], *The Gospel of Sri Ramakrishna*, trans., Swami Nikhilananda (New York: Ramakrishna-Vivekananda Center, 1942), p. 593.

[63]Vivekananda, *Raja Yoga*, p. 50.

[64]Vivekananda, *Raja Yoga*, pp. 60-61.

[65]Vivekananda, *Raja Yoga*, p. 89.

[66]Vivekananda, *Raja Yoga*, p. 71.

[67]Vivekananda, *Raja Yoga*, pp. 57, 70.

[68]Vivekananda, *Raja Yoga*, p. 62.

[69]Vivekananda, *Raja Yoga*, pp. 15-26.

[70]Vivekananda, *Raja Yoga*, p. 192.

[71]Vivekananda, *Raja Yoga*, p. 46.

[72]Vivekananda, *Karma Yoga and Bhakti Yoga*, pp. 51-52.

[73]Vivekananda, *Raja Yoga*, p. 62.

CHAPTER 11

Sick Man and God-Seeker

The title "Seymour—An Introduction" suggests that this story is to be seen as the opening chapter of a composite novel about Seymour Glass. In describing the contradictory aspects of the main character's life, the "Introduction" makes us aware of the central conflict and the major theme in the six Glass stories. We learn that Seymour is a God-seeker who devoted his life to a quest for enlightenment but also a Sick Man who eventually committed suicide. And the major theme in the narrative series is clarified when the narrator, Buddy Glass, explains that it was Eastern philosophy which guided Seymour in his quest for God.

When we read the "Introduction" as an account of Seymour's influence on Buddy, then what stands out are Seymour's positive qualitites. But when we read it as part of the story of Seymour's life, then his negative traits become more prominent. Buddy never describes any incidents that illustrate these negative traits of Seymour's character, but he mentions his suicide several times and suggests that Seymour had serious problems: "*Had* Seymour no grievous faults, no vices, no meannesses, that can be listed, at least in a hurry? What was he, anyway? A *saint*?" But then Buddy implies that Seymour was no saint when he says: "Thankfully, it isn't my responsibility to answer that one. (Oh, lucky day!)."

Although Buddy says that he is writing the "Introduction" not "to bury but to exhume and, most likely, to praise," he does shed some light on the nature of Seymour's problems. He explains that like many great artists Seymour was a Sick Man, and he says in a memorable run-on sentence:

. . . the curiously-productive-though-ailing poet or painter . . .
is invariably a kind of super-size but unmistakably "classic" neurotic, an aberrant who only occasionally, and never deeply, wishes
to surrender his aberration; or, in English, a Sick Man who not at
all seldom, though he's reported to childishly deny it, gives out
terrible cries of pain, as if he would wholeheartedly let go both
his art and his soul to experience what passes in other people
for wellness, and yet (the rumor continues) when his unsalu-
tary-looking little room is broken into and someone—not infre-
quently, at that, someone who actually loves him—passionately
asks him where the pain is, he either declines or seems unable
to discuss it in any constructive clinical length, and in the morning, when even great poets and painters presumably feel a bit
more chipper than usual, he looks more perversely determined
than ever to see his sickness run its course, as though by the
light of another, presumably *working* day, he had remembered
that all men, the healthy ones included, eventually die, and usually with a certain amount of bad grace, but that *he*, lucky man,
is at least being done in by the most stimulating companion,
disease or no, he has ever known ("Introduction," pp. 102-103).[1]

Although Buddy suggests that Seymour is a classic neurotic, he
believes that any attempts to identify the source of Seymour's
pain in purely psychoanalytic terms must fail, because people
trained in psychoanalysis "don't listen properly to cries of
pain when they come. They can't, of course. They're peerage
of tin ears. With such faulty equipment, with *those* ears, how
can anyone possibly trace the pain, by sound and quality alone,
to its source." The source of Seymour's pain, so Buddy assures
us, was not "a troubled childhood or a disordered libido." Instead, Seymour's pain came from his eyes. After all, he was an
artist-seer who was able to see more than others. And it was
this special vision, according to Buddy, which eventually killed
Seymour: "I say that the true artist-seer, the heavenly fool who
can and does produce beauty, is mainly dazzled to death by his
own scruples, by the blinding shapes and colors of his own
sacred human conscience." Buddy here suggests that the vision
that distinguishes the artist-seer from the average individual
is a moral vision. Hence, whatever it was that caused Seymour
to commit suicide must have something to do with Seymour's
religious attitudes which were shaped by his study of Eastern
philosophy.

Near the end of the "Introduction," Buddy explains that his and Seymour's roots in Eastern philosophy were "planted in the New and Old Testaments, Advaita Vedanta, and classical Taoism." In this connection, Buddy also mentions Zen Buddhism but stresses his own and Seymour's "extreme Zen-lessness." What attracted them both to Zen was not the philosophy but "classical Zen literature." This becomes apparent particularly in Buddy's discussion of Seymour's fondness for Chinese and Japanese haiku poetry.

Buddy's reference to Zen archery in connection with Seymour's marble shooting advice might suggest that Zen played a more imortant role in Seymour's outlook than Buddy wants to admit. But the notion of performing one's actions with detachment, of "Aiming but no aiming," is also a central concept in Hinduism. This is illustrated in a quote from the *Bhagavad Gita* which Seymour inscribed on the door of his and Buddy's room:

> You have the right to work, but for the work's sake only. You have no right to the fruits of work. Desire for the fruits of work must never be your motive in working . . . ("Zooey," p. 177).

Besides, the principle of Zen archery has its origin in a Hindu text, the *Mundaka Upanishad:*

> Take the Upanishad as the bow, the great weapon, and place upon it the arrow sharpened by meditation.
> Then, having drawn it back with a mind directed to the thought of Brahman, strike that mark, O my good friend—that which is the Imperishable.

> Om is the bow; the Atman is the arrow. Brahman is said to be the mark. It is to be struck by an undistracted mind. Then the Atman becomes one with the Brahman, as the arrow with the target.[2]

Moreover, Buddy explains that when he told him to "try not aiming so much," Seymour was unfamiliar with the principle of Zen archery and that he developed his marble-shooting technique "by sheer intuition." Since Seymour was, at that time of his life (1927), familiar with Hinduism (See "Hapworth,"

p. 92) and since the book on Zen Archery to which Buddy alludes had not yet been published, it seems that the idea behind his marble shooting technique must have come from his readings in Vedanta.[3]

Indeed, Advaita Vedanta references play a more important role throughout the "Introduction" than ideas from Zen Buddhism, the New and Old Testaments, or classical Taosim. Some Vedanta ideas are used playfully, but others can help us understand the nature of Seymour's character and of his quest for God. When describing how Seymour bought his clothes, Buddy, for instance, compares him to "a young *brahmacharya*, or Hindu religious novice, picking out his first loincloth," and when remembering how Seymour played ping pong, Buddy says, "It was like having Mother Kali herself on the other side of the net, multi-armed and grinning" ("Introduction," pp. 188, 194). More revealing than these two comments is Buddy's description of himself as "a fourth class Karma Yogin, with perhaps a little Jnana Yoga thrown in to spice up the pot" ("Introduction," p. 208). Buddy here describes himself according to the Hindu concepts of the four stages in life, and the four *yogas*, or paths to God. This suggests that Seymour also saw himself in these terms. But while Buddy considers himself a *Karma Yogin*, a person following the path of service with perhaps one toe on the path of knowledge (*jnana yoga*), we see in the "Introduction" that Seymour was essentially a *jnana yogin*, a man of knowledge who also practiced the meditation exercises of *raja yoga* (See Chapter 10). This comes out in the many references to Seymour's extraordinary erudition and in a letter in which he reveals that he is able to see into past incarnations when he reaches the trance-like state of *samadhi* during *raja yoga* meditation. Seymour writes: "That time, two summers ago, when I was out so long, I was able to trace that you and Z [Zooey] and I have been brothers for no fewer than four incarnations, maybe more" ("Introduction," p. 158).

An even more revealing Vedanta reference in that same letter concerns the concept of *karma*. Seymour is troubled by the fact that Buddy sees him as an authority figure, and he thinks that he must "have done something very wrong that this situation should be." He says that his guilt in the matter "can't even be fully understood, I'm certain—its roots run too deep into private and long-standing karma" ("Introduction," p. 158). This means that he sees his guilt as a result of his actions or yearnings in previous incarnations.

But the most important Vedanta concept in the "Introduction" is that of *mukti*. It explains the nature of Seymour's life-long quest and the central theme of the composite novel. At the beginning of the "Introduction," Buddy says about Seymour:

> . . . with or without a suicide plot in his head, he was the only person I've ever habitually consorted with, banged around with, who more frequently than not tallied with the classical conception, as I saw it, of a *mukta*, a ringding enlightened man, a God-knower ("Introduction," p. 106).

According to Sri Ramakrishna, one of Seymour's spiritual heroes, a *mukta* is a person "who firmly believes that God alone is the Doer and he is merely the instrument." Such a man is "liberated while living in the body," and does not have to wait for full knowledge of God until he dies.[4] The "classical conception" of the *mukta* or *jivanmukta*, is perhaps best expressed in the *Brihadaranyaka Upanishad*:

> This is the eternal glory of Brahman: It never increases nor decreases through work. [Therefore] one should know the nature of That alone. Knowing It one is not touched by evil action. Therefore he who knows It as such becomes self-controlled, calm, withdrawn into himself, patient and collected; he sees the Self in his own self (body); he sees all as the Self. Evil does not overcome him, but he overcomes all evil. Evil does not afflict him, but he consumes all evil. He becomes sinless, taintless, free from doubts, and a true Brahamana (knower of Brahman).[5]

Salinger's teacher Nikhilananda clarifies these ideas by explaining that a *jivanmukta*, a true God-knower, is a person who is "free from desires . . . free from the illusion of individuality . . . free from the binding effects of past action [*karma*]"; therefore "he can never perform any evil action. All his evil instincts were destroyed when he practiced spiritual discipline. Only good comes out of him—and that, too, without any effort."[6]

If we now consider the picture of Seymour that Buddy draws in the "Introduction," then we will realize that Seymour does not quite measure up to the "classical conception" of a *jivanmukta* and that he could not have achieved full enlightenment and knowledge of God in his current incarnation. In fact, as we can see from Seymour's letter to Buddy, Seymour was aware that he was not "free from the binding effects of past action" but was suffering the negative effects of his "private and longstanding karma" from previous incarnations. Moreover, Buddy's oblique references to Seymour's suicide and to his "grievous faults," "vices," and "meannesses" suggests that Seymour was indeed not completely "sinless, taintless, free from doubts."

But even if Seymour was not quite a *mukta*, the "Introduction" shows that *mukti*, full enlightenment and knowledge of God, was Seymour's life-long goal. This is apparent when Buddy refers to him as a "God-lover," one of those individuals "who look for God, and apparently with enormous success, in the queerest imaginable places." And Buddy illustrates Seymour's pervasive quest for God with this example:

> My brother, for the record, had a distracting habit, most of his adult life, of investigating loaded ashtrays with his index finger, clearing all the cigarette ends to the sides—smiling from ear to ear as he did it—as if he expected to see Christ himself curled up cherubically in the middle, and he never looked disappointed ("Introduction," pp. 108-109).

Buddy here wants to make the point that "the hallmark of the advanced religious . . . person is that he frequently behaves like a fool, even an imbecile." But since Seymour accepted the Vedanta belief in the immanence of God in all things ("All that exists is Brahman," *Chandogya Upanishad*, III, xvi, 1), his searching for God in queer places like loaded ashtrays does indeed identify him as an advanced God-seeker.

The more Buddy makes us understand Seymour's quest for God, the more he also makes us wonder why Seymour chose to kill himself. We might speculate, for instance, that he wanted to give up his body in order to achieve immediate union with God, a theory that has been advanced by some commentators.[7]   But such an interpretation of Seymour's death would only make sense if he had actually achieved *mukti*. As Sri Ramakrishna explains: "Suicide is a heinous sin, undoubtedly. A man who kills himself must return again and again to this world . . . ." However, if a person has achieved *mukti* and if his suicide does not have any negative effects on others, then the case is different. As Ramakrishna says, "after the attainment of Knowledge, the realization of God, some give up their bodies. But such a thing is rare indeed . . . . I don't call it suicide if a person leaves his body after having the vision of God. There is no harm in giving up one's body that way."[8]   In short, if a true *jivanmukta* takes his own life, he will go straight to *Brahman*, but if anyone else commits suicide, he will have to work out the negative *karma* created by this act in subsequent incarnations. Since Buddy tells us that Seymour was not quite a *mukta*, his suicide cannot be seen as a giving up of the body and a merging with *Brahman*. And Seymour's behavior during the last days of his life bears that out. His conflicts with his in-laws, his nastiness toward Muriel, and the way in which he killed himself all show that he did not die as a detached, sinless *jivanmukta*. In fact, on the day of his death he was further away from his goal of *mukti* than ever before in his life. This suggests that his suicide was not motivated by his hope of immediate union with God but by his despair about the sickness which had reversed his spiritual progress.

While the "Introduction" does not clearly explain the nature of Seymour's sickness, it does establish that it had less to do with his psyche than with his soul. According to Buddy, the symptoms of this sickness were the "scruples" that were caused by his "sacred human conscience." These symptoms suggest that his sickness was mainly caused by his moral perfectionism, that is, by his single-minded quest for God. The "Introduction" hints, moreover, that Seymour's sickness was complicated by the effects of his "private and longstanding karma." This negative *karma* manifested itself in the "grievous faults," "vices," and "meannesses" which Buddy refuses to discuss in the "Introduction" but which are well illustrated in "Hapworth 16, 1924," "Raise High the Roof Beam, Carpenters," and "A Perfect Day for Bananafish."

Seen as the opening chapter of the composite novel, "Seymour—An Introduction" establishes that Seymour was an artist-seer and God-lover, that his quest for God is the pervasive theme of his life story, but that he failed in this quest. The reasons for Seymour's failure are not explained in the "Introduction," and this raises the questions whether we are to see him as a positive or a negative model and whether we are to accept or to reject his teachings. The answers to these questions determine the religious meaning of the composite novel. But to find these answers we need to analyze the Eastern ideas in the other five stories.

NOTES

[1] All my quotations from the Glass stories come from the Bantam paperback editions of *Raise High the Roof Beam, Carpenters and Seymour—An Introduction* (New York, 1965); *Franny and Zooey* (New York: 1964); and from "Hapworth, 16, 1924" as it appears in the *New Yorker*, June 19, 1965, pp. 32-113.

[2] *Mundaka Upanishad*, 11, ii, 3-4, in Swami Nikhilananda, trans. *The Upanishads* (New York: Harper Brothers, 1949), I, 289-290. See also "Zooey," p. 60.

[3] Eugen Herrigel, *Zen in the Art of Archery*, trans. R.F.C. Hull (New York: Pantheon Books, 1953); originally published in German as *Zen in der Kunst des Bogenschiessens* (Konstanz, 1948).

[4] M. [Mahendranath Gupta], *The Gospel of Sri Ramakrishna*, trans. Swami Nikhilananda (New York: Ramakrishna-Vivekananda Center, 1942), pp. 719, 893.

[5] *Brihadaranyaka Upanishad*, IV, iv, 23, in Nikhilananda, *The Upanishads* I, 105-106.

[6] Swami Nikhilananda, "Discussion of Brahman in the Upanishads,"

in *Upanishads* I, 105-106.

[7]See for instance, Gordon E. Slethaugh, "Seymour: A Clarification," *Renascence*, 23 (1971), 115-128; Anthony Quagliano, "Hapworth 16, 1924: A Problem in Hagiography," *University of Dayton Review*, 8 (1971), 35-43; and Humayun Ali Mirza, "The Influence of Hindu-Buddhist Psychology and Philosophy on J.D. Salinger's Fiction," Unpubl. Dissertation, State University of New York at Binghamton, 1976, p. 182.

[8]*The Gospel of Sri Ramakrishna,* pp. 164-165.

CHAPTER 12

Study and Meditation

When we read "Hapworth 16, 1924" as part of Seymour's
life story, then it makes more sense to treat it as a letter that
was actually written by Seymour himself rather than as an
attempt by Buddy to come to an understanding of what went
on in Seymour's mind in the summer of 1924. Seen that way,
"Hapworth" clarifies why Seymour chose to pursue his quest
for God along the paths of study and meditation.

Religious ideas are more prominent in "Hapworth" than
in any other Seymour story. Although some of these ideas
seem to be Christian, they are highly unorthodox. For example, Seymour rejects the notion of the divinity of Christ
and merely sees Him as a fully enlightened man, as one of the
many human beings whom he "respect[s] without countless
reservations" ("Hapworth," p. 106).[1] Moreover, Seymour
believes in reincarnation and says that "Judgment Day, in my
forward opinion quite regularly occurs between bodies" ("Hapworth," p. 94). He also makes many references to "lights"
that he sees during meditation and to "glimpses" that he has of
previous incarnations and of the future. These comments reveal
the Eastern origin of Seymour's religious ideas and create difficulties for the reader who is only familiar with the Judaeo-
Christian tradition. And while Eastern ideas in other Seymour
stories are important but not vital to an understanding of their
meaning, Eastern ideas form the core of "Hapworth" and must
therefore be examined in detail.

In "Seymour—An Introduction," Buddy Glass tells us that
it was Seymour's lifelong quest to become "a *mukta,* a ringding enlightened man, a God-knower," and Buddy's transcription
of a letter that the seven-year-old Seymour wrote home from
summer camp further illustrates Seymour's "consuming

admiration for God." The letter confirms that the goal
of Seymour's striving was indeed union with God and
that he saw his progress toward this goal in terms of
Vedanta ideas.

Near the beginning of his letter from Camp Hapworth,
Seymour talks about his "karmic responsibility," the nature
of the duties he must perform in order to compensate for his
negative actions in previous lives. Vivekananda, a major exponent of Advaita Vedanta, defines this concept by saying that
"the action one has done cannot be destroyed until it has borne
fruit; no power in nature can stop it from yielding its results.
If I do an evil deed I must suffer for it; there is no power in
this universe to stop or stay it. Similarly, if I do a good deed
there is no power in the universe which can stop its bearing
good results."[2] Since the effects of our actions extend beyond one lifetime, so Vedanta teaches, we are all affected by
our actions from previous incarnations. If we are to make
spiritual progress in our current lives, we must therefore first
work out whatever negative *karma* still clings to us from previous lifetimes. This is one of the problems that Seymour
faces. Capable of limited clairvoyance, he is nevertheless unable
to determine the exact nature of his karmic responsibilities.
It would be nice, he says, if one could know "exactly where
one's everlasting duty lies. Quite to my regret and secret delight, my glimpses are ludicrously helpless to aid me in these
matters" ("Hapworth," p. 105). His "glimpses" do reveal
to him, however, two major obstacles to his spiritual progress.
Both are the results of his actions and omissions in previous
incarnations. They are his sensuality and his emotional instability.

The lesser of the two problems is his "heritage of sensuality." He says that he will not "harp on the subject of karma" because he knows that his parents do not sympathize with
his "absorbing and quite accidental interest in this subject."
He insists, however, that his sensuality is a "karmic responsibility" and says: ". . . one meets it, one conquers it, or if one
does not conquer it, one enters into honorable contest with it,
seeking and giving no quarter." Because of his precocious sensuality, Seymour is attraced to the young wife of the camp
director, Mrs. Happy, who rouses all of his "lusts of the body.

and genitals, despite their youthful size." Seymour frequently goes to chat with Mrs. Happy and looks forward "with mounting pleasure," as he puts it, "to the possibility, all too slight for words, of her opening the door, quite unwittingly, in the raw." "Considering my absurd age," so Seymour admits, "the situation has its humorous side." But he nevertheless takes the problem very seriously, for he says: "I intend, to be sure, to work on this sensual problem without ceasing [because] I for one do not look forward to being distracted by charming lusts of the body, quite day in and day out, for the few blissful, remaining years allotted to me in this appearance." He is quite confident, however, that "the problem of Mrs. Happy will pass into oblivion as the summer draws to a close."

The major obstacle to his spiritual advancement, so Seymour realizes, is his emotional instability. He says that this problem has troubled him in previous incarnations, particularly in the "last two tough ones." It makes it very difficult for him to get along with people who have "picayune, stunted attitudes toward everything in the universe and beyond," and this has been a major problem during his first sixteen days at Camp Hapworth. He says, "I am working on this emotional tendency while I am here, but am doing quite poorly." After reporting how he lost control of himself in a confrontation with the camp's head counsellor and threatened to kill the counsellor or to commit suicide, Seymour explains:

> I believe I could have curbed this criminal urge at the crucial moment, but one must painfully remember that a vein of instability runs through me quite like some turbulent river; this cannot be overlooked; I have left this troublesome instability uncorrected in my previous two appearances, to my folly and disgust; it will not be corrected by friendly, cheerful prayer. It can only be corrected by dogged effort on my part ("Hapworth," p. 44).

In a second confrontation, this time with the camp director, Mr. Happy, Seymour's instability again makes him lose his temper. Because he injured his leg during one of the scheduled activities, he threatens the camp director that his father will sue him for every dime he has. Seymour explains his outburst by saying that it is very hard for him "to be less than contemp-

tuous and scathing around Mr. Happy personally. I am working on it, but that man brings to the fore supplies of hidden
malice I thought I had worked out of my system years ago."
These two incidents show that in order to make spiritual progress toward his goal of enlightenment and oneness with God,
Seymour must find a way of overcoming the instability which
makes him behave in ways that are bound to result in negative *karma*. Seymour must decide what paths of spiritual advancement, what methods of serving God would help him most
in overcoming this major obstacle on his way toward *mukti.*

There is evidence in "Hapworth" which confirms that
Seymour saw his spiritual advancement in terms of the four
paths, or *yogas*, of Advaita Vedanta. In the "Introduction,"
Buddy Glass says that he himself is following *karma yoga,*
the path of service to others, and *jnana yoga*, the path of study
and knowledge ("Introduction," p. 208), and in "Hapworth,"
Seymour mentions two Vedanta texts about the paths of religious devotion and meditation. Among the books that he
wants to have sent to camp, he requests: "Raja-Yoga and Bhakti-
Yoga, two heartrending, handy quite tiny volumes, perfect
for pockets of any average, mobile boys our age, by Vivekananda
of India" ("Hapworth," p. 92).

Why Seymour requests Vivekananda's book on *bhakti
yoga* is not easy to understand, since the path of devotion to
a personal God is clearly not compatible with his ideas. Vivekananda defines this path when he says: "Bhakti-Yoga is a
real, genuine search after the Lord, a search beginning, continuing, and ending in love."[3] *Bhakti* is love for one of the personal manifestations of God, for what Advaita Vedanta calls
Saguna Brahman, the God with attributes. Seymour, however,
preferred to see God as *Nirguna Brahman*, as an abstract God
without attributes. This is evident from his comment that
the notion of a personal God, "adorned with an impressive
charming beard, stinks to high heaven" ("Hapworth," p. 105).
He says, however: "I am convinced God will kindly wear a
human head, quite capable of nodding, for the benefit of some
admirer who enjoys picturing Him that way, but I personally
am not too partial to His wearing a human head and would
perhaps turn on my heel and walk away if He put one on for
my dubious benefit" ("Hapworth," p. 62). Instead, Seymour's

"beloved, shapeless God" is a "nameless hallmark, preferably without shape and ridiculous attributes" ("Hapworth," p. 90). *Bhakti yoga*, the path of devotion to a personal God, is therefore out of the question for Seymour. Perhaps he requested the book on *bhakti yoga* because he wanted it for his brother Buddy, or perhaps because he wanted to make absolutely sure that *bhakti yoga* was not a path he could possibly pursue.

The other path of spiritual advancement that Seymour rejects is that of service, *karma yoga*. But he does not reject it as easily as the path of devotion, for in the early part of the letter, Seymour is much concerned with helping others. While commenting on his and Buddy's special gifts, he asks, for example: "Who can prevent us from doing a little good in this appearance?" His notion of "doing a little good" is illustrated by his desire to help Griffith Hammersmith, John Kolb, and Mrs. Happy, whose future lives, as he knows from his "glimpses," are likely to be miserable. He wants to adopt Griffith Hammersmith into the Glass family so that his materialistic mother can't ruin his life, and he wants to seek out John Kolb in later years and save him from alcoholism. He also wants to save the "rotten marriage" of Mr. and Mrs. Happy. By talking to Mrs. Happy as often as he can, he hopes to exert sufficient spiritual influence to prevent her from committing adultery. He knows that he should also try to influence Mr. Happy, but he claims: "He is not too approachable in this or in any other matter under the sun." Seymour realizes: "I am not at liberty to excuse myself from keen repsonsibility," but since he has nothing but contempt for Mr. Happy, he never even tries to help him. Nor does Seymour worry about the spiritual well-being of the dull and uncaring cooks, Mr. and Mrs. Nelson, or about that of Roger Pittman, the detestable head counsellor. While reviewing his confrontations with the staff at the camp, Seymour realizes that he simply cannot help those he cannot stand. As a result, he decides to be content with serving his immediate family. This becomes obvious in the section of the letter that contains his advice to his parents and his siblings. Moreover, he feels a special sense of responsibility for Buddy, because he knows that Buddy "will be swiftly and subtly guiding every child in the family long after I am quite burned out and useless or out of the picture."

But *karma yoga* requires more than service to one's immediate family. It requires helping everybody one comes in contact with, whether one likes the person or not. Vivekananda explains: "If you wish to help a man, never think of what that man's attitude should be towards you."[4] Seymour realizes this when he gives the following example: "I am utterly convinced that if A's hat blows off while he is sauntering down the street, it is the charming duty of B to pick it up and hand it to A without examining A's face or combing it for gratitude!" ("Hapworth," p. 32). Seymour here shows that he understands the *karma yoga* ideal, which is to serve others no matter what their attitudes are. But although he realizes that the cooks, the head counsellor, and the camp director are all unspiritual people who could use some guidance, he finds their attitudes toward him too irritating to consider helping them.

Seymour is also unable to accept another important part of *karma yoga*, the notion that one must do one's duty according to the position in life that one is in. As Vivekananda explains, in *karma yoga* "different rules are laid down for the different classes of men," the student, the householder, the retired person, and so on. "The life of every individual, according to the Hindu scriptures, has its peculiar duties apart from those common to humanity."[5] Seymour's duties as a young boy are to respect his parents and his teachers and to follow their guidance. But Seymour rebelled when his parents decided to send him to camp, for he talks about "the difficult days prior to our departure for this place" and mentions several times that he wishes he and Buddy didn't have to be at Camp Hapworth and "two other, quite unknown boys had this opportunity to stay off the streets." Apparently, his parents sent him and Buddy to camp because they felt the boys were beginning to turn into intellectual freaks and needed to be exposed to the activities of normal boys. This is suggested when Seymour tells his father: "Try your utmost not to mind too much when we don't remind you freely and movingly of other regular boys." But although they know their parents expect them to act like "regular boys," Seymour and Buddy resist camp discipline and avoid camp activities whenever they can in order to pursue their intellectual goals. This shows that Seymour does not accept one of the cardinal rules of *karma yoga*, namely to perform the duties appropriate to his position in life. It seems therefore that *karma yoga* is not a path of spiritual advancement that Seymour wants to follow.

A path more congenial to Seymour is that of *jnana yoga*, the path of study and knowledge. In defining this path, Vivekananda quotes Sri Krishna, the divine charioteer in the *Bhagavad Gita*, who says that *jnana yogins* are "those who worship the Absolute, the Indescribable, the Undifferentiated, the Omnipresent, the Unthinkable, the All-Comprehending, the Immovable, and the Eternal . . . ."[6] And Nikhilananda explains that *jnana yoga* demands withdrawal from normal, average life:

> The path of knowledge is steep and austere, and the search for impersonal reality is extremely difficult for those who are constantly aware of their duties to the world. This path, therefore, is usually pursued by monks who have renounced the world.[7]

But since Seymour was born with extraordinary intellectual powers, *jnana yoga* seemed to him the logical path to follow. He started out on this path at the age of six when he began his studies at a branch of the New York Public Library. And when he calls himself a "private scholar" in his letter from camp, this is no exaggeration. The booklist at the end of the letter shows that his studies in literature, religion, and history have concentrated on works that reveal the workings of "the human heart and brain" because "industrious absorption with the human brain and heart" is his way of searching for God. The letter also shows that Seymour pursues this quest so singlemindedly that he doesn't want to spend time on anything else. This is why he tries to escape from the scheduled activities at Camp Hapworth whenever he can in order to continue his studies. As a result, he and Buddy are ostracized by the other campers and the staff.

A second path toward God that Seymour has been following every since he was six years old is that of *raja yoga*, or meditation. His letter shows that he has been familiar with Vivekananda's *raja yoga* manual for over a year. This becomes apparent when he reminds his mother of a conversation he had with her in May of 1923. In this conversation, he tried to teach her a breathing exercise from Vivekananda's book which was supposed to have a calming effect on her nerves. He now reviews this breathing exercise for her:

> . . . please try very hard to breathe through the left nostril exclusively, at other times going back swiftly to the right nostril. To get the breath started in the proper nostril, to review slightly, warmly lock your fist in the opposing armpit, bearing down with friendly pressure, or simply lie down for several minutes on the side of the body opposing the desired nostril . . . As I mentioned . . . this nostril business can be abandoned in a trice at the very instant that one takes utter and complete reliance upon God with regard to breathing, seeing, hearing, and the other maddening functions . . . ("Hapworth, " pp. 77-78).[8]

When he explained this breathing exercise to his mother a year earlier, Seymour had mentioned to her the "lights" that he had been seeing as a result of his practice of *raja yoga*. And in his letter from camp, he tells his mother that when he meditates after taps, he can again see "the magnificent light I mentioned to you last May" ("Hapworth," p. 58). But more important than the lights he sees during *raja yoga* meditation are the "glimpses" he has of events in previous incarnations and in the future.

When Seymour describes his "glimpses," it becomes clear that they come to him against his wish. One is an "abominable glimpse" that he had "at recess period after Christmas vacation." It revealed to him, so Seymour tells his father, that "my and Buddy's intimacy with you, dear Les, in our last appearance, was fairly slight and fraught with discordance" ("Hapworth," p. 50). Seymour says therefore that he is "trying like hell to cut down on getting any glimpses" while he is at Camp Hapworth, and he says about his latest one:

> I would far from object if that were practically the last glimpse of my life. However, those two, tantalizing, tiny portals in my mind I mentioned last year are still far from closed . . . . If it were up to me, I would gladly shut the portals myself; in only three or four cases . . . is the nature of the glimpses worth the wear and tear on one's normalness and blessed peace of mind . . . ("Hapworth," p. 62).

It is particularly his ability to see into the future which Seymour finds upsetting. He knows, for instance, that he himself will not live much longer than a "generous matter of thirty (30) years"; but that bothers him much less than what he knows about the future of others. About Griffith Hammersmith, a boy at camp, he says, "His future, I am fairly sick to death to say, looks abominable." His life will be ruined, so Seymour explains, by his vain and prestige-conscious mother, who is doing "such a maddening, crappy job as a mother and woman." Another fellow camper, John Kolb, so Seymour knows, will become an alcoholic when he grows up, since "he has a waiting tendency to drink himself into a soothing stupor." And about Mrs. Happy, the wife of the camp director, Seymour knows that she is "in future danger of immorality; a quite subtle downfall and dégringolade from mere flirtation and girlish conversation is foreseeable."

But some of Seymour's "glimpses" are more cheerful and "quite uplifting." For instance, Seymour tells his parents:

> Either this coming winter or the winter which briskly follows, you, Bessie, Les, Buddy, and the undersigned will all be going to one of the most pregnant and important parties that Buddy and I will ever attend . . . . At this party, entirely in the night time, we will meet a man, very overweight, who will make us a slightly straightforward business and career offer . . . . it will involve our easy, charming prowess as singers and dancers, but this is very far from all it will involve. He, this corpulent man, will not too seriously change the regular, normal course of our childhood and early, amusing youth by this business offer, but I can assure you that the surface upheaval will be quite enormous ("Hapworth," p. 61).

What Seymour predicts here is that he and Buddy will be signed up for the national radio quiz show "It's a Wise Child" on which they will appear for a long time. But even more stunning than this prediction is the second half of this "glimpse." He predicts that Buddy, "at a later date by innumerable years," will be writing a short story about this party. And as we know from Buddy's note at the beginning of "Hapworth," Buddy was just working on that story when his mother sent him Seymour's letter from Camp Hapworth which he had never seen before.

Raja yoga not only explains.Seymour's glimpses but also his extraordinary mental powers. Seymour tells us that he and Buddy have "certain abilities, prowesses, knacks, and facilities" which are "warmly attached to [them] like cement from previous appearances" ("Hapworth," p. 40), and Seymour's practice of *raja yoga* allowed him to develop these abilities even further. Vivekananda explains that when the *raja yogin* reaches the super-conscious state of *samadhi*, he "will have seen the foundations of his mind, and it will be under his perfect control. Different powers will come to the yogi . . . and the yogi will find himself as he is and as he always was, the Essence of Knowledge, the Immortal, the All-Pervading."[9] That is to say, since *samadhi* is temporary absorption in *Brahman*, and since *Brahman* is, among other things, the Essence of Knowledge, the practitioner of *raja yoga* will be able to enlarge the scope of his knowledge beyond what seems humanly possible. Seymour's unbelievable erudition is thus due in part to his having been born with a superior mind and in part to his having begun to pursue *jnana* and *raja yoga* at the age of six.

But while Seymour's pursuit of the paths of knowledge and meditation has allowed him to make rapid intellectual and spiritual progress, it has also made him feel contempt for normal, unspiritual people. At Camp Hapworth, this contempt has led to violent confrontations, and these conflicts have plunged Seymour into a crisis concerning the direction of his quest for oneness with God. He is no longer sure that he shouldn't pursue different paths toward God, perhaps those of devotion and service, *bhakti* and *karma yoga*. Seymour almost wishes that God would tell him in what direction to go. But then he says:

> While there is always a flimsy possibility that one's beloved, shapeless God will surprise one out of the blue with a charming, useful command, such as "Seymour Glass, do this," or "Seymour Glass, my young, foolish son, do that," I utterly fail to warm up to this possibility ("Hapworth," p. 105).

But then Seymour addresses God directly and tells Him: "Do not favor me with charming, personal commands and magnificent short cuts!" And he winds up thanking God for not playing favorites with him:

It is humorous and kindly of you, Your Grace, to allow me to remain absorbed in my own dubious methods, such as industrious absorption with the human heart and brain. My God, you are a hard one to figure out, thank God! I love you more than ever! Consider my services everlastingly at your disposal! ("Hapworth," p. 106).

As Seymour comes to the decision to continue his quest for God via the paths of *jnana* and *raja yoga*, he wonders if "the afternoon sun is shining in a very moving manner" or if his "brain is not merely shining in a very moving manner" ("Hapworth," p. 106). Although he is not sure that he is really experiencing a moment of illumination, he is able to overcome his doubt concerning the direction of his quest for God. The rest of the letter shows that his inner struggle is over. By writing the letter, and particularly by ending it with advice to his family and a very erudite discussion of a long list of books, he is able to suppress the misgivings about *jnana* and *raja yoga* that still plagued him when he began to write.

Thus the crux of Seymour's letter from Camp Hapworth is his decision to continue in his quest for enlightenment and union with God along the paths he had chosen when he was six years old. As we have seen, he rejects *bhakti* and *karma yoga,* the paths of devotion and of service, and reaffirms his decision in favor of *jnana* and *raja yoga,* the paths of study and of meditation. It is significant that the paths he rejects are other-directed ones while those he adopts are self-directed ones. Study and meditation are not likely to help Seymour overcome the emotional instability which often surfaces in his dealings with others. Instead, these two paths are likely to increase the difficulties he has in getting along with normal people. His violent confrontations with the staff at Camp Hapworth have shown him that his instability is a major obstacle to his spiritual progress, and that it "can only be overcome by dogged effort on [his] part." But he is not willing to make this effort. Instead of confronting the problem, he tries to circumvent it by withdrawing from normal people. Eventually, however, this problem caught up with Seymour. As we can see in "Raise High the Roof Beam, Carpenters," Seymour came to realize that his decision to pursue his quest for God via the self-directed paths of knowledge and meditation was a wrong one because it did not help him overcome his instability.

NOTES

[1] The quotations from the Glass stories in this chapter come from "Hapworth 16, 1924," *New Yorker,* June 19, 1965, pp. 32-113 and from *Raise High the Roof Beam, Carpenters and Seymour—An Introduction* (New York, Bantam, 1965).

[2] Swami Vivekananda, *Karma Yoga and Bhakti Yoga* (New York: Ramakrishna-Vivekananda Center, 1955), p. 69.

[3] Vivekananda, *Karma Yoga*, p. 117.

[4] Vivekananda, *Karma Yoga*, p. 11.

[5] Vivekananda, *Karma Yoga*, p. 20.

[6] Vivekananda, *Karma Yoga*, p. 178.

[7] Swami Nikhilananda, *Hinduism: Its Meaning for the Liberation of Spirit* (New York: Harper, 1958), p. 123.

[8] Swami Vivekananda, *Raja Yoga* (New York: Ramakrishna-Vivekananda Center, 1955).

[9] Vivekananda, *Raja Yoga*, pp. 85-86.

CHAPTER 13

A New Beginning

"Raise High the Roof Beam, Carpenters" not only deals with the events on Seymour's wedding day, it also reveals what happened to him as a result of his decision to pursue his quest for enlightenment along the paths of study and meditation. In "Carpenters," Seymour tries to make a new beginning, for he has come to realize his mistake in trying to advance his spiritual development in ways which have estranged him from average humanity, and this realization has made him give up *jnana* and *raja yoga*, the paths of study and meditation, in favor of *karma yoga*, the path of service. This is why he did not mind being drafted into the military service, unlike his brother Waker who was a conscientious objector, and this is also why he decided to marry the simply Muriel Fedder.

Although the narrator, Buddy Glass, insists that Seymour's decision to marry Muriel was an admirable one, he nevertheless makes us wonder if Seymour's relationship with Muriel might not have something to do with his suicide. Right at the beginning of the story, Buddy mentions that Seymour "committed suicide in 1948 while on vacation in Florida with his wife." This piece of information suggests that despite his best intentions, Seymour was unable to derive any spiritual benefits from his marriage and that his decision to marry Muriel was therefore ultimately a mistake.

To understand why Seymour believed he needed to marry Muriel, we have to examine his religious ideas in some detail. These ideas will also help us understand three other puzzling questions in "Carpenters": Why Seymour deliberately injured Charlotte Mayhew; what Muriel's resemblance to Charlotte has to do with Seymour's attraction to her; and why Seymour made a suicide attempt in 1941, several months before he met Muriel.

The climactic passage of "Carpenters" reveals that Seymour saw his marriage in terms of the Vedanta view of life. Buddy suddenly understands why Seymour married Muriel when he reads in Seymour's diary that on the day before the wedding, Seymour had "been reading a miscellany of Vedanta all day" and that he felt as though he was "about to be born. Sacred, sacred day!" ("Carpenters," pp. 90-91).[1] The reference to the Vedanta view of marriage reveals that Seymour saw his wedding day as the point in his life where he left the student stage and entered that of the householder. In order to understand this, we must review the Hindu concept of the four *asramas* or stages of life. This is how Salinger's teacher, Swami Nikhilananda, explains this ancient concept:

> The full life period [of a Hindu] was divided into four stages, namely, brahmacharya, garhasthya, vanaprasthya, and sannyasa. The first stage was devoted to study. The celibate student led a life of chastity and austerity and served his teacher with humility. He learnt [sic] the Mantra and Brahmana sections of the Vedas. And when he left the teacher's house, after completing his studies, he was commanded not to deviate from truth and not to forget to presevere in the study of the Vedas. The second stage was devoted to household duties. The young man took a wife. Both together performed the Vedic sacrifices with the hymns of the Mantra and in accordance with the rules laid down in the Brahmanas. The third stage commenced when the hair turned grey and the face began to wrinkle. The householder consigned the responsibility of the home to his children and retired with his wife into the forest. He was then known as a vanaprashta or aranyaka, a forest dweller. The Aranayaka portions of the Vedas prescribed for him sacrifice by meditation and symbolic worship
>
> The final stage, called sannyasa, was the culmination of the strictly regulated life [of a Hindu]. During this stage, having renounced the world, he became a sannyasin, a wandering monk, free from worldly desires and attachments and absorbed in the uninterrupted contemplation of Brahman . . . . The Sannyasin took the vow of dedicating his life to Truth and to the service of humanity, and was honored as a spiritual leader of society.[2]

In each of the four stages, different *yogas* or paths of spiritual advancement are to be followed. In the student stage it is predominantly *jnana yoga*, the path of study and knowledge. But in the householder stage it is *karma yoga*, the path of service to others and of scrupulous fulfillment of everyday duties. Thus a Hindu who leaves the student stage and enters the householder stage is expected to give up his quest for knowledge temporarily—he will resume it again in the third stage—and devote himself single-mindedly to the performance of his household duties.

Up to his twenty-third year, Seymour Glass saw himself as being in the *brahmacharya*, or student stage. The "Introduction" and "Hapworth" show that he had been following *jnana yoga*, the path of study and knowledge, ever since he was six years old. "Hapworth," moreover, illustrates Seymour's concern about the primary requirement of the student stage, that of absolute chastity. In this letter from camp he mentions that his "heritage of sensuality" had affected his spiritual progress in previous incarnations and that it was again causing him difficulties. He says: "I for one do not look forward to being distracted by charming lusts of the body, quite day in and day out, for the few blissful, remaining years allotted to me in this appearance." And he therefore vows to "work on this sensual problem without ceasing" ("Hapworth," p. 36). But the Charlotte Mayhew incident, which occurred when Seymour was twelve, suggests that he continued to be "distracted by charming lusts of the body."

If we see the incident in the light of Charlotte's uncanny resemblance to Muriel and of Seymour's limited clairvoyance, then Seymour's fear of being distracted from his pursuit of spiritual progress can explain why he hurt Charlotte. In the "Introduction," Buddy reports that Charlotte had a crush on Seymour and that she pursued him in a most uninhibited manner. The Glass children therefore called her "Charlotte the Harlot" ("Introduction," p. 179). Apparently, Seymour could not resist Charlotte, for it was he who invited her to stay at the Glasses' lake cottage where the stone-throwing incident took place. His decision to injure her may have been prompted by one of his "glimpses." Since the age of six, he had been able to see events in his own and other people's future, and it may well be that he also had a glimpse of Muriel and recognized her to be the person who would bring about a big change in the way in which he was pursuing his quest for God. Because some of Seymour's glimpses were rather indistinct—he predicted inaccurately, for instance, that Buddy would be present when he died—Seymour may have thought that Charlotte and Muriel were the same person. After all, Charlotte looked so much like Muriel that one of Muriel's relatives said she "could have doubled for Muriel at that age." Besides, the two girls were both very sensual. Buddy later underlines this particular similarity by calling Muriel a "Spiritual Tramp," a name reminiscent of "Charlotte the Harlot." Thus when Seymour threw the stone at Charlotte, he threw it at the person who he thought would make him relinquish the paths of study and meditation. And since he was unwilling to stop following these paths at the age of twelve, he decided to do something drastic to break off their relationship for the time being. If this was indeed his plan, then it succeeded; for after he injured Charlotte, her parents promptly took her off the radio quiz show "It's a Wise Child."

Seymour knew, of course, that his cruelty toward Charlotte was bound to produce much negative *karma*. But he must have believed that this would, in the long run, be less of a hindrance to his spiritual progress than the sensuality that Charlotte aroused in him. Once Charlotte was out of the picture, he apparently hoped to make up for the negative *karma* by increasing his efforts to advance along the spiritual paths of study and meditation.

However, as Seymour reached adulthood, he gave up *jnana* and *raja yoga* because he found that he was making less and less progress along these paths. In 1940, when he was twenty-one, he wrote a memo to Buddy which reveals that he was worried about the effects of his "private and long-standing karma." And as we know from "Hapworth," his long-standing karma expressed itself chiefly in terms of his sensuality and his instability, two problems he says he had "left uncorrected in [his] previous two appearances." In his memo, Seymour says that he has realized that his *karma* can't be nullified: "The hard thing to do is to put it to practical use before it gets around to paralyzing you." To prevent his *karma* from paralyzing him, that is, from stopping his spiritual progress completely, Seymour therefore decided to shift from the paths of study and meditation to the path of service, or *karma yoga*.

Seymour's decision to become a *karma yogin* explains why he registered for military service. This is an unlikely thing to do for a God-seeker, and Seymour's attitude contrasts sharply with that of his brother Waker who spent the war years in a conscientious objector's camp in Maryland. Seymour and Waker had different attitudes toward military service because Waker was a Christian (he later became a Carthusian monk) and Seymour was basically a Vedantist. For while Christ preached non-violence, the *Bhagavad Gita* teaches that a man's duty to his community may require him to violate even the most sacred religious duty of *ahimsa*, non-injury to all living things. This is well illustrated in the second chapter of the *Gita*, when the warrior Arjuna does not want to go into battle because he abhors the idea of killing. He says to Sri Krishna, an incarnation of God who has taken on the form of his chariot driver:

> I shall not struggle,
> I shall not strike them.
> Now let them kill me,
> That will be better.[3]

But Sri Krishna tells him: ". . . if you refuse to fight in this righteous war, you will be turning aside from your duty." And then Sri Krishna explains that the act of killing does not have much significance when it is done as part of one's duty:

> Bodies are said to die, but That which possesses the body is eternal. It cannot be limited, or destroyed. Therefore you must fight.

> Some say that Atman [The Godhead that is within every being]
> Is slain, and others
> Call it the slayer:
> They know nothing.
> How can It slay
> Or who shall slay It.[4]

There can be no doubt that Seymour was familiar with these ideas, for in the story "Zooey" we find that he had inscribed a key passage from the *Gita* on the door of his and Buddy's room. And the passage that he picked for this inscription is the one that describes the essence of *karma yoga*, the path of service, which he had decided to follow when he registered for the draft (See "Zooey," p. 177).

However, Seymour apparently found that rendering military service did not result in further spiritual progress but in conflicts which created more negative *karma*, and he therefore attempted to kill himself. Seymour mentions his first suicide attempt in his diary when he gently chides Muriel for having told her mother "where I got the scars on my wrists" ("Carpenters," p. 70). This comment shows that the suicide attempt must have occurred before Seymour first met Muriel, in the winter of 1941. And since Buddy never mentions Seymour's first attempt to kill himself, he apparently did not know about it until he read Seymour's diary. Hence, the suicide attempt must have occurred after Seymour was drafted and began basic training at Fort Monmouth, New Jersey, sometime in 1941.

When we consider Seymour's instability and his unwillingness to get along with normal people as revealed in his letter from Camp Hapworth, then it becomes clear why his decision to serve in the Army was bound to cause conflicts. For at Camp Hapworth, Seymour had decided that he simply could not get along with people who had "picayune, stunted attitudes toward everything in the universe and beyond." And during one confrontation with a camp counsellor, he had in fact threatened "to kill him or myself, possibly before nightfall." Since that time, Seymour had avoided contact with un-intellectual and un-spiritual people. This was easy for him, since he led the life of a poet, a student of literature and philosophy, and an English professor at a major university. Moreover, since he had been pursuing his quest for God via the self-directed paths of study and meditation, he had never learned to control his instability and to relate to normal people. Undoubtedly, the attitudes of his drill instructors and fellow draftees at Fort Monmouth were even more "picayune" and "stunted" than those of the people at Camp Hapworth. Hence Seymour's emotional instability and estrangement from ordinary humanity must have led to conflicts as violent as those at Camp Hapworth. But while he only threatened to kill himself at Camp Hapworth, he now actually slashed his wrists. He attempted to kill himself because his inability to get along with people made him realize that his spiritual progress had stopped, and because he hoped that he would be able to pursue his quest for God under better conditions in his next incarnation.

Shortly after his suicide attempt, Seymour met Muriel, and she gave him new hope since he saw marriage as a way of rejoining average humanity and resuming his spiritual progress. This comes out in the passage in Seymour's diary in which he explains the Vedanta view of marriage. On the day before his wedding, Seymour writes:

> I've been reading a miscellany of Vedanta all day. Marriage partners are to serve each other. Elevate, help, teach, strengthen each other, but above all *serve*. Raise their children honorably, lovingly, and with detachment. A child is a guest in the house, to be loved and respected—never possessed, since he belongs to God. How wonderful, how sane, how beautifully difficult, and therefore true. The joy of responsibility for the first time in my life ("Carpenters," p. 91).[5]

This statement is the key to an understanding of Seymour's decision to marry Muriel since it is after reading this passage in Seymour's diary that Buddy finally accepts Seymour's choice of Muriel as a marriage partner. The ideas in this passage must therefore be examined in detail.

The view of the responsibilities of marriage partners that Seymour here paraphrases is not the traditional Hindu view but that of modern Advaita Vedanta. While Seymour's statement implies spiritual equality of husbands and wives, the traditional Hindu view sees wives as definitely inferior and therefore unable to teach and elevate their husbands. This notion is strikingly illustrated in the most authoritative of the *shastras*, *The Laws of Manu*:

> . . . women must be kept in dependence by the males (of) their (families), and, if they attach themselves to sensual enjoyments, they must be kept under one's control . . . .

> (When creating them) Manu allotted to women (a love of their) bed, (of their) seat and (of) ornament, impure desires, wrath, dishonesty, malice, and bad conduct.
>
> For women no (sacramental) rite (is performed) with sacred texts, thus the law is settled; women (who are) destitute of strength and destitute of knowledge (of) Vedic texts, (are as impure as) falsehood (itself), that is a fixed rule.[6]

This traditional notion of the inferiority of women which, among orthodox Hindus, has persisted into the twentieth century,[7] is certainly not the view which Seymour calls "wonderful" and "sane."

The view of the relationship of marriage partners that modern Vedanta advocates goes back to the ideas of the oldest Indian scriptures, the Vedas. Contrary to *The Laws of Manu*, the Vedas prescribe that marriage partners must perform all religious ceremonies together. Man and wife are described as two halves of one being, and they are expected to support and sustain each other in their common quest for spiritual advancement. This is reflected in the old Sanskrit word for marriage, *vivaha*, which comes from the verb for "to lift, to hold up, to sustain."[8] The marriage ceremonies of the Vedas clearly illustrate this notion of partnership. The *Rig Veda*, for example, contains a marriage ceremony in which the marriage partners say: "May the Universal gods unite both of our hearts. May the waters unite them; may Matarisvan, Dahtri and the bountiful unite both our hearts."[9] And in the *Baudhayana Grihyasutra*, which is based on Vedic texts, there is this wedding prayer: "May thy heart be in mine, May thy thoughts be mine, Mayst thou listen to me with one heart and follow me and be my friend."[10] Commenting on this *Baudhayana* passage, Shakuntala Shastri writes:

> The marriage ritual of the Mantra-Brahmana [sections of the Vedas] is based on the co-operation of the wife in all the *Vratas* (i.e. duties) of her husband, and as such she is his companion in religious life as well as in the domestic life; this higher and more intimate relationship is lost in later times [i.e. when *The Laws of Manu* became the authoritative code].[11]

Modern Vedanta returns to this Vedic conception of the relationship between marriage partners and sees the wife as her husband's *dharmapatni*, her partner in a common spiritual quest. This idea is well expressed by one of Seymour's spiritual heroes, Sri Ramakrishna, when he says that "a wife endowed with spiritual wisdom is a real partner in life. She greatly helps her husband to follow the religious path . . . . Both of them are devotees of God—His servant and His handmaid."[12]

The idea of mutual service that Seymour's diary entry stresses probably comes from one of the many accounts of the marriage of Sri Ramakrishna and Sarada Devi. Their relationship illustrates well the service ideal and the notion of the immanence of God in the marriage partner. The story of this marriage appears, for instance, in a miscellany of essays by and about Vivekananda from which Buddy quotes in the "Introduction" ("Introduction," p. 109). Vivekananda explains that the marriage of Sri Ramakrishna and Sarada Devi was arranged by their parents when the girl was only five years old and that the girl continued to live with her parents until she came of age. The following is Vivekananda's account of what happened when she turned eighteen and went to claim her husband:

> In her far-off home the girl had heard that her husband had become a religious enthusiast and that he was even considered insane by many. She resolved to learn the truth for herself; so she set out and walked to the place where her husband was. When at last she stood in her husband's presence, he at once admitted her rights as his wife—although in India, any person, man or woman, who embraces a monastic life is thereby freed from all worldly obligation. The young man said to her: "As for me, the Divine Mother has shown me that She resides in every woman, and so I have learnt to look upon every woman as the Divine Mother [Kali]. But if you wish to draw me into the world, since I have been married to you, I am at your service."
>
> The maiden was a pure and noble soul and was able to understand her husband's aspirations and sympathize with them. She quickly told him that she had no wish to drag him down to the life of worldliness, but that all she desired was to remain near him, to serve him, and to learn from him.[13]

While Seymour was no Ramakrishna and did not expect Muriel to be a Sarada Devi, the passage nevertheless illustrates Seymour's notion that the primary responsibility of marriage partners is to elevate and to serve one another. And as Ramakrishna's response to Sarada Devi shows, the idea of service is based on the notion that God—in this case personified by Kali—is immanent in the partner. This idea is also illustrated in the *Brihadaranyaka Upanishad* as summarized by Vivekananda:

> "Never, O Beloved, is the husband loved on account of the husband, but because the Lord is in the husband." The Vedanta philosophy says that even in the love of husband and wife, although the wife is thinking that she is loving the husband, the real attraction is the Lord, who is present there. He is the only attraction; there is no other. But the wife in most cases does not know that it is so; yet ignorantly she is doing the right thing, which is loving the Lord . . . . Similarly, no one loves a child or anything else in the world except on account of Him who is within.[14]

That Seymour did indeed see God in Muriel is suggested in the "Introduction" when Buddy says that Seymour "looked for God in the queerest imaginable places," for instance even in "radio announcers, in newspapers, in taxicabs with crooked meters, literally everywhere." And in the story "Zooey" we learn that he also saw God in the imaginary "Fat Lady" who represents all that is repulsive about the radio audience for whom the Glass children were performing on the quiz show "It's a Wise Child."

While all this may clarify Seymour's views of the relationship of marriage partners, it does not explain why he chose Muriel and not someone who was more interested in things spiritual and intellectual. Two reasons offer themselves. One is that Seymour apparently believed that it was the will of God that he marry Muriel and nobody else, and the other is that he believed that Muriel had precisely what he needed to continue his progress toward spiritual perfection and union with God.

When Seymour first met Muriel in the winter of 1941, he must have been startled by her resemblance to Charlotte Mayhew. But when he came to know her better, he probably realized that it was she, and not Charlotte, whom he had seen in his "glimpses" as his future wife. Moreover, Muriel was, as Boo Boo puts it, "terrific-looking," and her unlikely attraction to a grotesque, ugly introvert like himself must have seemed a miracle to Seymour, an indication that they were indeed destined for each other. And when we examine Muriel's character, we realize that she had qualities that could be very helpful to Seymour in continuing his spiritual progress.

Even Muriel's sensuality did not present a problem to Seymour because he had by now overcome his own sensuality. This is suggested when, on the day before his wedding, he wants to talk to Muriel and asks her to meet him in the lobby of a hotel rather than at his own apartment. "The morality of this invitation," so Buddy points out, "was by no means out of character" ("Carpenters," p. 23). For another thing, sensuality was no longer an obstacle to Seymour's spiritual progress, for now that he was about to get married and to enter the householder stage of life, it would ensure the consummation of a sacrament. Eventually, however, so Seymour knew, Muriel would have to overcome her sensual tendencies, hopefully with his help since, according to Vedanta, sex is only justified when procreation is the aim. As Ramakrishna says about the partners in an ideal, spiritual marriage: "After the birth of one or two children, they live like brother and sister."[15] It is doubtful that the sensual Muriel would have found that acceptable; but then, Seymour hoped to teach and elevate her in spiritual matters, just as he expected her to help and strengthen him in other ways.

Muriel's most important quality, the one that Seymour hoped to profit from most in his quest for God, was her simplicity and lack of discrimination. By marrying Muriel and by giving up meditation and the quest for knowledge, Seymour hoped to overcome his estrangement from normal people and learn to respond to life naturally and uncritically. This is suggested in his diary, when he says about Muriel, "How I love and need her undiscriminating heart" and "How I worship her simplicity" ("Carpenters," pp. 67-68, 73).

In terms of Eastern philosophy, what Seymour wanted to achieve is the kind of indiscrimination and childlike simplicity which is called *viveka* in Hinduism and "the way of the Tao" in Taoism. Seymour comments on this concept in a conversation with a psychiatrist whom Mrs. Fedder had invited to dinner to get a free opinion on Seymour. The psychiatrist, Dr. Sims, aptly diagnosed Seymour's problem as a "perfection complex of some kind." He told Seymour that in order to be a happier person, he ought to be less discriminating and "accept the virtues of living the imperfect life." In commenting on this conversation, Seymour writes in his diary:

> I agree with him, but only in theory. I'll champion indiscrimination till doomsday, on the ground that it leads to health and a kind of very real, enviable happiness. *Followed purely*, it's the way of the Tao, and undoubtedly the highest way. But for a discriminating man to achieve this, it would mean that he would have to dispossess himself of poetry, go *beyond* poetry. That is, he couldn't possibly learn or drive himself to *like* bad poetry in the abstract, let alone equate it with good poetry. He would have to drop poetry altogether. I said it would be no easy thing to do ("Carpenters," p. 74).

"The way of the Tao" to which Seymour refers is the way of realizing the Absolute by giving up all intellectual striving and by submitting to a simpler life. This concept of the Tao, the Nameless Absolute, is very similar to the Hindu concept of *Brahman*. Lao-tse explains it in the opening lines of the *Tao Teh Ching*: "The Tao that can be told of / Is not the Absolute Tao; / The names that can be given / Are not Absolute Names."[16] Ramakrishna defines *Brahman* in a similar way: "What Brahman is cannot be described. Speech stops there."[17] Taoism and Hinduism agree that this Nameless Absolute cannot be understood via rational thought or study. In fact, book-learning is pointed out as a potential obstacle by both systems of thought. Lao-tse says: "Banish wisdom, discard knowledge, / and the people shall profit a hundredfold"; / "Banish learning, and vexations end."[18] Similarly, Ramakrishna often stressed that mere learning does not help man perceive the Absolute: "Books, scriptures and things like that only point the way to reach God. After finding the way, what more need is there of books and scriptures? Then comes the time for action."[19] This idea is elaborated by Vivekananda who says: "We may all read the Vedas and yet not realize anything; but when we practice their teachings, then we shall attain to that state in which we realize what the scriptures say, which penetrates where no reason nor perception nor inference can go."[20] Only when he goes beyond his intellect and his learning, so Vivekananda says, "then a man transcends the oridnary limits of reason and directly perceives things which are beyond all reason."[21]

This perception of "things which are beyond all reason" requires a kind of discrimination which Taoists and Hindus equate with indiscrimination. This indiscrimination leads to the highest form of knowledge which is very much like no-knowledge. Vivekananda explains this when he says: "You may ask what that state would be in which there is no mind, no knowledge. What we call knowledge is a lower state than one beyond knowledge . . . . ignorance is the lowest state; the two extremes seem the same."[22] Thus, according to both Taoism and Vedanta, somebody who is very close to full enlightenment might appear to be an extremely simple, undiscriminating person.

It was therefore because he felt he was about to be reborn into a new and simple life that Seymour was so overjoyed on the day of his wedding and did not want to share his happiness with anyone but Muriel: "I feel as though I am about to be born," he writes in his diary "Sacred, sacred day." Unable to make further spiritual progress via the paths of study and meditation, he was eager to leave the student stage of life, enter the stage of the householder, and continue his quest for God via the simple path of service, *karma yoga*. With Muriel's help, he hoped to transcend his erudition and discrimination, to find "the way of the Tao," and to attain *viveka*, the highest state of discrimination, which is indistinguishable from indiscrimination.

But Seymour also realized that this would not be easy for him. He says in his diary that for a discriminating man to achieve indiscrimination "would mean that he would have to dispossess himself of poetry, go *beyond* poetry. That is, he couldn't possibly learn or drive himself to *like* bad poetry in the abstract, let alone equate it with good poetry." He suggests here that he is afraid he might not be able to dispossess himself of the intellectual and spiritual habits he had acquired during the student stage of his life and that this might jeopardize his spiritual progress in the householder stage. But he knew that he must overcome these habits because they gave Muriel a feeling of estrangement and uncloseness. And since his "glimpses" had convinced him that it was God's will that he marry Muriel and serve her as best he could, he joyfully gave up the paths of study and meditation in order to become a householder and *karma yogin*. The radical change that Seymour was willing to make in his life is perhaps best illustrated by his promise to see a psychiatrist and to have himself "slightly overhauled" ("Carpenters," p. 75).

But despite his best intentions, Seymour found that his marriage did not help him resume his spiritual progress, and six years after he married Muriel, he committed suicide. Nevertheless Buddy insists that in marrying Muriel, Seymour had made the right decision, and he compares Seymour's judgment to that of the sage Chiu-fang Kao in the Taoist tale that Seymour once read to Franny. Kao was a superlative judge of horses because he was able to see "the spiritual mechanism" behind all things. And Buddy says that since Seymour's "permanent retirement from the scene, I haven't been able to think of anybody whom I'd care to send out to look for horses in his stead" ("Carpenters," p. 5). By stressing Seymour's ability as a seer, Buddy suggests that his suicide had nothing to do with his choice of Muriel as a marriage partner. The next chapter will examine what happened to Seymour in the six years between his wedding and his suicide and show why Seymour was unable to resume his spiritual progress in the householder stage of his life.

NOTES

[1] The quotations from the Glass stories in this chapter come from the Bantam paperback editions of *Raise High the Roof Beam, Carpenters and Seymour—An Introduction* (New York, 1965); *Franny and Zooey* (New York, 1964); *Nine Stories* (New York, 1964); and from "Hapworth 16,

1924," *New Yorker*, June 19, 1965, pp. 32-113.

[2] Swami Nikhilananda, "General Introduction" to *The Upanishads* (New York: Harper Brothers, 1949), I, 4-5.

[3] Swami Prabhavananda and Christopher Isherwood, trans., *The Song of God: Bhagavad Gita* (Hollywood: Vedanta Press, 1944), pp. 43-44.

[4] *Bhagavad Gita*, p. 41.

[5] Seymour's comments give the impression that he is summarizing a specific passage from a Vedanta text. But I have been unable to find any direct parallel in the two dozen Vedanta anthologies I have examined. Swami Adiswarananda of the Ramakrishna-Vivekananda Center in New York does not recognize the passage, either, and Professor Agehananda Bharati of Syracuse University is sure that it is "a concocted passage." I still think that there may be such a passage somewhere, but it is also possible that Seymour's ideas come from several different sources.

[6] George Bühler, trans., *The Laws of Manu* (Oxford: Clarendon Press, 1882), Sacred Books of the East Series, XXV, 327-328, 330.

[7] See for instance the description of a Brahman marriage in Sinclair Stevenson, *The Rites of the Twice-Born* (London: Oxford University Press, 1920), p. 98.

[8] Ray Bali Pandy, *Hindu Samskaras* (Delhi: Motilal Banarasidass, 1949), p. 233.

[9] *Rig Veda*, X, 85, 47. Quoted in Shakuntala Rao Shastri, *Women of the Vedic Age* (Bombay: Bharatiya Vidya Bhavan, 1952), p. 15.

[10] *Baudhayana Grihyasutra*, I, 4, 1. Quoted in Shastri, p. 172.

[11] Shastri, p. 136.

[12] M. (Mahendranath Gupta), *The Gospel of Sri Ramakrishna*, trans. Swami Nikhilananda (New York: Ramakrishna-Vivekananda Center, 1942), pp. 401-402.

[13] Swami Vivekananda, *Inspired Talks* (New York: Ramakrishna-Vivekananda Center 1958), pp. 167-168.

[14]Swami Vivekananda, *Karma Yoga and Bhakti Yoga* (New York: Ramakrishna-Vivekananda Center, 1955), pp. 175, 250.

[15]*The Gospel of Sri Ramakrishna*, p. 108.

[16]Lin Yutang, *The Wisdom of Laotse* (New York: Random House, 1948).

[17]*The Gospel of Sri Ramakrishna*, p. 835.

[18]*The Widsom of Laotse*, pp. 119, 128.

[19]*The Gospel of Sri Ramakrishna*, p. 729.

[20]Swami Vivekananda, *Raja Yoga* (New York: Ramakrishna-Vivekananda Center, 1955), p. 139.

[21]Vivekananda, *Raja Yoga*, p. 140.

[22]Vivekananda, *Raja Yoga*, pp. 116-117.

CHAPTER 14

Spiritual Deterioration

When we read "A Perfect Day for Bananafish" as an independent story, Seymour's suicide appears to be that of a man who was driven to despair by the lack of spirituality in everyone around him, especially his superficial and materialistic wife. But when we read it as part of the Glass series, we find that his death is not that of a victim or martyr at all but of someone who was in despair about his own shortcomings.

But interpreting "Bananafish" as part of the composite novel about Seymour's quest for God poses some problems because when Salinger wrote the story, he had not yet decided to make Seymour the God-seeker who would become the main character in a whole series of stories, nor had he formulated any particular religious philosophy for Seymour to follow. In fact, textual and biographical evidence shows that Salinger did not begin to study Advaita Vedanta, which forms the basis of the Glass philosophy, until several years after the publication of "Bananafish" (See Chapter 10: The Eastern Roots of the Glass Philosophy).

The decision to write a narrative series about Seymour and his spiritual influence on his siblings confronted Salinger with the problems of how to explain the character differences between the Seymour in "Bananafish" and in the later Glass stories and, above all, how to reconcile Seymour's suicide with his religious aspirations. He solved one of these two problems by making Buddy Glass claim authorship of "Bananafish" and by having him admit that he gave "the 'Seymour' in the story" some qualities that "the Seymour in Real Life" did not have. And he solved the other problem by suggesting in the later Glass stories that Seymour's suicide was due to his emotional instability and his spiritual deterioration. To determine what

"Bananafish" tells us about Seymour's quest for God, we must therefore consider the story in the light of Buddy's unreliability as a narrator and of the information that the other stories give us about Seymour's psychological and spiritual problems.

It seems that Buddy misrepresented Seymour in "Banana-fish" because he considered his brother a near-saint and wanted to blame his suicide on Muriel rather than on Seymour's own faults and weaknesses. Buddy admits in "Seymour—An Intro-duction" that the "Seymour" in "Bananafish" is "not Seymour at all but, oddly, someone with a striking resemblance to . . . myself" ("Introduction," p. 113).[1] This resemblance is particu-larly obvious when Buddy makes Seymour call Muriel a "Spiri-tual Tramp" and when he makes him tell Sybil Carpenter that Muriel is probably "at the hairdresser's. Having her hair dyed mink" ("Bananafish," pp. 4, 12). These comments show that Buddy saw Seymour as a victim of Muriel's superficiality and materialism, but they are at odds with Seymour's own attitude toward Muriel as expressed in his diary in "Raise High the Roof Beam, Carpenters." For when he married Muriel, Seymour found her concern for appearances and material things "human-size and beautiful" ("Carpenters," p. 72). In that diary, Seymour even predicted that Buddy would "despise" Muriel for her lack of spirituality. And Buddy's contempt for Muriel is quite apparent in the opening scene of "Bananafish" where Buddy stresses Muriel's obsessive concern with her own appear-ance and that of other people. By presenting Muriel as a crass materialist and by making Seymour seem resentful of her, Buddy tries to detract the reader's attention away from those "facts" which suggest that Seymour's suicide is due to his own shortcomings. Foremost among these facts are Seymour's psy-chological problems, which kept him in psychiatric wards of Army hospitals for three years, and his spiritual deterioration, which is revealed in his decision to shoot himself in his hotel room while sitting on a bed near the sleeping Muriel.

Seymour's psychological problems are mentioned in all but one of the six Glass stories.[2] In "Seymour—An Introduc-tion," Buddy refers to Seymour as a "Sick Man," a "classical neurotic," and an "unbalanced type" but refuses to report any incidents that would illustrate the nature of Seymour's prob-lems. Two other stories describe such incidents. In "Hap-

worth 16, 1924," the seven-year-old Seymour has a run-in with
a counsellor at summer camp and gets so upset that he threatens
to kill him or to commit suicide. In "Raise High the Roof Beam,
Carpenters," we learn that at the age of twelve, Seymour deliberately threw a rock at a little girl, injuring her so badly that she
needed nine stitches in her face. In that story, we find
out that, at the age of twenty four, Seymour slashed his
wrists in a suicide attempt and that, one year later, he
refused to show up for his own wedding because he was
too happy. But in "Carpenters," we also read in Seymour's diary that he was aware of his problems, for he
promised his bride to see an analyst. However, in "A
Perfect Day for Bananafish" we find that the psychiatric
treatment Seymour received in the Army did him more
harm than good. After all, he killed himself a week after his
release from an Army hospital. That these treatments
had something to do with Seymour's suicide is suggested by
Zooey when he tells his mother not to consult a psychiatrist
concerning Franny's nervous breakdown. He says: "Just think
of what analysis did for Seymour," and he warns Bessie that
Franny might "come out of analysis in even worse shape than
Seymour" ("Zooey," pp. 105-106, 110). The reason why Zooey
thinks that Seymour came out of analysis in bad shape is that
Seymour did not need psychiatric help because his problems,
like Franny's, were essentially spiritual rather than psychological in nature.

Several stories confirm that it was indeed spiritual and
not psychological problems which drove Seymour to suicide.
In the "Introduction," Buddy says that Seymour's death was
not due to such reasons as "a troubled childhood or a disordered
libido" but that he was "dazzled to death by his own scruples,
the blinding shapes and colors of his own sacred human conscience" ("Introduction," pp. 104-105). These scruples, so
we understand when we consider Seymour's suicide in the light
of his letter from Camp Hapworth, are his inability to love Muriel
and others who have "picayune, stunted attitudes toward everything in the universe and beyond." In this letter, Seymour is
worried that his inability to control his malice toward such
people might lead to his "utter dégringolade in this appearance."
By "dégringolade" Seymour not only means his physical but also
his spiritual undoing, for he knows that he has left his instability

uncorrected in his last two incarnations and says "it will not be corrected by friendly, cheerful prayer. It can only be corrected by dogged effort on my part" ("Hapworth," p. 44). But instead of making this effort and trying to learn how to get along with those whose values are less spiritual than his own, Seymour decided to withdraw from normal people as much as possible and to pursue his quest for enlightenment along the paths of study and meditation. These self-directed religious practices estranged him so much from common humanity that his spiritual progress came to a halt by the time he was twenty-four, and this is why Seymour made his first suicide attempt. But then he met Muriel and married her because he hoped that her normalness would help, teach, and strengthen him and that by serving her as her husband he would be able to resume his spiritual progress. But as we see in "Bananafish," he was unable to derive any spiritual benefits from his marriage.

Seymour's spiritual deterioration becomes particularly apparent when we compare his attitude toward Muriel just before he married her in 1942 and just before he killed himself in 1948. When he married Muriel, he said he "loved" and "needed" her "simplicity" and her "undiscriminating heart." At that time, he found her superficiality and materialism "humansize and beautiful" and said that he could not think of them "without being deeply, deeply moved" ("Carpenters," pp. 66-67, 72-73). But six years later, he could no longer love Muriel and only felt malice toward her, or else he would not have decided to sneak into the room where she was sleeping and blow his brains out while sitting next to her.

There are two reasons why Seymour was unable to reverse his spiritual deterioration. One has to do with his own shortcomings and the other with external circumstances. For one thing, Seymour only made an effort to overcome his instability when he noticed that it had stopped his spiritual progress. He realized too late that by withdrawing from those whose attitudes irritated him, he did nothing to correct his instability and instead became even less able to relate to normal people. And when he finally tried to rejoin common humanity by allowing himself to be drafted into the military service, he was unable to cope with the sudden change and tried to commit suicide.

However, he continued his efforts to overcome his instability
by marrying Muriel and by trying to make himself love all
those qualities that used to provoke his malice. But external
circumstances doomed him to failure.

The external circumstances that explain Seymour's continued spiritual deterioration all have to do with the war. When
Seymour married Muriel in 1942, he was stationed at a B-17
base in California while Muriel was living in New York; later
he was transferred to the European Theater of Operations; and
he did not come home until 1948, three years after the end of
the war. Thus in the six years that he was married to Muriel,
he did not spend much time with her and therefore could not
serve her or be strengthened by her. Instead, he had to deal
with Army people all this time, with the result that he had
a nervous breakdown which was so severe that he was treated
in Army hospitals for three years. These treatments increased
his instability rather than curing it, probably because he resent-
ed the concept of "normalcy" with which the Army psychia-
trists were operating, and these feelings of resentment may
have accelerated his spiritual deterioration.

When Seymour was reunited with Muriel, he apparently
hoped that she might still help him reverse his spiritual deterioration. He tried to make a new start with her by agreeing to a second honeymoon at the same hotel in Florida where they had
stayed during their first one.[3] But Seymour and Muriel had different ideas as to what this new beginning should be like. While
Muriel was hoping for a regular, romantic honeymoon, Seymour
did not want to have any sexual intimacy with her. This is suggested by the fact that their hotel room had twin beds and that
Muriel is reading a magazine article entitled "Sex is Fun—or
Hell."

Seymour's refusal to sleep with Muriel indicates that he
believed his spiritual deterioration was so far advanced that a
normal marital relationship could not reverse it. He probably
wanted his relationship with Muriel to be the kind of intense
spiritual union that Vedanta Hinduism considers the ideal marriage. According to Vedanta, marriage should not be seen as
an opportunity for the unrestrained gratification of sexual
desires. Instead, as one Vedanta text puts it: "Restraint of
one's lustful tendencies, finally resulting in their thorough

eradication, is the aim of the Hindu marriage."[4] This means that the sex act should be seen only as a sacrament, as the means of procreation. And Seymour apparently did not want Muriel to conceive a child before she had become a more spiritual person, a *dharmapatni*, or helpmate in his spiritual quest. For it is a Hindu belief that the soul, or *jiva* of a child that is about to be conceived is strongly affected by the spiritual tendencies of both parents. As Ramananda Saraswati explains: "The coming Jeeva [sic] is first conceived by the father and sojourns in his body for about two months before the mother receives him. For the preservation and development . . . of the Jeeva, both the places of sojourn, the father and mother, must be in a condition of *similar* purity."[5]

Clearly, Seymour expected too much from Muriel. Had they lived together during the six years since they were married, Seymour might have elevated Muriel with his religious ideas and Muriel might have helped him to resume his spiritual progress by teaching him how to enjoy a simple, undiscriminating life and how to relate to normal people. But during their six years of separation, Muriel remained as superficial and materialistic as she was on the day of her wedding, and Seymour became more unstable and less capable of getting along with normal, unspiritual people. Thus, while Seymour had originally found Muriel's simplicity and her undiscriminating heart very touching and lovable, he finally developed so much resentment and malice toward her that he decided to make his suicide as upsetting to her as he possibly could.

If we see Seymour's death in the context of his quest for God, then it shows that during the last years of his life, Seymour had not only stopped making any spiritual progress but had actually experienced a severe spiritual decline. His decision to shoot himself in the room where Muriel was sleeping is an act of malice, an attempt to hurt Muriel, which suggests that Seymour may even have been so blinded by his despair about his spiritual deterioration that, like Buddy, he blamed Muriel for it.

Thus Buddy's characterization of Seymour in "Bananafish" is perhaps not as far off the mark as Buddy's brothers and sisters believed when they told him that the Seymour in the story is not the real Seymour at all but someone with a striking resemblance to Buddy himself. After all, Buddy often points out that he is spiritually not as far advanced as Seymour was. Therefore, Buddy's slip of the pen, his involuntary misrepresentation of Seymour's personality in "Bananafish," actually makes sense, because by the time Seymour killed himself, he had sunk, as it were, to Buddy's level.

Seen as part of the religious novel about Seymour's quest for God, "Bananafish" shows that Seymour was definitely not a saint when he died. This is especially apparent from the nasty way he chose to kill himself. In the context of the other parts of the Glass series, "Bananafish" suggests that the reason for Seymour's suicide was his despair about his spiritual deterioration, and particularly about his inability to love those who don't share his values. And he was unable to love people such as Muriel because he has thoroughly alienated himself from them by pursuing his quest for God, for most of his life, in too selfish a manner.

But despite his faults, vices, and meannesses, Seymour exerted a powerful influence on his siblings, both during his lifetime and after his death. In part, this influence was positive and in part negative. The dual nature of this influence is best illustrated in the stories "Franny" and "Zooey."

NOTES

[1] The quotations from the Glass stories in this chapter come from the Bantam paperback editions of *Nine Stories* (New York, 1964); *Raise High the Roof Beam, Carpenters and Seymour—An Introduction* (New York, 1965); *Franny and Zooey* (New York, 1964); and from "Hapworth 16, 1924," *New Yorker*, June 19, 1965, pp. 32-113.

²"Franny" is the only Glass story that doesn't mention Seymour's suicide.

³Actually, Seymour and Muriel cannot have stayed at the same hotel in Florida during their honeymoon "before the war" because they did not get married until June of 1942, when the war was well under way. Thus, Muriel's comment is another indication that Salinger had not yet outlined Seymour's life story when he wrote "Bananafish."

⁴Ramanada Saraswati, *The Hindu Ideal* (Madras: Patanjali & Co., 1933), p. 189.

⁵Saraswati, p. 197.

CHAPTER 15

Seymour's Example

Like "A Perfect Day for Bananafish," "Franny" was written at a time when Salinger had not yet worked out his plans for a narrative series about Seymour's life and teachings. The story does not mention Seymour and his suicide, nor does it mention any of the other Glasses; in fact, it does not even mention that Franny's last name is Glass. But unlike "Bananafish" and like the later Glass stories, "Franny" has as its central theme the quest for enlightenment. The way in which Franny pursues this quest appears positive when we consider the story as a self-contained account and negative when we consider it in the context of other parts of the Glass series. When we read the story by itself, we sympathize with Franny's decision to use the Jesus Prayer in order to withdraw from the crass, materialistic world of people like her boyfriend, Lane Coutell. But when we read the story as part of the composite novel, we will see her withdrawal into the Jesus Prayer as negative because we can't help wonder if Franny is not going to become as estranged from common humanity as Seymour and if her nervous breakdown is not an indication that she may eventually wind up killing herself just like her older brother.

Seen as part of the narrative series about Seymour and his influence on his siblings, "Franny" illustrates the negative effects that Seymour's example had on his sister. In order to understand the nature of Seymour's influence, we must examine the religious ideas that guided Franny, particularly we must determine what *The Way of a Pilgrim* and various Eastern texts have to say about the practice and effects of incessant prayer. This information shows that Seymour is indeed responsible for Franny's religious crisis because by withdrawing into a self-directed way of striving for enlightenment, Franny is following Seymour's example. Moreover, their means of with-drawal, Franny's Jesus Prayer and Seymour's *raja yoga*, are quite similar.

There can be no doubt that Franny's religious crisis is a result of the religious training to which Seymour subjected her. Zooey complains that the younger Glass children were "funnel-fed on religious philosophy," and this religious train-ing began practically in infancy. In "Carpenters," for example, we find Seymour reading a Taoist tale to the ten-month-old Franny, and in "Zooey," we learn that Seymour and Buddy began Zooey's and Franny's religious education very early because, as Buddy explains, "we thought it would be wonder-fully constructive to at least . . . tell you as much as we knew about the men—the saints, the arhats, the bodhisattvas, the jivanmuktas—who knew something or everything about this state of being. That is, we wanted you both to know what Jesus and Gautama and Lao-tse and Shankaracharya and Hui-neng and Sri Ramakrishna etc., were before you knew too much or anything about Homer or Shakespeare or even Blake or Whitman, let alone George Washington and his cherry tree or the definition of a peninusla or how to parse a sentence" ("Zooey," pp. 65-66).[1] But when Zooey tries to convince Franny that her nervous breakdown is due to the "freakish education" she received in Seymour's "home seminars," Fran-ny rejects this analysis of her problem. Instead she wishes Sey-mour were still alive to give her advice, for she says: "I want to talk to Seymour." This makes it clear that Franny's religious attitudes were decisively shaped by Seymour and that she con-tinued to follow his teachings even after his suicide.

But Seymour is not only responsible for the "freakish standards" which are at the bottom of Franny's religious crisis, he is also responsible for her withdrawal into mysticism. He taught his siblings that man's highest purpose is the quest for God and he acquainted them with various ways of pursuing this quest. One of these ways is outlined in *The Way of a Pilgrim* and its sequel *The Pilgrim Continues His Way*, two books which Franny claims to have discovered at college but which she actually got from Seymour. As Zooey tells his moth-er: ". . . she got *both* books out of Seymour and Buddy's old room, where they'd been sitting on Seymour's desk for as long as I can remember." These two books advocate a path toward God-consciousness which requires withdrawal from all normal, everyday activities. They provide the rationale for Franny when she decides that she can no longer live in the world of the Lane Coutells. And as we know from the story "Zooey," Franny is unable to go through with her plans for her weekend with Lane and instead takes refuge at her parents' apartment where she does little else but lie on a couch "crying and mumbling to herself for forty-eight hours."

An examination of the story in the light of *The Way of a Pilgrim* and *The Pilgrim Continued His Way* explains why Franny feels the need to say the Jesus Prayer, and it also shows that a more important theme in the story than that of the conflict between spiritual and material values is that of the quest for God.

Both pilgrim books explain again and again that the purpose of the Jesus Prayer is to achieve "union with God."[2] That is the long range goal. But first, the God-seeker must develop "detachment from all earthly things" and to "cleanse the soul from all sensuality."[3] And he can do that by reciting the Jesus Prayer. Among the many examples that the two pilgrim books give of the effects of the prayer, *The Way of a Pilgrim* mentions the case of "a pleasure loving girl [who] prayed on her return home, and the prayer showed her the way to the virginal life and obedience to the teachings of Christ."[4] This example explains why Franny is so attracted to the prayer. She wants "to purify [her] whole outlook and get an absolutely new conception of what everything is about" and ultimately, so she hopes, she will "get to see God" ("Franny," pp. 37, 39). And as we can tell from her decision to go home to her parents' apartment rather than to go through with Lane's plans for a tryst at her rooming house, she has definitely taken the first step in the direction of purifying her outlook.

In order to understand what is involved in Franny's plan to pray incessantly, we must examine what is said about the Jesus Prayer in the *Philokalia*, a collection of mystical writings by the Fathers of the Eastern Orthodox Church. The ideas of the *Philokalia* have much in common, as Franny mentions to Lane, with Buddhist and Hindu teachings, for the *Philokalia* not only advocates incessant prayer but also controlled breathing and meditation. This is how the pilgrim summarizes the instructions of the *Philokalia*:

> "picture to yourself your heart . . ., turn your eyes to it just as though you were looking at it through your breast, and picture it as clearly as you can. And with your ears listen closely to its beating, beat by beat. When you have got into the way of doing this, begin to fit the words of the Prayer to the beats of the heart one after the other, looking at it all the time. Thus with the first beat, say or think 'Lord,' with the second 'Jesus,' with the third 'Christ,' with the fourth 'have mercy,' and with the fifth, 'on me.' And do it over and over again. This will come easily to you, for you already know the groundwork and the first part of praying with the heart. Afterwards, when you have grown used to what I have just told you about, you must begin bringing the whole Prayer of Jesus into and out of your heart in time with your breathing, as the Fathers taught. Thus, as you draw your breath in, say, or imagine yourself saying, 'Lord Jesus Christ,' and as you breathe again, 'have mercy on me.' Do this as often and as much as you can, and in a short space of time you will find a slight and not unpleasant pain in your heart, followed by a warmth. Thus by God's help you will get the joy of self-acting inward prayer of the heart. But then, whatever you do, be on your guard against imagination and any sort of visions. Don't accept any of them whatever, for the holy Fathers lay down most strongly that inward prayer should be kept free from visions, lest one fall into temptation."[5]

A *starets,* a spiritual guide or Christian *guru,* is necessary to help the beginner overcome such temptations. As the pilgrim explains: " . . . the inward process could not go on properly and successfully without the guidance of a teacher."[6] The visions that the pilgrim is referring to are side effects of spiritual progress. In the two *Pilgrim* books, we find that those who practice the Jesus Prayer often experience several such supersensory phenomena. In one case, a blind man not only finds himself "flooded . . . with light" but even has a vision of a church that is actually burning in a distant village. Others, as his *starets* tells the pilgrim, "see light in the darkest rooms, as though it streamed from every article in it, and see things by it; who see their doubles and enter into the thoughts of other people."[7]

But the God-seeker must reject all these manifestations of his spiritual progress, for "God would have the Christian absolutely renounce all his desires and delights and attachments, and submit himself entirely to His divine will."[8]   Delight about signs of spiritual progress and eagerness for such progress are, in the word of the *starets*, evidence of "spiritual covetousness" which is a major obstacle on the way to God.   Thus one reason why the Jesus Prayer isn't helping Franny to overcome her ego may be that she is too intent on seeing results, on feeling a change in her outlook.   Another reason may be that she is not practicing the prayer under the supervision of a spiritual guide.   And this is probably why Franny shows up at her parents' apartment.   She hopes to get some spiritual guidance, either by talking to Zooey or by calling up Buddy.

But most important to the practice of incessant prayer is withdrawal from all distractions.   Throughout the first of the two pilgrim books, the pilgrim seeks out secluded places where he prays and meditates.   And during his several pilgrimages, he usually takes side roads through deep forests so as not to be disturbed by people.   And the second volume, *The Pilgrim Continues His Way*, ends with a discussion in which a hermit and a monk maintain that serious God-seekers must withdraw from society.   A professor asks: "But the silent hermit who has withdrawn from human society, in what way can he, in his inactivity, be of service to his neighbor and what contribution can he make to the well-being of human society? He completely destroys in himself that law of the Creator which concerns union in love of one's kind and beneficient influence upon the brotherhood."   But the hermit denies this and argues that the God-seeker who withdraws from society and devotes himself entirely to his own spiritual advancement performs an important service to humanity: "His experience and teaching pass on from generation to generation, as we see ourselves and of which we avail ourselves from ancient times to this day. And this in no sense differs from Christian love; it even surpasses it in its results [because] by his very life he benefits, edifies and persuades to the search for God."[9]   This argument in favor of the solitary quest for God is the essence of the two *Pilgrim* books and it explains Franny's withdrawal from the world of ordinary people.

The Way of a Pilgrim and *The Pilgrim Continues His Way*
make it clear that Franny's religious crisis marks a turning point
in her life.   The religious training she has received from Seymour and Buddy has not only led to a conflict between her
values and the values of people like Lane Coutell but also to
an inner conflict between the demands of her physical nature
and her spiritual aspirations.   Her brother Zooey is aware of
this inner conflict.   Zooey suggests that Franny really knows
that Lane is "a big nothing" and when he hears that Franny
has referred to Lane as "brilliant," Zooey says, "That's just
sex talking . . . ."   Because of her simultaneous feelings of attraction and revulsion, Franny has "to strain" when she tells Lane
that she loves him.   And when she collapses at Sickler's Restaurant, this is a sign that she can no longer make this kind of
effort.   At the end of the story she has come to believe that
the opposite demands of her physical and spiritual nature are
irreconcilable and that she must make a choice.   And that
she has made a choice is clear at the end of the story when
she is saying the Jesus Prayer.   She has decided to withdraw
from the world and follow the teachings of the *Pilgrim* books.
This would seem a radical decision for any other twenty-year-
old girl to make, but not for Franny Glass.

By withdrawing into the Jesus Prayer, Franny is following
the example of her dead brother Seymour who also withdrew
from the world to pursue his quest for God.   Moreover, Seymour used a similar method of turning inward.   This becomes
clear when Zooey explains to his mother that Franny's method
of incessant prayer, combined with controlled breathing and
meditation, is very similar to *raja yoga*, which Seymour practiced for most of his life:

> The idea, really, is that sooner or later, completely on its own,
> the prayer moves from the lips and the head down to a center
> in the heart and becomes an automatic function in the person,
> right along with the heartbeat.   And then, after a time, once
> the prayer *is* automatic in the heart, the person is supposed to
> enter into the so-called reality of things.   The subject doesn't
> really come up in either of the [two *Pilgrim*] books, but, in East-
> ern terms, there are seven subtle centers in the body, called *chak-
> ras*, and the one most closely connected with the heart is called
> *anahata*, which is supposed to be sensitive and powerful as hell,

and when it's activated, it, in turn, activates another of these
centers, between the eyebrows, called *ajna*—it's the pineal gland,
really, or, rather, an aura around the pineal gland—and then, bingo,
there's an opening of what mystics call the 'third eye.' It's nothing
new, for God's sake. It didn't just start with the little pilgrim's
crowd, I mean. In India, for God knows how many centuries,
it's been known as *japam*. *Japam* is just the repetition of any of
the human names of God. Or the names of his incarnations—his
avatars, if you want to get technical. The idea being that if you
call out the name long enough and regularly enough and *lit*erally
from the heart, sooner or later you'll get an answer. Not exactly an answer. A *response*" ("Zooey," pp. 113-114).

The similarities between Franny's Jesus Prayer and Seymour's
raja yoga become even clearer when we examine what Vedanta
texts have to say about the practice of incessant prayer.

Zooey compares Franny's saying the Jesus Prayer to the
Hindu practice of *japam*. This is how one of Seymour's idols,
Sri Ramakrishna explains that practice:

> "Japam means silently repeating God's name in solitude. When
> you chant His name with single-minded devotion you can see
> God's form and realize Him. Suppose there is a piece of timber
> sunk in the water of the Ganges and fastened with a chain to the
> bank. You proceed link by link, holding to the chain, and you
> dive into the water and follow the chain. Finally you are able
> to reach the timber. In the same way, by repeating God's name
> you become absorbed in Him and finally realize Him."[10]

If one's chosen form of God is *Nirguna Brahman*, the God
without attributes, then the "name" of God that his *guru* is
likely to make him repeat is the holy syllable "OM." Vivekananda says about this syllable that it is "the Sound-Brahman,"
or "the word representative of the thought out of which the
universe has become manifested."[11] That Franny was familiar
with the Hindu parallels to the Jesus Prayer, becomes apparent
when she tells Lane Coutell: "In India, they tell you to meditate on the 'Om,' which means the same thing, really [as saying
the Jesus Prayer], and the exact same result is supposed to
happen . . . . Something happens in some absolutely non-physical part of the heart [the *anahata*, or fifth *chakra*] where the

Hindus say that Atman [*Brahman* in the form of man's soul]
resides . . . and you get to see God" ("Franny," p. 39).

Even more similar to the Jesus Prayer than meditation on
the word OM, is the practice of repeating a *mantra* or prayer,
during *raja yoga* meditation. According to Vivekananda, the
purpose of *raja yoga* is to liberate the divine energy, or life
force, which is thought to be coiled up at the bottom of the
spine, and to make it travel along the spine and strike in turn
all seven subtle centers or *chakras* until it hits the highest one,
"the thousand petalled lotus of the brain." The *raja yogin*
does this through meditation, controlled breathing, and synchronization of a *mantra*, such as the Jesus Prayer, with his
breathing. When he is able to activate the subtle center in the
brain, so Vivekananda explains, then "the whole brain, as it
were, reacts, and the result is the full braze of illumination."[12]
As one is making progress in the practice of *raja yoga*, one will
first see lights, and after a while one will experience other supersensory phenomena. Vivekananda says: "For instance after
the first few months of practice you will begin to find that you
can read another's thoughts; they will come to you in picture
form. Perhaps you will hear something happening at a long
distance when you concentrate your mind with a wish to hear.
These glimpses will come, by little bits at first. . . . "[13] And
as we can see in "Hapworth," Seymour was fully familiar with
the "lights" and the "glimpses" mentioned by Vivekananda.
These effects of the practice of *raja yoga* are strikingly similar to the effects of the Jesus Prayer as described in the *Pilgrim* books: The advanced practitioners of the Jesus Prayer
also see lights, can read thoughts of others, and have glimpses
of things happening far away (See Chapter 10, pp. 123-164).

Another similarity between the practice of *raja yoga* and
the Jesus Prayer is that both of these paths toward God require
withdrawal from everyday life. And Franny's withdrawal is the
most important similarity between her quest for God and Seymour's. As in the case of Seymour, we must ask if this withdrawal is not an escape, an evasion of her responsibility to
others, for it seems that it is her inability to love those whose
values she can't accept which makes Franny retreat into the
Jesus Prayer.

When we consider what happened to Seymour as a result of his withdrawal, we realize that Franny is following a dangerous example. After all, Seymour became so estranged from normal people that his conflicts with others eventually resulted in spiritual deterioration and suicide. But Franny did not recognize this. For one thing, she did not see much of Seymour during the last eight years of his life. This is because Seymour and Buddy moved away from the family and into their own apartment in 1940; a year later, Seymour joined the Army; and he remained in the Army until shortly before his suicide in 1948. Moreover, as Buddy mentions in his letter to Zooey, the Glass siblings "all agreed not to say a word" about Seymour's suicide ("Zooey," p. 67). Consequently, Franny was unaware of Seymour's spiritual decline. And she saw his suicide as the death of a martyr, because this is how Buddy portrayed it in "A Perfect Day for Bananafish." Franny therefore did not hesitate to follow Seymour's example.

As I have shown in an earlier chapter, when we read "Franny" as an independent story, we are made to sympathize with Franny's spiritual values because they stand in such sharp contrast to the crass materialism of Lane Coutell. Hence we understand why she escapes into the Jesus Prayer. But when we see the story in the context of Seymour's similar withdrawal and its consequences, then we realize that she uses the Jesus Prayer as an escape from her responsibilities to others and that she offers her love to God so that she doesn't have to bother with people. The crux of her problem is that she pursues her quest for God in a way that is so self-directed that it is bound to fail. This is precisely why Seymour's quest for God failed. And as I will show in the next chapter, Zooey recognizes this and tries to set Franny straight by pointing out to her the difference between Seymour's example and Seymour's teachings.

NOTES

[1] The quotations from the Glass stories in this chapter come from the Bantam paperback edition of *Franny and Zooey* (New York, 1964).

[2] R. M. French, trans. *The Way of a Pilgrim* and *The Pilgrim Continues His Way* (New York: Seabury Press, 1952), pp. 102-103.

[3] *The Way of a Pilgrim*, pp. 15, 23.

[4] *The Way of a Pilgrim*, p. 207.

[5] *The Way of a Pilgrim*, pp. 102-103.

[6] *The Way of a Pilgrim*, p. 105.

[7] *The Way of a Pilgrim*, p. 105.

[8] *The Way of a Pilgrim*, p. 103.

[9] *The Way of a Pilgrim*, pp. 224-225.

[10] M. (Mahendranath Gupta) *The Gospel of Sri Ramakrishna*, trans. Swami Nikhilananda (New York: Ramakrishna-Vivekananda Center, 1942), pp. 878-879.

[11] Swami Vivekananda, *Karma Yoga and Bhakti Yoga* (New York: Ramakrishna-Vivekananda Center, 1955), p. 151.

[12] Swami Vivekananda, *Raja Yoga* (New York: Ramakrishna-Vivekananda Center, 1955), p. 57.

[13] Vivekananda, *Raja Yoga*, pp. 25-26.

CHAPTER 16

Seymour's Teachings

"Zooey" is the final chapter in the composite novel about Seymour's quest for God and his spiritual influence on his siblings. It is the only Glass story that contains explicit criticism of Seymour's religious ideas, but it also explains that the core of his later teachings is valid, even though Seymour was unable to practice what he preached and even though he killed himself in despair. Zooey at first attacks Seymour and his teachings when he blames him for having turned Franny and himself into "freaks." But at the end of the story, Zooey uses an idea of Seymour's to help Franny pull out of her religious crisis. This apparent contradiction is due to Zooey's realization that there is a difference between Seymour's earlier and his later teachings.

Franny and Zooey were unaware of the shift in the direction of Seymour's quest for God because it occurred gradually and was not completed until after Seymour had left home. Zooey did not have an inkling of it until Buddy repudiated Seymour's earlier teachings in a letter he wrote three years after Seymour's suicide. And even then, Zooey did not quite understand Seymour's change. He comes closer to comprehending it four years later, when he re-reads Buddy's letter in search for advice on how to help Franny overcome her crisis. And even then, his realization occurs only gradually. He approached his insight when he meditates on some inscriptions on the door of Seymour's and Buddy's old room, but it does not hit him with full force until he remembers that Seymour once told him to shine his shoes for the Fat Lady. At this point Zooey suddenly understands that Seymour had the same problem in getting along with others as Franny and himself and that these problems made Seymour change his outlook.

Zooey explains Seymour's negative influence to his mother

when he tells her that Seymour and Buddy have turned Franny and himself into "freaks":

> "We're *freaks*, the two of us, Franny and I . . . I'm a twenty-five-year-old freak and she's a twenty-year-old freak, and both those bastards are responsible . . . . The symptoms are a little more delayed in Franny's case than mine, but she's a freak, too, and don't you forget it. I swear to you, I could murder them both without even batting an eyelash. The great teachers. The great emancipators. My God. I can't even sit down to lunch with a man any more and hold up my end of a decent conversation. I either get so bored or so goddam preachy that if the son of a bitch had any sense, he'd break his chair over my head" ("Zooey," pp. 103-104).[1]

And in his conversation with Franny, Zooey says something very similar:

> "We're freaks, that's all. Those two bastards got us nice and early and made us into freaks with freakish standards, that's all. We're the Tattooed Lady, and we're never going to have a minute's peace, the rest of our lives, till everybody else is tattooed, too . . . . On top of everything else . . . we've got 'Wise Child' complexes. We've never really got off the goddam air. None of us. We don't talk, we hold forth. We don't converse, we expound" ("Zooey," pp. 139-140).

The nature of the education that made Zooey and Franny into freaks is revealed in Buddy's letter to Zooey. In this letter, Buddy tells Zooey: ". . . I know how bitterly you resent the years when S. and I were regularly conducting home seminars, and the metaphysical sittings in particular" ("Zooey," p. 66). Part of Buddy's purpose in writing the letter is, so he says, to tell Zooey "*why* S. and I took over your and Franny's education as early and as highhandedly as we did" ("Zooey," p. 64).

Buddy explains that the education that they gave Zooey and Franny was more religious than academic since Seymour had begun to feel that academic knowledge might only be an obstacle on the path to God-consciousness. By the time Zooey and Franny were able to read, Buddy says he and Seymour "had no real urge even to push our favorite classics at the two of you—not, anyway, with the same gusto that we had at the twins [Walter and Waker] or Boo Boo." They didn't because they were afraid that Zooey and Franny might turn into "child pedants and academic weisenheimers." Instead, Seymour decided to emphasize Zooey and Franny's religious education. Buddy writes:

> ". . . Seymour had already begun to believe (and I agreed with him, as far as I was able to see the point) that education by any name would smell as sweet, and maybe much sweeter, if it didn't begin with a quest for knowledge at all but with a quest, as Zen would put it, for no-knowledge. Dr. Suzuki says somewhere that to be in a state of pure consciousness—*satori*—is to be with God before he said, Let there be light. Seymour and I thought that it might be a good thing to hold back this light from you and Franny (at least as far as we were able), and all the many lower, more fashionable lighting effects—the arts, sciences, classics, languages—till you were both able to at least conceive of a state of being where the mind knows the source of all light. We thought it would be wonderfully constructive to at least (that is, if our own 'limitations' got in the way) tell you as much as we knew about the men—the saints, the arhats, the bodhisattvas, the jivanmuktas—who knew something or everything about this state of being. That is, we wanted you both to know who and what Jesus and Gautama and Lao-tse and Shankaracharya and Hui-neng and Sri Ramakrishna, etc., were before you knew too much or anything about Homer or Shakespeare or even Blake or Whitman, let alone George Washington and his cherry tree or the definition of a peninsula or how to parse a sentence" ("Zooey," pp. 65-66).

But it seems that the religious training which Seymour and Buddy gave Zooey and Franny did more harm than the academic knowledge they had earlier pushed at Walter, Waker, and Boo Boo. For while Zooey and Franny both experienced religious crises, there is no indication in any of the Glass stories that Walter, Waker, or Boo Boo had nervous breakdowns or ulcers.

In the last years before he relinquished the guidance of his younger siblings, Seymour apparently began to realize that a preoccupation with religion can have just as negative an effect as too much academic knowledge. This is why he urged Zooey to shine his shoes and why he told Franny to be funny for the Fat Lady. Seymour first mentioned the Fat Lady in 1937, when Zooey was seven. At that time, Zooey did not understand "what the hell he was talking about," but he did what Seymour told him because somehow "it made *sense.*" It is not until eighteen years later, when he tries to help Franny overcome her religious crisis that Zooey understands that shining one's shoes for the Fat Lady is a metaphor for a particular way of life and a particular path toward God, for the life of action and the path of service.

Seymour's gradual change of outlook, his advocating *karma yoga,* the path of action and service, instead of *jnana* and *raja yoga,* the paths of study and meditation, is further illustrated in a letter he wrote to Buddy, three years after he told Zooey to shine his shoes for the Fat Lady. In this letter, Seymour talks about Buddy's career as a writer. He tells him to trust his inborn talent when he says: "Follow your heart, win or lose." And then he asks: "When was writing ever your profession? It's never been anything but your religion." And since writing is Buddy's religion, he will only be asked two questions at the end of his life: *"Were most of your stars out? Were you busy writing your heart out?"* ("Introduction," p. 160). What Seymour means here is that Buddy should make his work his means of spiritual development by writing with all his might and by writing only when he is truly inspired.

Three years after Seymour's death, Buddy passed the same advice on to Zooey. At the time, Zooey tried to decide whether to continue his formal education beyond the M.A. degree or to pursue a career in show business. Buddy urged him not to follow his head and become a Ph.D. but to follow his heart and become an actor. He tells him: "*Act,* Zachary Martin Glass, when and where you want to, since you feel you must, but do it *with all your might*" ("Zooey," p. 68). Buddy gives this advice to Zooey as an antidote to the religious training that he and Seymour had given to Zooey in his childhood and adolescence. Seymour's death has pointed out to Buddy the dangers of following the paths of study and meditation, and he had become worried about Zooey because Zooey had a reputation in his college dorm "for going off and sitting in meditation for ten hours at a time," and *that*, so Buddy says, made him worry ("Zooey," p. 67).

After re-reading Buddy's letter, Zooey tries to pass along Buddy's advice to Franny. But he fails since he does not quite understand this advice and because he can only put it in negative terms. He tells Franny that it is wrong to quit college just because she is disgusted with the self-centeredness of people like Professor Tupper and that it is equally wrong to give up her acting career just because she is disgusted with her own desire for applause and recognition. Withdrawal into the Jesus Prayer is wrong, so Zooey tells his sister, because he suspects that she is "using it as a substitute for doing whatever the hell your duty is in life or just your daily duty" ("Zooey," p. 169). Rather than telling her in positive terms that doing her duty is the only religious thing she can do, Zooey berates Franny for what she is doing wrong. When Franny reacts negatively to his criticism, Zooey has to give up his attempt to talk her out of the Jesus Prayer.

But after Zooey goes to Seymour's and Buddy's old room, reads some inscriptions on the door and meditates on them, he is able to understand Seymour's and Buddy's advice. In particular, it is a passage from the *Bhagavad Gita* which helps Zooey understand Seymour's teachings. This passage is considered to be the core statement of the *Gita* because it expresses the principle of *karma yoga*, the path of service. Seymour apparently inscribed it on the door of his and Buddy's room as the "top entry" after he had come to see the path of service as superior to the paths of study and meditation:

> You have the right to work, but for the work's sake only. You have no right to the fruits of your work. Desire for the fruits of work must never be your motive in working. Never give way to laziness, either.
>
> Perform every action with your heart fixed on the Supreme Lord. Renounce attachment to the fruits. Be even tempered . . . in success and failure; for it is this evenness of temper which is meant by yoga.
>
> Work done with anxiety about results is far inferior to work done without such anxiety, in the calm of self-surrender. Seek

refuge in the knowledge of Brahman. They who work selfishly for results are miserable.

—"Bhagavad Gita" ("Zooey," p. 177).[2]

After reading this and several other quotes on the door, Zooey sits down at Seymour's old desk and meditates. He sits, with his face in his hands, "inert but not asleep, for a good twenty minutes." Then he reads an entry from Seymour's diary which dates to 1938, just before Seymour's change in direction. It is an account of Seymour's twenty-first birthday, and Zooey stops in the middle of it: ". . . again he leaned forward on his elbows and buried his face in his hands. This time he sat motionless for almost a half hour" ("Zooey," pp. 181-182). Apparently Zooey is trying to get in touch with Seymour's spirit in order to help Franny. He does this because a few minutes earlier, during their conversation, Franny had whimpered: "I want to talk to Seymour." Zooey's attempt to put himself in touch with Seymour seems to be successful because when he makes his phone call to Franny, he appears to be controlled by Seymour's spirit: "When he moved again, it was as though marionette strings had been attached to him and given an overzealous yank. He appeared to be given just enough time to pick up his cigar before another jerk of the invisible strings swung him over to the chair at the second desk in the room—Buddy's desk— where the phone was" ("Zooey," p. 182). Then he calls Franny, and this time he manages to convice Franny that the other-directed path of service is superior to all self-directed religious practices.

The key to Zooey's success is that he now interprets Buddy's advice in terms of the *Bhagavad Gita.* He tells Franny:

> "You can say the Jesus Prayer from now till doomsday, but if you don't realize that the only thing that counts in the religious life is de*tach*ment, I don't see how you'll ever move an *inch.* Detachment, buddy, and only detachment. Desirelessness. 'Cessations from all hankerings' " ("Zooey," p. 198).

Here Zooey is echoing the passage in the *Gita* that urges us: "Renounce attachment to the fruits [of your actions]." And then he refers to another concept from the *Gita,* the concept

of *karma,* the effects that our actions and desires in previous
incarnations have on our present lives. He tells his sister: "Somewhere along the line—in one damn incarnation or another, if
you like—you not only had a hankering to be an actor or an
actress but to be a *good* one. You're stuck with it now. You
can't just *walk out* on the results of your hankerings. Cause
and effect, buddy, cause and effect. The only thing you can
do now, the only re*lig*ious thing you can do, is *act.* Act for
God, if you want to—be *God's* actress" ("Zooey," p. 198).
These ideas are a paraphrase of another passage in the *Bhagavad
Gita:*

> Now you shall hear how a man may become perfect if he
> devotes himself to the work which is natural to him. A man
> will reach perfection if he does his duty as an act of worship
> to the Lord, who is the source of the universe, prompting all
> actions, everywhere present.
>
> A man's own natural duty, even if it seems imperfectly done,
> is better than work not naturally his own even if it is well per-
> formed. When a man acts according to the law of his nature,
> he cannot be sinning. Therefore, no one should give up his natural
> work, even though he does it imperfectly. For all action is in-
> volved in imperfection, like fire in smoke.
>
> When a man has achieved non-attachment, self-mastery and
> freedom from desire through renunciation, he reaches union
> with Brahman, who is beyond all action.[3]

This passage explains Zooey's idea that we are all born for a
specific natural duty and that the most religious thing we can
do is to perform this duty with detachment, that is, to perform
it not for ourselves but for God. As the *Gita* quote on Seymour and Buddy's door says: "Perform every action with your
heart fixed on the Supreme Lord." And it is when he expresses
this idea to Franny that Zooey remembers Seymour's Fat Lady
parable.

After he tells Franny to "act for God," and to "be *God's*
actress," Zooey suddenly realizes that acting for God is the
same as shining one's shoes for the Fat Lady. When Zooey reports how he once wanted to go to the broadcast studio with
unpolished shoes and Seymour told him "to shine them for
the Fat Lady," Franny remembers that Seymour told her some-

thing very similar, that he told her to "be funny for the Fat Lady." At this point, a realization hits Zooey, and he tells his sister:

> "I don't care where an actor acts. It can be in summer stock, it can be over a radio, it can be over *tele*vision, it can be in a goddam Broadway theatre, complete with the most fashionable, most well-fed, most sunburned-looking audience you can imagine. But I'll tell you a terrible secret—Are you listening to me? *There isn't anyone out there who isn't Seymour's Fat Lady.* That includes your Professor Tupper, buddy. And all his goddam cousins by the dozens. There isn't anyone *any*where that isn't Seymour's Fat Lady. Don't you know that? Don't you know that goddam secret yet? And don't you know—*listen* to me, now—*don't you know who that Fat Lady really is*? . . . Ah, buddy. Ah, buddy. It's Christ Himself. Christ Himself, buddy" ("Zooey," pp. 201-202).

Zooey's excitement indicates that this is the moment of his epiphany. He realizes that Buddy's advice to act with all his might and Seymour's advice to shine his shoes for the Fat Lady are essentially identical with the idea of the *Bhagavad Gita* that the best path to God is simply that of performing one's natural duty without attachment to its fruits.

But since Franny's religious crisis revolves around Christian and not Hindu ideas, Zooey couches the ideas of the *Gita* in Christian terms. By doing that, he is able to help her pull out of her crisis. Zooey's notion that acting for the Fat Lady is acting for Christ recalls Christ's statement: "Inasmuch as ye have done it unto one of the least of these my brethren, ye have done it unto me" (Matthew xxv, 40). Because of their intensive religious training, Zooey and Franny must have been familiar with this concept and with the very similar teachings of the *Bhagavad Gita*, but they never realized that it held the key to their problem of how to get along with unspiritual people.

When Zooey explains the significance of the Fat Lady parable, he and Franny finally come to terms wth Seymour's legacy. They now realize that the religious education that Seymour had given them made them greedy for "spiritual treasure," for spiritual advancement toward union with God, and more importantly, that it also made them despise those who don't share their spiritual values. As a result of their inability to get along with normal people, Zooey wound up with a bleeding ulcer and Franny with a nervous breakdown. But as Zooey ponders Seymour's teachings, he realizes that Seymour eventually gave up the self-directed paths of study and meditation, and began to advocate *karma yoga,* the other-directed path of service recommended by the *Bhagavad Gita.*

The story "Zooey" thus clarifies Seymour's teachings and explains the discrepancy between what he practiced and what he preached. By showing what problems Zooey and Franny have as a result of the religious education Seymour gave them, the story corroborates what other parts of the composite novel suggest, namely that Seymour's spiritual deterioration was due chiefly to his single-minded pursuit of his quest for God via the self-directed paths of study and meditation, *jnana* and *raja yoga.* The story shows that by following Seymour's example, Zooey and Franny have become unable to love unspiritual people or even to get along with them.

However, the story also confirms that Seymour eventually recognized his mistake and tried to correct it by shifting to *karma yoga,* the path of service which is advocated by the *Bhagavad Gita.* But as it turned out, Seymour was unable to become a successful *karma yogin,* partly because of external circumstances and partly because his spiritual deterioration had already progressed too far. Nevertheless, he tried to pass his changed outlook on to his siblings, and Zooey and Franny belatedly realize that they should not follow Seymour's example but his teachings.

"Zooey" spells out these teachings more clearly and comes closer to summing up the overall meanings of the Glass series than any other part of the composite novel. The story suggests that the essence of Seymour's teachings is identical with the central idea of the *Bhagavad Gita,* with the idea that for most people the best path of spiritual advancement is not accumulation of abstract knowledge or withdrawal into self-directed religious practices but selfless performance of everyday duties. And this idea is expressed most memorably and concisely when Seymour tells Zooey to shine his shoes for the Fat Lady.

NOTES

[1] The quotations from the Glass stories in this chapter come from the Bantam paperback editions of *Franny and Zooey* (New York, 1964) and *Raise High the Roof Beam, Carpenters and Seymour—An Introduction* (New York, 1965).

[2] *Bhagavad Gita*, II, 47-49; in Swami Prabhavananda and Christopher Isherwood, trans., *The Song of God: Bhagavad Gita* (Hollywood: Vedanta Press, 1944), p. 40.

[3] *Bhagavad Gita*, XVIII, 46-49; in Prabhavananda, p. 127.

PART III

FORM AND MEANING

CHAPTER 17

The Unity of the Composite Novel

Beginning with "Raise High the Roof Beam, Carpenters" (1955), the later Glass stories all show that they are parts of a larger whole, of a narrative series or composite novel. They all contain references to events in earlier stories and they are all related by two interdependent thematic concerns, Buddy's development as a writer and Seymour's life and teachings. But what the composite novel has to say about these two themes is difficult to understand, because unlike other authors of short story cycles, Salinger did not impose any definite pattern on his series. Thus while the arrangement of the parts in Anderson's *Winesburg, Ohio,* Hemingway's *In Our Time,* or Faulkner's *Go Down Moses* clarifies their overall meanings, the lack of any definite arrangement suggests that Salinger's composite novel has remained uncompleted, and this has discouraged attempts to interpret it as a composite novel.[1]

Statements by Salinger himself provide contradictory clues concerning his plans. When he published the stories "Franny" and "Zooey" in one volume in 1961, Salinger referred to the Glass stories as a "narrative series" and stressed the role of Buddy Glass by calling him his "alter-ego and collaborator." He also mentioned that "a couple of stories in the series besides FRANNY and ZOOEY have already been published in *The New Yorker,* and some new material is scheduled to appear there soon, or Soon."[2] The two stories that had already been published are "Raise High the Roof Beam, Carpenters" and "Seymour—An Introduction," and he paired them off in another volume in 1963. It is curious that Salinger should mention only two other Glass stories besides "Franny" and "Zooey," and omit "A Perfect Day for Bananafish," the story of Seymour's suicide which was also published in *The New Yorker.*

This is particularly odd since Seymour's suicide is mentioned in all Glass stories except "Franny" and because the "Introduction" lists "Bananafish" as a story written by Buddy Glass. Salinger's failure to mention "Bananafish" in his dust jacket notes for *Franny and Zooey* suggests that, in 1961, he did not consider the story to be part of the Glass series, just as he had omitted some early Holden Caulfield stories from *The Catcher in the Rye*.[3]

After *Franny and Zooey* had been published, a cover story on Salinger in *Time* magazine reported an unnamed "friend" of Salinger's as saying that "Salinger intends to write a Glass trilogy."[4] If this is indeed what Salinger intended at that time, then *Franny and Zooey* is the first part and *Raise High the Roof Beam Carpenters and Seymour—An Introduction* the second part of that trilogy. And if the first two parts are any indication, the remaining part could be expected to consist of a third pair of stories in one volume. But in the dust jacket notes for *Carpenters* (1963), Salinger made a comment suggesting that his plans for the Glass series called for a format larger than a trilogy. He said that he decided to publish "Carpenters" and the "Introduction" in something of a hurry "to avoid unduly or undesirably close contact with new material in the series," and he mentioned that he had "several new Glass stories coming along."[5]

However, Salinger published only one more Glass story, "Hapworth 16, 1924," and this fact has some interesting ramifications as far as the form of the Glass series is concerned: For one thing, it can be taken as an indication that Salinger returned to his concept of the Glass series as a trilogy. It has been reported that after "Hapworth" Salinger submitted another Glass story to the *New Yorker* but withdrew it at the last minute.[6] The preface to "Hapworth" suggests that this might have been the story that Buddy says he was working on when his mother sent him Seymour's letter from Camp Hapworth: "a long short story about a particular party, a very consequential party, that she [Bessie] and Seymour and my father and I all went to one night in 1926." It may well be that Salinger decided not to publish this story because he realized that "A Perfect Day for Bananafish" makes a better companion story for "Hapworth," and that he stopped publishing after

"Hapworth" not only because he feels that publishing is a terrible invasion of his privacy, as he said in an interview, but also because "Hapworth" completes the Glass trilogy.[7]

Ultimately, what matters is not what Salinger's plans for the form of the Glass series may have been but what effect he has created by deciding not to publish any more Glass stories and not to arrange the already published ones in a definite pattern. This decision forces the reader to read the stories very carefully if he wants to understand their interrelationships and their overall meaning as a narrative series. By this decision, Salinger also limits his readership to those who are willing to make a greater effort to expand their understanding than does the average reader; for by not arranging the stories in a specific way, Salinger makes his reader an active participant in the process that gives shape to the composite novel. The reader must decide for himself, for instance, whether he wants to see the series as uncompleted and fragmentary or as a completed but unassembled trilogy. And the view he takes of the form of the composite novel will influence his interpretation of its overall meaning.

Salinger's decision not to impose a final shape on the Glass series—or his decision not to complete it—suggests that we ought not to interpret the significance of the stories in terms of any preconceived notions about the relationship between form and meaning in conventional short story cycles. This is also underlined by statements in the last three parts or the series which reveal that these pieces are not short stories at all but deliberate attempts to transcend conventional narrative forms. In trying to understand the unique form of the Glass series, we must therefore pay special attention to what its narrator Buddy Glass has to say about it.

In "Seymour—An Introduction," Buddy Glass comments at length on his plans for a narrative series about Seymour. He says that Seymour's character "lends itself to no legitimate sort of narrative compactness that I know of, and I can't conceive of anyone, least of all myself, trying to write him off in one shot or in one fairly simple series of sittings, whether arranged by the month or by the year." Then he goes on to explain:

> My original plans for this general space were to write a short
> story about Seymour and call it "SEYMOUR ONE," with the
> big "ONE" serving as a built-in convenience to me, Buddy Glass,
> even more than to the reader—a helpful, flashy reminder that
> other stories (a Seymour Two, Three, and possibly Four) would
> logically have to follow. Those plans no longer exist. Or, if
> they do—and I suspect that this is much more likely how things
> stand—they've gone underground, with an understanding, per-
> haps, that I'll rap three times when I'm ready ("Introduction,"
> pp. 106-107).[8]

Elsewhere in the "Introduction," Buddy says that he had written about Seymour before, and he refers specifically to "A
Perfect Day for Bananafish" and to "Raise High the Roof Beam,
Carpenters." In fact, so Buddy says, there has seldom been a
time when he hasn't written about his brother, and if he were
forced to write a story about a dinosaur, he would probably
"give the big chap one or two small mannerisms reminiscent
of Seymour" ("Introduction," pp. 111-112).

In writing the "Introduction," Buddy discovers why he
feels compelled to write story after story about Seymour
and why his account of Seymour's life and of his influence on
his family has to be open-ended. When he recalls how his brother
Waker once gave away his brand-new Davega bicycle just because some boy wanted it, Buddy comes to the "sudden realization that Seymour is my Davega bicycle" ("Introduction,"
p. 204). By this he means that his purpose as a writer is to
give away whatever insights he has concerning the meaning of
Seymour's life and death. And six years later, Buddy explains
this idea once more when he says in the prefatory note to "Hapworth": ". . . for a good many years of my life—very possibly,
all forty-six—I have felt myself installed, elaborately wired, and,
occasionally plugged in, for the purpose of shedding some light
on the short, reticulate life and times of my late, eldest brother,
Seymour Glass, who died, committed suicide, opted to discontinue living, back in 1948, when he was thirty-one" ("Hapworth," p. 32). Even though seventeen years have elapsed
since Seymour's suicide, Buddy still cannot "write him off"
because there is too much to say and because he still is not

sure that he fully understands his brother. Therefore, the only form that is appropriate for Buddy's biography of Seymour is that of the open-ended composite novel.

Despite its fragmentary plot and despite the radical differences between the form of the early and the later stories, Buddy's composite novel has a special kind of unity. Objective elements that pull the stories together are the voice of the narrator Buddy Glass and a web of shared references to events in the lives of the Glasses, particularly in the life of Seymour. These events reveal two lines of narrative development: one is the story of Buddy's growth as a writer and the other is that of Seymour's quest for God and his spiritual influence on his siblings. Moreover, the composite novel is also unified by two questions that take shape in the mind of every reader who reads more than one or two of the stories. One is the question why an advanced God-seeker such as Seymour killed himself and the other is why his siblings consider him a near-saint despite his suicide. Since these questions are never explicitly answered, the composite novel has the character of a puzzle from which several pieces are missing. But just as a puzzle completes itself in our minds, whether or not we put the last pieces in their places, so the Glass novel assumes a kind of subjective unity in our imagination, no matter how fragmentary it remains in objective fact.

This unity is not a matter of mechanical completeness but of organic harmony. William Blake, one of Seymour's and Buddy's favorite poets, describes this kind of unity when he writes: "But when a Work has unity, it is as much in a Part as in the Whole: the Torso is as much a unity as the Laocoon."[9] What mattered to Blake and to other Romantics was not that a work be complete but that its parts work toward a common purpose and that each part reflect a common spirit. This view derives from the conviction that form is secondary to idea, that substance is less important than essence. And as I have shown, Buddy's composite novel reveals the same belief that form should grow organically out of idea and that a writer is likely to do violence to his inspiration if he forces it into a mechanical unity.

It is tempting to speculate that the disjointed form of

the Glass novel may have a meaning similar to that of the frag-
mented structures of such short story cycles as Hemingway's
In Our Time and Faulkner's *Go Down Moses.* The stories of
Hemingway and Faulkner are based on the existentialist assumption that the world is chaotic and that man is the only possible
source of order. The characters in these stories are defeated
by the forces of disorder, and this is reflected in the deliberate
lack of unity of the short story cycles. By contrast, the Glass
stories are based on the assumption of a divine order and they
describe characters whose lives are quests guided by the belief
that man's highest goal is union with God. The disjointedness
of Salinger's composite novel therefore seems to be at odds
with the wholeness of its vision of life.

The apparent disjointedness of the Glass series can be
explained in terms of Salinger's religious and aesthetic ideas.
Like his alter ego and collaborator, Buddy Glass, Salinger seems
to believe that an artist should not consciously shape the structure of his work but allow his inspiration free rein. The structure of his work should come from his heart, that part of him
that is in touch with the source of all Beauty and Truth, rather
than from his head. If the artist works in this way, as a mere
instrument of a divine creative force, then his work, like any
organic thing, will grow its own shape. He may not understand that shape himself but he must not tamper with it (See
Chapter 8: Buddy's Philosophy of Composition).

Thus Salinger left the Glass series alone after he published
"Hapworth," rather than forcing it into any definite arrangement. By doing that, or, rather, by not doing anything, he gave
the reader the freedom to arrange its parts for himself. In this
way, paradoxically, Salinger gave the Glass series a much greater
latitude of meaning than it would otherwise have. The lack of
any apparent order in the composite novel therefore does not
express a negative but a positive view of life, a belief in a deeper unity which lies behind the apparent disjointedness of appearances.

NOTES

[1] As far as I know, there are no previous studies of the form of the Glass series as a short story cycle or composite novel. However, there are a number of good essays on thematic elements that unite the stories. See the section on "Overviews" in the bibliography.

[2] The full text of the dust cover notes for the 1961 Little and Brown edition of *Franny and Zooey* runs as follows:

> *The author writes:* FRANNY came out in *The New Yorker* in 1965, and was swiftly followed, in 1957, by ZOOEY. Both stories are early, critical entries in a narrative series I'm doing about a family of settlers in twentieth-century New York, the Glasses. It is a long-term project, patently an ambitious one, and there is a real-enough danger, I suppose, that sooner or later I'll bog down, perhaps disappear entirely, in my own methods, locutions, and mannerisms. On the whole, though, I'm very hopeful. I love working on these Glass stories, I've been waiting for them most of my life, and I think I have fairly decent, monomaniacal plans to finish them with due care and all-available skill.
>
> A couple of stories in the series besides FRANNY and ZOOEY have already been published in *The New Yorker,* and some new material is scheduled to appear there soon or Soon. I have a great deal of thoroughly unscheduled material on paper, too, but I expect to be fussing with it, to use a popular trade term, for some time to to come. ("Polishing" is another dandy word that comes to mind.) I work like greased lightning myself, but my alter-ego and collaborator, Buddy Glass, is insufferably slow.
>
> It is my rather subversive opinion that a writer's feelings of anonymity-obscurity are the second-most valuable property on loan to him during his working years. My wife has asked me to add, however, in a single explosion of candor, that I live in Westport with my dog.

[3] The five Caulfield stories that preceded the publication of *The Catcher in the Rye* (1951) are: "The Last Day of the Furlough," *Saturday Evening Post,* July 15, 1944, pp. 24+; "The Stranger," *Collier's,* December 1, 1945, pp. 13+; "This Sandwich Has No Mayonnaise," *Esquire,* 24 (Octo-

ber, 1945), pp. 54+; "I'm Crazy," *Collier's,* December 22, 1945, pp. 36+; "Slight Rebellion Off Madison," *New Yorker,* December 21, 1946, pp. 82+. Only the last two stories actually became parts of *The Catcher.*

[4] John Skow, "Sonny: An Introduction," *Time,* September 15, 1961, pp. 84-90; rpt. in Anatole Grunwald, ed. *Salinger: A Critical and Personal Portrait* (New York: Harper, 1962), p. 16.

[5] The full text of the dust cover notes for the 1963 Little and Brown edition of *Raise High the Roof Beam, Carpenters and Seymour—An Introduction* runs as follows:

> *The author writes:* The two long pieces in this book originally came out in *The New Yorker*—RAISE HIGH THE ROOF BEAM, CARPENTERS in 1955, SEYMOUR—*An Introduction* in 1959. Whatever their differences in mood and effect, they are both very much concerned with Seymour Glass, who is the main character in my still-uncompleted series about the Glass family. It struck me that they had better be collected together, if not deliberately paired off, in something of a hurry, if I mean them to avoid unduly or undesirably close contact with new material in the series. There is only my word for it, granted, but I have several new stories coming along—waxing, dilating—each in its own way, but I suspect the less said about them, in mixed company, the better.
>
> Oddly, the joys and satisfactions of working on the Glass family peculiarly increase and deepen for me with the years. I can't say why, though. Not, at least, outside the casino proper of my fiction.

[6] James Bryan, "Salinger and His Short Fiction," Unpubl. Diss. University of Virginia: Charlottesville, 1968, p. 75.

[7] Lacey Fosburgh, "J. D. Salinger Speaks About His Silence," *New York Times,* November 3, 1974, pp. 1, 69.

[8] The quotations from the Glass stories in this chapter come from the Bantam paperback edition of *Raise High the Roof Beam, Carpenters and Seymour—An Introduction* (New York, 1965) and from "Hapworth 16, 1924," *The New Yorker,* June 19, 1965, pp. 32-113.

[9] William Blake, "On Homer's Poetry & On Virgil," in *The Complete Writings of William Blake,* ed. Geoffrey Keynes (London: Oxford University Press, 1966), p. 778.

CHAPTER 18

Art and Religion

The overall meaning of the Glass series can be interpreted on at least three different levels. On the most basic level, the stories are related to one another by their concern with the lack of spiritual values in contemporary America and they develop this theme in terms of conflicts between the Glasses and the people around them. On a deeper level, the narrative series deals with Buddy's development as a writer and explores the problems of the nature and purpose of art. But the core of the Glass series is the religious theme that emerges from Seymour's quest for enlightenment.[1]

Whether we see the meaning of the composite novel as primarily philosophical, aesthetic, or religious depends on our own interests. But how much of this meaning we will be able to understand depends on how much time and effort we are willing to devote to the stories, because an understanding of Glass series as a composite novel requires a considerable intellectual and emotional commitment. It requires, first of all, a willing suspension of disbelief, for we cannot possibly come to terms with the meaning of the Glass novel unless we are willing to accept Seymour's superhuman intellect and his supernatural psychic powers. But accepting Seymour is not enough. If we really want to understand him, we must be willing to re-read the stories again and again until the complicated web of his life and his ideas grows into an organic shape in our minds, or rather, in our hearts. Furthermore, in order to grasp as much as possible of the overall meaning of the composite novel, we must also familiarize ourselves with the works of literature, aesthetics, and religious philosophy to which Seymour, Buddy, and Zooey refer in the stories. In short, an understanding of the Glass novel requires as much effort as do, for instance, T. S. Eliot's

"The Waste Land," James Joyce's *Ulysses,* William Faulkner's *The Sound and the Fury,* or, more recently, Thomas Pynchon's *Gravity's Rainbow.*

If we only read the texts of the stories themselves and do not care to expand our knowledge of aesthetics and religion, then we will find that the meaning of the Glass series is essentially philosophical because the stories are all concerned with the values by which people live and they all advocate a particular value system and vision of life. The values of Glasses are developed in terms of such conflicts as that of Seymour and Muriel in "A Perfect Day for Bananafish," Franny and Lane Coutell in "Franny," and Buddy and the Matron of Honor in "Raise High the Roof Beam Carpenters." These conflicts and the characters in the stories are so designed that we are made to sympathize with the intellectual and spiritual values of the Glasses and to condemn the superficiality and materialism of their antagonists. And the values of the Glasses reveal a vision of life according to which the physical world is merely a transitory world of appearances while the metaphysical world—the eternal world of ideas and essences—is the ultimate reality. Thus the vision of life in the Glass stories is one which, to a reader more familiar with Western than Eastern thought, will appear to be very similar to the philosophical idealism of the British and American Romantics. And the favorable comments that several stories make about such figures as Blake, Wordsworth, Keats, Shelly and the American Transcendentalists suggest that there is indeed a kinship between the vision of life of the Glass series and of Romantic Literature. This kinship becomes even more apparent when we read the stories as a *Künstler-Roman,* a composite novel about Buddy's struggle to come to terms with his art.

Buddy's development as a writer, his growing understanding of Seymour's ideas and the changes in the form of his work, reveal the aesthetic meaning of the Glass series. The form of Buddy's early stories shows that he was initially very much concerned with turning out polished products which follow conventional story patterns and please large audiences. Gradually, however, the form of Buddy's work became less rigid and its content more esoteric and less appealing to the average reader. These changes are due to the influence of Seymour's ideas. Buddy eventually came to adopt Seymour's belief that all great

art is created spontaneously, from the heart rather than the head, with the artist serving as the instrument of divine inspiration, a notion very similar to the Romantic concept of the artist as an Aeolian harp. In this view of the nature of art, inspiration determines form, for since the work originates with God, the artist should not impose any arbitrary form on it but should allow the form to grow organically out of the content. But the belief that the artist should follow his heart and not his head explains not only the irregular form of the later Glass stories, it also explains their religious preoccupation.

Related to Seymour's and Buddy's view that the nature of all great works of art is determined by divine inspiration is the idea that the purpose of art is to communicate the truths that the artist grasps when "all his stars are out," when he is truly inspired. The Glasses' view of the purpose of art is well expressed in Buddy's statement that the best poems are "utterances that please or enlighten or enlarge the invited eavesdropper to within an inch of his life." This statement reveals Buddy's acceptance of the time-honored concept that art should delight and instruct and that it is the function of the artist to serve his fellow man. And like Plato and the Romantics, Seymour and Buddy believed that the instruction that art provides should be philosophical or religious in nature. It should point out the divine essence of all things, the *Tao* of the Taoists or the *Brahman* of the Hindus, something that Seymour once called "the main current of poetry that runs through things, all things." Thus, according to the Glasses, great art is always religious, and true artists are God's servants and spokesmen. Because of the connection that Seymour and Buddy saw between art and religion, a full understanding of the aesthetic meaning of the Glass series depends on an understanding of its religious ideas.

The religious meaning of the Glass novel lies, paradoxically, both in the failure of Seymour's quest for God and in his teachings. Because Seymour killed himself in despair, he clearly serves as a negative example, and yet the stories all present his ideas as extraordinary insights. This apparent contradiction resolves itself when we realize that Seymour's mistakes and shortcomings prevented him from practicing what he preached, and that his life is therefore a negative illustration of the positive ideas contained in his teachings.

Seymour's failure as a God-seeker is chiefly due to his estrangement from common humanity, and this estrangement in turn is a result of the self-directed ways in which he pursued his spiritual development. Born a genius, Seymour made the quest for enlightenment the purpose of his life when he was still a child. At the age of six, he discovered Vedanta Hinduism and began to pursue his quest along the paths of study and meditation, *jnana* and *raja yoga*. By the age of seven, he found that his precociousness as "poet and private scholar" and his "consuming admiration for God" had estranged him from normal people to such a degree that his interactions with them led to conflicts which brought out his most negative tendencies. This problem was complicated by his emotional instability which he had said he had left uncorrected in his previous two incarnations. Although he knew that only dogged effort on his part would help him correct this instability and avoid the negative *karma* that his conflicts with others were bound to produce, he did not make that effort. Instead, he continued his quest for enlightenment in the self-directed manner in which he had begun it. By the time he was in his early twenties, he realized that his contempt and malice toward others had brought his spiritual progress to a halt, and he attempted to kill himself by slashing his wrists. But then he tried to correct his mistake by giving up *jnana* and *raja yoga*, the self-directed paths of study and meditation, and to continue his quest for God by following *karma yoga*, the other-directed path of action and service. Hoping to overcome his instability and his estrangement from common humanity and to reverse his spiritual deterioration by serving others rather than himself, Seymour tried to make a new beginning by signing up for military service and by getting married. But this change came too late, for he was unable to give up his habit of intellectual and spiritual discrimination, to follow his heart instead of his head. As a result, his deterioration continued until it made him commit suicide.

Thus the failure of Seymour's quest for God contains the warning that if we want to lead spiritual lives, we should not withdraw into self-directed religious practices because they will estrange us from common humanity. And since God is immanent in man, such practices will eventually also estrange us from God rather than bring us close to It.

When Seymour realized the negative effects that his self-directed quest for enlightenment had on him, he began to advocate *karma yoga,* the path of action and service is taught by the *Bhagavad Gita.* At that time, he inscribed a key passage from the *Gita* as the top entry on a panel of quotations on the door of his and Buddy's room:

> You have the right to work, but for the work's sake only. You have no right to the fruits of work. Desire for the fruits of work must never be your motive in working. Never give way to laziness, either.
>
> Perform every action with your heart fixed on the Supreme Lord. Renounce attachment to the fruits. Be even-tempered . . . in success and failure; for it is this evenness of temper which is meant by yoga.
>
> Work done with anxiety about results is far inferior to work done without such anxiety, in the calm of self-surrender. Seek refuge in the knowledge of Brahman. They who work selfishly for results are miserable.

The *karma yoga* concept expressed in this passage contains the essence of Seymour's teachings and of the religious meaning in the composite novel. This concept consists of three related ideas which are all illustrated in the later Glass stories, "Raise High the Roof Beam, Carpenters," "Zooey," "Seymour—An Introduction," and "Hapworth 16, 1924." These three ideas are that our work becomes an act of worship and a means of spiritual development if we perform it for God or for others; if we perform it as best as we can; and, above all, if we perform it with detachment.

"Carpenters" illustrates the basic notion of service to others as a means of spiritual development. In his diary, Seymour explains his hope that his marriage will help him resume his spiritual progress when he summarizes ideas from a miscellany of Vedanta: "Marriage partners are to serve each other. Elevate, help, teach, strengthen each other, but above all *serve.*" And by serving each other, so Vedanta teaches, the marriage partners are serving God. The service ideal of *karma yoga* also comes out in the story "Zooey," when Zooey tells Franny that she is so concerned with her own spiritual development that she is missing out on every single religious action going on around her. She doesn't even realize that the only kind of chicken soup that her mother ever offers anyone is "consecrated chicken soup," that Bessie is in fact serving God by serving others. Zooey therefore tells Franny not to use the Jesus Prayer as a substitute for doing her duty in life or just her daily duty but to make her work on the stage her religion and become "God's actress."

The second aspect of the *karma yoga* concept, the idea that our work becomes our means of spiritual advancement if we perform it to the best of our abilities, is expressed both in the "Introduction" and "Zooey." In the "Introduction," Seymour tells Buddy that writing is not really his profession: "It's never been anything but your religion." Therefore Buddy's duty is to "write his heart out" whenever he is writing anything. Buddy passes this advice on to Zooey when he tells him that since he had decided to become an actor, he should "act with all his might." And Zooey, in turn passes this idea along to Franny, telling her that since she wants to be "God's actress," she should "shoot for some kind of perfection" whenever she is on the stage.

But the most important aspect of *karma yoga* and of Seymour's teachings is the idea of detachment. This idea is illustrated in all four later Glass stories. In "Carpenters," the idea of detachment appears when Seymour summarizes the Vedanta view of marriage and says that marriage partners should "raise their children honorably, lovingly, and with detachment. A child is a guest in the house, to be loved and respected, never possessed, since he belongs to God." And Zooey also stresses the importance of the concept when he tells Franny that "the only thing that counts in the religious life is de*tach*ment." And then he defines detachment in the same terms as the *Bhagavad Gita* as "Desirelessness. 'Cessation from all hankerings'." That detachment means desirelessness is also illustrated in Seymour's letter from Camp Hapworth, when he writes that he would like to be able to miss his family without hoping that they miss him in return. He says: "I am utterly convinced that if A's hat blows off while he is sauntering down the street, it is the charming duty of B to pick it up and hand it to A without examining

A's face or combing it for gratitude."

But the best illustration of the concept of detachment occurs in "Seymour—An Introduction" when Seymour gives Buddy advice on how to shoot marbles. He asks him: "Could you try not aiming so much?" And then he explains that if Buddy aims too much, that is, if he is more interested in winning than making a perfect shot, then it will be pure accident if he hits the other marble. But if he can overcome his hankering for winning then his chances of making a perfect shot are much greater. And Buddy later gives a further illustration of the concept when he compares Seymour's marble shooting method with "the fine art of snapping a cigarette end into a small waste basket from across a room." Buddy says that most people will only be able to hit the waste basket "if they either don't care a hoot whether or not the butt goes in the basket or the room has been cleared of eyewitnesses, including, quite so to speak, the cigarette snapper himself." Thus the detachment that Seymour advocates is detachment from the tangible results of one's actions. Buddy drives this point home when he says that after Seymour heard his marble hit its target "it never seemed to be clear to him whose winning click it was. And it is also a fact that someone almost invariably had to pick it up and *hand* it to him."

Seymour's teachings and the religious meaning of the Glass novel are perhaps best summed up in Seymour's advice to Zooey to shine his shoes for the Fat Lady before performing on the radio quiz show "It's a Wise Child." Seen in the light of Seymour's Vedanta beliefs, and particularly in the light of the ideas of the *Bhagavad Gita*, the Fat Lady comment suggests that for most people the best path of spiritual development is service to others; and that by serving others we are serving God. However, to make this service a religious act, we should perform it to the best of our abilities—we should shine our shoes even though nobody sees them—and, above all, we should perform it without attachment to the fruits of our actions, that is, we should do our work for the sake of doing it well rather than for any applause or reward.

These ideas inform both the aesthetic meaning of the Glass series and the general meaning that the stories have for the amateur reader who just reads and runs. This becomes particularly clear in Buddy's discussion of Seymour's marble shooting advice; for in explaining what Seymour meant by telling him not to aim so much, Buddy points out the significance that this idea has for his own work as a writer and for the lives of his readers. Buddy's comments suggest that the artist will find the greatest satisfaction in his work when he concentrates on the creative act itself rather than worrying about its results, when he does not aim at any specific form and meaning but allows his intuition to shape his work and lead him to new insights. Only in that way will he be able to put himself in touch with the divine, with the essence of beauty and truth, and communicate a sense of it to his audience. Similarly, the average person will achieve the greatest sense of personal contentment when he performs his duty in life, or just his daily duty, with his heart fixed on doing it well rather than aiming for any tangible rewards; for as the *Bhagavad Gita* says: "They who work selfishly for results are miserable."

Thus Salinger's Glass series, despite the difficulty of its form and the complexity of its meaning, is not only addressed to those who are already in touch with the spiritual world of art and religion but also to those who are caught up in the material world of getting and spending. The Glass stories tell us, the mass of men who lead lives of quiet desperation, that we can achieve the meaning and contentment in life that has eluded us if we learn to look beyond appearances. Salinger's Glasses extend our vision and give us intimations of the divine essence hidden in the most common objects and incidents of everyday life, of the main current of poetry that runs through all things.

NOTES

[1] Most interpretations of the overall meaning of the Glass series were written before the publication of "Hapworth 16, 1924" (1965) and are of

a very general nature. The most notable ones are: Warren Hinkle, "J. D. Salinger's Glass Menagerie," *Ramparts,* 1 (1962), 48-51; Alfred Chester, "Salinger: How to Love Without Love," *Commentary,* 35 (1963), 467-474; Kenneth Hamilton, "J. D. Salinger's Happy Family," *Queens Quarterly,* 71 (1964), 176-187; and Lyle Glazier, "The Glass Family Saga: Argument and Epiphany," *College English,* 27 (1965), 248-251.

The best of the more recent general interpretations are Howard Harper, "J. D. Salinger—through the glasses darkly," in *Desperate Faith* (Chapel Hill: University of North Carolina Press, 1967), pp. 65-95; James Lundquist, "A Cloister of Reality: The Glass Family," in *J. D. Salinger* (New York: Ungar, 1979), pp. 115-150; and Dennis L. O'Connor, "J. D. Salinger: Writing as Religion," *The Wilson Quarterly,* 4 (Spring 1980), 182-190.

The aesthetic meaning of the Glass series has been discussed by Arthur Mizener in "The American Hero as Poet: Seymour Glass," in *The Sense of Life in the Modern Novel* (Boston: Houghton-Mifflin, 1964), pp. 217-246, and Kenneth Hamilton, "The Interplay of Life and Art," in *J. D. Salinger: A Critical Essay* (Grand Rapids: Eerdmans, 1967), pp. 11-21.

The two most detailed religious interpretations of the Glass series are Sumitra Paniker, "The Influence of Eastern Thought on 'Teddy' and the Seymour Glass Stories of J. D. Salinger," Unpubl. Diss. University of Texas: Austin, 1971; and Humayun Ali Mirza, "The Influence of Hindu-Buddhist Psychology and Philosophy on J. D. Salinger's Fiction," Unpubl. Diss. State University of New York: Binghamton, 1976.

EPILOG

Salinger as a Neo-Romantic Writer

Some critics have written Salinger off because they believe that his later fiction has turned away from the main highway of American literature and run into a dead end. Stanley Edgar Hyman, for instance, objects to the content and the form of the later Glass stories and calls them a "turgid hagiography" characterized by "anarchy and incoherence."[1] Hyman expresses the sentiments of several other critics when he advises Salinger that he had better return to the more conventional themes and forms of his earlier work in *The Catcher in the Rye* and *Nine Stories*.[2] Such negative assessments do not recognize that Salinger's later fiction represents, better than the work of many other writers, the typical traits of a major trend in recent American literature, a trend that can best be described as Neo-Romanticism.

Neo-Romantic elements in contemporary American fiction have been noted by such astute observers as Robert Scholes, Ray Olderman, and Arthur Mizener, but these critics do not agree at all on the major traits that distinguish this type of fiction, nor do they even agree on the authors whose work can be considered Neo-Romantic.[3] They do agree, however, that this trend is a revival of what nineteenth century Romantics called the Romance, a form of fiction that is not strictly mimetic but has as its special latitude, in Hawthorne's words, the "neutral territory, somewhere between the real world and fairy-land, where the Actual and the Imaginary may meet and each imbue itself with the nature of the other."[4] And indeed, much contemporary fiction creates fictional worlds which are not mirror images but symbols of the real world. Consequently, a reader who wants to enjoy and understand Neo-Romantic fiction must not only be willing to suspend his disbelief but, more importantly, he must be willing to adopt a symbolic and idealistic vision of life, or else he may find this kind of fiction turgid and incoherent.

Although analyses of individual contemporary novels and short stories have pointed out specific Romantic elements, in the works of Kerouac, Nabokov, Bellow, Mailer, Updike, Vonnegut, and Pynchon, no extended study has yet described the traits of content and form that are common to Neo-Romantic fiction in general.[5] Because Salinger's Glass novel contains more Romantic elements than the work of most contemporary writers, it may serve as a paradigm.

Like much contemporary fiction, Salinger's later Glass stories, "Raise High the Roof Beam, Carpenters," "Zooey," "Seymour—An Introduction," and "Hapworth 16, 1924," are Romances not only because they repudiate the Realistic tradition of mimetic representation in their plots and characters, but above all because their themes, their vision of life, and their view of art reflect philosophical Idealism rather than common-sense pragmatism. The plots in the Glass stories, for instance, do not consist of everyday incidents, as is the case in Realistic fiction, but of incidents that are unusual and often improbable. Remember, for instance, Seymour's "glimpses" of future events or of incidents in past incarnations and his taking ten stitches in his leg without anesthesia; or Buddy's memorizing a whole book in half an hour; or Zooey's communing with Seymour's spirit. As these incidents suggest, Salinger's characters are not average, typical people, as the personages in Realistic fiction usually are, but extraordinary people with almost unbelievable mental powers. Moreover, their problems are not those of average Americans but problems that will trouble only highly intellectual and spiritual people. Consequently, the themes in the Glass stories are also quite unlike those in Realistic fiction. They do not concern the individual's relationship to his society but his relationship to his art, to his *karma*, and to his God. In short, they are not the economic or psychological themes typical of Realism but the philosophical or religious themes typical of Romantic literature. These philosophical and religious themes reveal a vision of life that is, like that of many nineteenth century Romantics, an amalgam of Neo-Platonic and oriental ideas. And the view of art expressed in the Glass stories is also shaped by this ideology. Like Blake,

Emerson, and Hindu aestheticians, Salinger sees the artist not as a self-willed creator but as an instrument of the divine will. This divine will expresses itself through the artist's inspiration. And the purpose of the works that it makes the artist create is to enlighten and enlarge the reader by communicating to him a vision of the divine, to make him see more than he would see on his own.

Most of these Neo-Romantic traits of Salinger's later fiction have parallels in the work of such writers as Bellow, Mailer, Vonnegut, and Updike. But there is also an opposite trend in contemporary American fiction, represented by such writers as John Barth, Raymond Federman, William Gass, and Ronald Sukenick, a trend that has come to be labelled Post-Modernism. Like the Neo-Romantics, the Post-Moderns also repudiate the Realistic tradition, but their fiction is more deliberately non-mimetic. Also, they often include in their works shrill arguments against conventional fiction because it presents a world that has wholeness and meaning, while, in their minds, the real world is chaotic and meaningless. And this points to the essential difference between these two trends of contemporary American fiction. The vision of life of the Post-Moderns is, typically, existentialist or nihilistic and that of the Neo-Romantics is, typically, idealistic or religious.

There is considerable dispute among critics as to which of these two trends represents the mainstream of American literature. The general readers, however, have long since decided the question. They just do not find post-modern fiction enjoyable. At least this is what I find when I assign post-modern novels and stories in my college literature classes. The average reader's negative reaction to this kind of fiction has two reasons: He finds it too difficult to read because of its lack of structure, and he finds its vision of life too depressing. Although the television news seems to confirm daily that the world is indeed a mechanism that is rapidly unmaking itself into entropic, meaningless chaos, most people do not want to accept that view and instead, consciously or subconsciously, search for a pattern of meaning in the apparent disorder. Neo-Romantic fiction confirms their intimations of a benign pattern, of a divine plan. This is why writers such as Salinger, Bellow, and Updike, who point out such patterns, continue to attract larger readerships than writers such as Barth, Federman, and Sukenick, who only tell us that our worst fears are justified. Because of works of art that reflect the hopes and aspirations of an age rather than its doubts and fears have always had a deeper impact on a nation's cultural tradition, the works of the Neo-Romantics will probably outlast those of the Post-Moderns.

That Neo-Romanticism is indeed the mainstream of contemporary American literature was apparently also the opinion of the Swedish Academy of Literature when they awarded the 1975 Nobel Prize to Saul Bellow. Like Salinger, Bellow began his career in the forties with fiction which was firmly rooted in the realistic tradition and in an existential world view. This is apparent in his first two novels, *Dangling Man* (1944) and *The Victim* (1948). But in the fifties, Bellow, began to move beyond Realism and Existentialism, and *Henderson the Rain King* (1957) is his first full-blown Romance. *Henderson* is Romantic not only because of its bizarre plot, its extraordinary protagonist, and the central theme of the quest for spiritual regeneration but also because of its vision of life which bears an uncanny resemblance to Emersonian Transcendentalism. And with *Humboldt's Gift* (1975), Bellow has even moved beyond Idealism into mysticism.

Humboldt's Gift has much in common with Salinger's Glass series. It deals with a God-seeker who, like Seymour Glass, believes in *karma* and reincarnation. Like Seymour, he also pursues his spiritual quest by studying esoteric religious texts and by doing involved mental exercises from obscure meditation manuals. But the similarities go even further, for Charles Citrine, Bellow's protagonist, is, like Seymour, a writer. This gives Bellow the opportunity to express his views on the nature of the creative process and the purpose of art, and these ideas are strikingly similar to those expressed by Salinger. Both authors believe that writers are ultimately only instruments of a divine will and that the purpose of their work is the cure of souls. This sketchy comparison of the work of Salinger and Bellow suggests that Salinger's Glass novel is by no means outside of the mainstream of contemporary American fiction. For if it is, then so is the work of Saul Bellow.

What makes Salinger's later fiction more unconventional than the work of Bellow is the structure of the three last Glass stories. "Zooey," "Seymour—An Introduction," and "Hapworth 16, 1924" are experimental pieces which, as James Lundquist has observed, show a considerable structural resemblance to some of the experimental works of the Post-Moderns.[6] This is especially apparent in the "Introduction." But this story's self-reflexiveness, Buddy's constant commentary on the way in which he is composing the "Introduction," and its lack of a conventional plot are the result of a view of life and art that has nothing whatsoever in common with the ideology of such Post-Modern works as Barth's "Lost in the Funhouse," Federman's *Double or Nothing*, and Sukenick's *The Death of the Novel*. For while the Post-Moderns refuse to develop well-ordered plots because they do not see any order in life, and while they try to destroy the illusion of fiction because they want to reflect the process of entropic unmaking that they think is going on in the world, Salinger, in his later stories, does not want to impose an arbitrary structure because he believes that a work will grow its own shape and its own meaning if the writer just follows his inspiration. And in his comments on how he is composing the "Introduction," Salinger's narrator shows that he sees the creation of a work of fiction as an activity that reveals the unpredictable, organic way in which the divine order of the world takes shape. Because this divine order is not clearly apparent in our daily lives, it should not be obvious in works of fiction, either. This order will become clear, however, to those who respond to fiction and to real life with their intuitive rather than their rational faculties. Thus the apparent formlessness of Salinger's later fiction is not the result of a pessimistic denial of order but of a religious faith in the mysterious workings of an order-giving creative force.

Now it should be clear why some critics do not appreciate and understand Salinger's later fiction and why they wish he would return to the more conventional themes and forms of *The Catcher in the Rye* and *Nine Stories*. What they really object to is not Salinger's experimentation with short story structure but the ideology underlying his later work. Realists and existentialists themselves, these critics have no sympathy for the Romantic tendencies and the religious world view in Salinger's later fiction. Accustomed to mechanical and objective analysis of literature, they are unable to respond to the Glass stories in the spirit in which they were written. As a result they cannot enjoy and understand them.

Fortunately, amateur readers are less prejudiced than critics and therefore respond more favorably to the Glass stories and other similar Neo-Romantic stories and novels. And the reason why most amateur readers find that this kind of fiction pleases, enlightens and enlarges them more than the Post-Modern variety is that it confirms their intuitive awareness of a transcendent meaning behind the appearances of everyday reality.

Since Salinger stopped publishing, almost two decades ago, the Neo-Romantic movement in fiction has gained momentum. Realizing that the reading public is more interested in symbolic than in photographic representation of reality, many writers have followed Salinger's example, turned away from the conventions of the Realistic novel, and turned to those of the Romance. Even John Barth, one of the leading figures in Post-Modernism, has recently moved in this direction when he published *Sabbatical: A Romance* (1982). But Neo-Romantic tendencies are not only apparent in American literature. They are also prominent, for example, in the stories and novels of the most recent recipient of the Nobel Prize, the Colombian writer Garbriel Garcia Marquez (1982). And while Salinger may not have published enough work to qualify for a similar distinction, *The Catcher in the Rye, Nine Stories,* and the Glass series have been enough to secure his place in literary history as one of the most distinctive representatives of Neo-Romantic fiction.

NOTES

[1]Stanley Edgar Hyman, "J. D. Salinger's House of Glass," in *Standards: A Chronicle of Books for Our Time* (New York: Horizon, 1966), pp. 123-127.

[2]See Maxwell Geismar, "J. D. Salinger: The Wise Child and the *New Yorker* School of Fiction," in *American Moderns* (New York: Hill & Wang, 1958), pp. 195-209; Warren French, *J. D. Salinger* (New York: Twayne, 1963), p. 170; and Max F. Schulz, "Epilogue to 'Seymour: An Introduction': Salinger and the Crisis of Consciousness," *Studies in Short Fiction*, 5 (1968), 137-138.

[3]Robert Scholes, "Fabulation and the Revival of Romance," in *The Fabulators* (New York: Oxford University Press, 1967), pp. 17-34; Ray Olderman, "The Problem of Reality and the New Rationale for Romance," in *Beyond the Waste Land* (New Haven: Yale University Press, 1972), pp. 1-29; and Arthur Mizener, "The New Romance," *Southern Review*, 8 (1972), 106-117.

Interpretations of the Glass stories that see them in the light of Romantic ideas are: John O. Lyons, "The Romantic Style of Salinger's 'Seymour: An Introduction'," *Contemporary Literature*, 4 (1963), 62-69; Carl F. Strauch, "Salinger: The Romantic Background," *Contemporary Literature*, 4 (1963), 31-40; and Klaus Karlstetter, "J. D. Salinger, R. W. Emerson and the Perennial Philosophy," *Moderna Sprak*, 63 (1969), 224-236.

[4]Nathaniel Hawthorne, *The Complete Novels and Selected Tales* (New York: Modern Library, 1937), p. 108.

[5]Attempts to define American Neo-Romanticism have been made in the following essays: Ronald L. Davis, "All the New Vibrations: Romanticism in 20th Century America," *Southwest Review*, 54 (1969), pp. 256-270; Frank McConnell, "The corpse of the dragon: notes on postromantic fiction," *Tri-Quarterly*, 33 (1975), 273-303; and Peter A. Brier, "Caliban Reigns: Romantic Theory and Some Contemporary Fantasists," *Denver Quarterly*, 13 (1978), 38-57.

[6]James Lundquist, *J. D. Salinger* (New York: Ungar, 1979), pp. 152-153. For a more general discussion of the self-reflexiveness that is typical of much contemporary fiction, see Robert Scholes, *Fabulation and Metafiction* (Urbana: University of Illinois Press, 1979), pp. 210-218.

Bibliography

I

Salinger's Fiction

"The Young Folks," *Story*, 16 (1940), 26-30.

"Go See Eddie," *University of Kansas City Review*, 7 (1940), 121-124.

"The Hang of It," *Collier's*, July 12, 1941, p. 22.

"The Heart of a Broken Story," *Esquire*, 16 (September 1941), pp. 32, 131-132.

"Personal Notes of an Infantryman," *Collier's*, July 12, 1942, p. 96.

"The Long Debut of Lois Tagget," *Story*, 21 (1942), 28-34.

"The Varioni Brothers," *Saturday Evening Post*, July 17, 1943, pp. 12-13, 76-77.

"Both Parties Concerned," *Saturday Evening Post*, February 16, 1944, pp. 14, 47-48.

"Soft Boiled Sergeant," *Saturday Evening Post*, April 15, 1944, pp. 18, 82, 84-85.

"Last Day of the Furlough," *Saturday Evening Post*, July 15, 1944, pp. 26-27, 61-62, 64.

"Once a Week Won't Kill You," *Story*, 25 (1944), 23-27.

"A Boy in France," *Saturday Evening Post*, March 31, 1945, pp. 21, 92.

"Elaine," *Story*, 25 (1945), 38-47.

"This Sandwich Has No Mayonnaise," *Esquire,* 24 (October, 1945), 54-56, 147-149.

"The Stranger," *Collier's,* December 1, 1945, pp. 18, 77.

"I'm Crazy," *Collier's,* December 22, 1945, pp. 36, 48, 51.

"Slight Rebellion Off Madison," *New Yorker,* December 21, 1946, pp.

"A Young Girl in 1941 with No Waist at All, *Mademoiselle,* 25 (May 1947), 222-223, 292-302.

"The Inverted Forest," *Cosmopolitan,* 112 (December, 1947), 73-80, 85-86, 88, 90, 92, 95-96, 98, 100, 102, 107, 109.

"A Perfect Day for Bananafish," *New Yorker,* January 31, 1948, pp. 21-25; see *Nine Stories.*

"A Girl I Know," *Good Housekeeping,* 126 (February 1948), 37, 186, 188-196.

"Uncle Wiggily in Connecticut," *New Yorker,* March 20, 1948, pp. 30-36; see *Nine Stories.*

"Just Before the War with the Eskimos," *New Yorker,* June 5, 1948, pp. 37-40, 42, 44, 46; see *Nine Stories.*

"Blue Melody," *Cosmopolitan,* 125 (September 1948), 51, 112-119.

"The Laughing Man," *New Yorker,* March 19, 1949, pp. 27-32; see *Nine Stories.*

"Down at the Dinghy," *Harper's,* 198 (April, 1949), 87-91; see *Nine Stories.*

"For Esmé—With Love and Squalor," *New Yorker,* April 18, 1950, pp. 28-36; see *Nine Stories.*

The Catcher in the Rye (Boston: Little and Brown, 1951).

"Pretty Mouth and Green My Eyes," *New Yorker,* July 14, 1951, pp. 20-24; see *Nine Stories.*

"DeDaumier-Smith's Blue Period," *World Review,* 39 (May 1952), 33-48; see *Nine Stories.*

"Teddy," *New Yorker,* January 31, 1953, pp. 26-36, 38; see *Nine Stories.*

Nine Stories (Boston: Little and Brown, 1953).

"Franny," *New Yorker*, January 29, 1955, pp. 24-32, 34-43.

"Raise High the Roof Beam, Carpenters," *New Yorker*, November 19, 1955, pp. 51-58, 60-116.

"Zooey," *New Yorker*, May 4, 1957, pp. 32-42, 44-139.

"Seymour—An Introduction," *New Yorker*, June 6, 1959, pp. 42-54, 54-111.

Franny and Zooey, (Boston: Little and Brown, 1961).

Raise High the Roof Beam, Carpenters and Seymour—An Introduction (Boston: Little and Brown, 1963).

"Hapworth 16, 1924," *New Yorker*, June 19, 1965, pp. 32-113.

II

Salinger's Sources

The following works form the basis of Seymour's eclectic religious philosophy. All of them are either quoted, mentioned, or alluded to in the Glass stories.

Blyth, R. H. *Zen and Zen Classics*. 5 vols. Tokyo: Hokuseido Press, 1955-1962.

Bynner, Witter, trans. *The Way of Life According to Laotzu*. New York: Capricorn, 1944.

French, R. M., trans. *The Way of a Pilgrim and The Pilgrim Continues His Way*. New York: Harper, 1954.

Giles, Lionel, trans. *Musings of a Chinese Mystic: Selections from the Philosophy of Chuang-Tzu*. New York: Dutton, 1909.

—. *Taoist Teachings: Translated from the Book of Lieh-Tzu*. London: Murray, 1947.

Kadloubovsky, E. trans. *Writings from the Philokalia*. London: Faber, 1952.

Kierkegaard, Soren. *Fear and Trembling and The Sickness Unto Death*, trans. Walter Lowrie. Garden City: Doubleday, 1954.

M [Mahendranath Gupta]. *The Gospel of Sri Ramakrishna*, trans. Swami Nikhilananda. New York: Ramakrishna-Vivekananda Center, 1942.

McCann, Justin, ed. *The Cloud of Unknowing and Other Treatises*. Westminster: Novena Press, 1952.

Nikhilananda, Swami, trans. *The Upanishads*, 4 vols. New York: Harper, 1949.

Prabhavananda, Swami. *The Sermon on the Mount According to Vedanta*. Hollywood: Vedanta Press, 1963.

Prabhavananda, Swami and Christopher Isherwood, trans. *The Song of God: Bhagavad Gita*. Hollywood: Vedanta Press, 1944.

—. *Shankara's Crest Jewel of Discrimination (Viveka Chudamani)*. Hollywood: Vedanta Press, 1947.

Senzaki, Nyogen and Paul Reps, *101 Zen Stories*. London: Rider, 1939.

Shankaracharya. *Self-Knowledge (Atmanodha)*, trans. Swami Nikhilananda. New York: Ramakrishna-Vivekananda Center, 1946.

Suzuki, Daisetz Teitaro. *Essays in Zen Buddhism*. 3 vols. London: Rider, 1949, 1950, 1953.

—. *Manual of Zen Buddhism*. London: Rider, 1950.

—. *Mysticism: Christian and Buddhist*. New York: Harper, 1957.

Vivekananda, Swami. *Inspired Talks*. New York: Ramakrishna-Vivekananda Center, 1958.

—. *Jnana Yoga*. New York: Ramakrishna-Vivekananda Center, 1955.

—. *Karma Yoga and Bhakti Yoga*. New York: Ramakrishna-Vivekananda Center, 1955.

—. *Raja Yoga*. New York: Ramakrishna-Vivekananda Center, 1955.

III

Glass Criticism

Bibliographies:

Beebe, Maurice and Jennifer Sperry, "Criticism of J. D. Salinger: A Selected Checklist," *Modern Fiction Studies,* 12 (1966), 377-390.

Fiene, Donald M., "J. D. Salinger: A Bibliography," *Contemporary Literature,* 4 (1963), 109-149.

Starosciak, Kenneth. *J. D. Salinger: A Thirty Year Bibliography, 1938-1968.* New Brighton, Minnesota: Starosciak, 1971.

Sublette, Jack R., *J. D. Salinger: An Annotated Bibliography, 1938-1981.* New York: Garland, 1983.

Books and Monographs:

French, Warren. *J. D. Salinger,* rev ed. Boston: Twayne, 1976.

Gwynn, Frederick and Joseph Blotner. *The Fiction of J. D. Salinger.* Pittsburgh: University of Pittsburgh Press, 1958.

Hamilton, Kenneth. *J. D. Salinger: A Critical Essay.* Grand Rapids: Eerdmans, 1967.

Lundquist, James. *J. D. Salinger.* New York: Frederick Ungar, 1979.

Miller, James E. *J. D. Salinger.* Minneapolis: University of Minnesota Press, 1965.

Dissertations:

Brinkley, Thomas E. "J. D. Salinger: A Study of his Eclecticism—Zooey as Existential Zen Therapist," Diss. Ohio State University, 1976.

Bryan, James E. "Salinger and his Short Fiction," Diss. University of Virginia, 1968.

Mirza, Humayun Ali. "The Influence of Hindu-Buddhist Psychology and

and Philosophy on J. D. Salinger's Fiction," Diss. State University of New York at Binghamton, 1976.

Paniker, Sumitra. "The Influence of Eastern Thought on 'Teddy' and the Seymour Glass Stories of J. D. Salinger," Diss. University of Texas at Austin, 1971.

Anthologies:

Belcher, William F. and James E. Lee, eds. *J. D. Salinger and the Critics.* Belmont: Wadsworth, 1962.

Grunwald, Henry Anatole, ed. *Salinger: A Critical and Personal Portrait.* New York: Harper, 1962.

Laser, Marvin and Norman Fruman, eds. *Studies in J. D. Salinger.* New York: Odyssey, 1963.

Marsden, Malcolm M., ed. *If You Really Want to Know.* Chicago: Scott and Foresman, 1963.

[See also the Salinger issues of *Contemporary Literature,* 4 (1963) and *Modern Fiction Studies,* 12 (1966)].

Selected Commentaries:

"Seymour—An Introduction"

French, Warren. "Resurrection," in *J. D. Salinger,* rev. ed. Boston: Twayne, 1976, pp. 155-160.

Goldstein, Bernice and Sanford. "'Seymour: An Introduction'—Writing as Discovery," *Studies in Short Fiction,* 7 (1970), 248-256.

Grunwald, Henry Anatole. "Introduction," in *Salinger: A Critical and Personal Portrait.* New York: Harper, 1962, pp. ix-xxviii.

Hassan, Ihab. "Almost the Voice of Silence: The Later Novelettes of J. D. Salinger," *Contemporary Literature,* 4 (1963), 5-20.

Lyons, John O. "The Romantic Style of Salinger's 'Seymour—An Introduction,'" *Contemporary Literature,* 4 (1963), 62-69.

Slethaugh, Gordon E. "Seymour: A Clarification," *Renascence,* 23 (1971), 115-128.

Wiegand, William. "The Knighthood of J. D. Salinger," *New Republic*, October 19, 1959, pp. 19-21; rpt. in the Grunwald and Laser anthologies.

"Hapworth 16, 1924"

Bellman, Samuel I. "New Light on Seymour's Suicide: Salinger's *Hapworth 16, 1924,*" *Studies in Short Fiction*, 3 (1966), 348-351.

Goldstein, Bernice and Sanford. "Ego and Hapworth 16, 1924," *Renascence* 24 (1972), 159-167.

Metcalf, Frank. "The Suicide of Salinger's Seymour Glass," *Studies in Short Fiction*, 9 (1972), 243-246.

Quagliano, Anthony. *"Hapworth 16, 1924:* A Problem in Hagiography," *University of Dayton Review*, 8 (1971), 35-43.

Schulz, Max F. "Epilogue to *Seymour: An Introduction:* Salinger and the Crisis of Consciousness," *Studies in Short Fiction*, 5 (1968), 128-138.

Slethaugh, Gordon. "Seymour: A Clarification," *Renascence*, 23 (1971), 115-128.

"Raise High the Roof Beam Carpenters"

Baskett, Sam S. "The Splendid/Squalid World of J. D. Salinger," *Contemporary Literature*, 4 (1963), 48-61.

Goldstein, Bernice and Sanford. "Some Zen References in Salinger," *Literature East and West*, 15 (1971), 83-87.

Gwynn, Frederick and Joseph Blotner. "Raise High the Roof Beam, Carpenters," in *The Fiction of J. D. Salinger*. Pittsburgh: University of Pittsburgh Press, 1958, pp. 45-46.

Hassan, Ihab. "Almost the Voice of Silence: The Later Novelettes of J. D. Salinger," *Contemporary Literature*, 4 (1963), 5-20.

Schwartz, Arthur. "For Seymour—With Love and Judgment," *Contemporary Literature*, 4 (1963), 88-99.

Wiegand, William. "J. D. Salinger: Seventy-Eight Bananas," *Chicago Re-*

view, 11 (1958), 3-19; rpt. in the Grunwald anthology.

"A Perfect Day for Bananafish"

Bellman, Samuel I. "New Light on Seymour's Suicide: Salinger's *Hapworth 16, 1924,*" *Studies in Short Fiction,* 3 (1966), 348-351.

Bryan, James E. "Salinger's Seymour's Suicide," *College English,* 24 (1962), 226-229.

Genthe, Charles. "Six, Sex, Sick: Seymour, Some Comments," *Twentieth Century Literature,* 10 (1965), 170-171.

Goldstein, Bernice and Sanford. "Zen and *Nine Stories,*" *Renascence,* 22 (1970), 171-182.

Hassan, Ihab. "J. D. Salinger: Rare Quixotic Gesture," in *Radical Innocence.* Princeton: Princeton University Press, 1961, pp. 259-289.

Lane, Gary. "Seymour's Suicide Again: A New Reading of J. D. Salinger's "A Perfect Day for Bananafish," *Studies in Short Fiction,*" 10 (1973), 27-33.

Metcalf, Frank. "The Suicide of Salinger's Seymour Glass," *Studies in Short Fiction,* 9 (1972), 243-246.

Slethaugh, Gordon. "Seymour: A Clarification," *Renascence,* 23 (1971), 115-128.

Wiegand, William. "J. D. Salinger: Seventy-Eight Bananas," *Chicago Review,* 11 (1958), 3-19; rpt. in the Grunwald anthology.

"Franny"

French, Warren. "Pilgrimage," in *J. D. Salinger,* rev. ed. Boston: Twayne, 1976, pp. 139-143.

Galloway, David. "The Love Ethic," in *The Absurd Hero in American Fiction.* Austin: University of Texas Press, 1966, pp. 140-169.

Gwynn, Frederick and Joseph Blotner. "Franny," in *The Fiction of J. D. Salinger.* Pittsburgh: University of Pittsburgh Press, 1958, pp. 46-48.

Panichas, George. "Salinger and the Russian Pilgrim," in *The Reverent Discipline.* Knoxville: Univ. of Tenessee Press, 1974, pp. 372-387.

Seitzman, Daniel. "Salinger's 'Franny': Homoerotic Imagery," *American Imago*, 22 (1965), 57-76.

"Zooey"

Detweiler, Robert. "J. D. Salinger and the Quest for Sainthood," in *Four Spiritual Crises in Mid-century American Fiction.* Gainesville: University of Florida Press, 1963, pp. 36-43.

Galloway, David. "The Love Ethic," in *The Absurd Hero in American Fiction.* Austin: University of Texas Press, 1966, pp. 140-169.

Green, Martin. "Franny and Zooey," in *Re-Appraisals* (New York: Norton, 1965), pp. 197-210.

Hassan, Ihab. "Almost the Voice of Silence: The Later Novelettes of J. D. Salinger," *Contemporary Literature*, 4 (1963), 5-20.

McIntyre, John. "A Preface to *Franny and Zooey*," *Critic*, 20 (1962) 25-28.

Updike, John. "Anxious Days for the Glass Family," *New York Times Book Review*, September 17, 1961. pp. 1, 52; rpt. in the Grunwald and Laser anthologies.

Overviews:

Chester, Alfred. "Salinger: How to Love Without Love," *Commentary*, 35 (1963), 467-474.

Glazier, Lyle. "The Glass Family Saga: Argument and Epiphany," *College English*, 27 (1965), 248-251.

Goldstein, Bernice and Sanford. "Zen and Salinger," *Modern Fiction Studies,* 12 (1966), 313-324.

Hamilton, Kenneth. "J. D. Salinger's Happy Family," *Queens Quarterly,* 71 (1964), 176-187.

Harper, Howard. "J. D. Salinger—through the glasses darkly," in *Desperate Faith.* Chapel Hill: University of North Carolina Press, 1967, pp. 65-95.

Hinkle, Warren. "J. D. Salinger's Glass Menagerie," *Ramparts,* 1 (1962), 48-51.

Lodge David. "Family Romances," *Times Literary Supplement,* June 13, 1975, p. 642.

Lundquist, James, "A Cloister of Reality: The Glass Family," in *J. D. Salinger,* New York: Ungar, 1979, pp. 115-150.

Mizener, Arthur. "The American Hero as Poet: Seymour Glass," in *The Sense of Life in the Modern Novel.* Boston: Houghton Mifflin, 1964, pp. 217-246.

O'Connor, Dennis L. "J. D. Salinger: Writing As Religion," *The Wilson Quarterly,* 4 (Spring 1980), 182-190.

Wiegand, William. "Salinger and Kierkegaard," *Minnesota Review,* 5 (1965), 137-155.

IV

Works Quoted

Abhedananda, Swami. *Doctrine of Karma.* Calcutta: Ramakrishna Vedanta Math, 1944.

Anand, Mulk Raj. *The Hindu View of Art.* Bombay: Asia Publishing House, 1957.

Blake, William. *The Complete Writings of William Blake,* ed. Geoffrey Keynes. London: Oxford University Press, 1966.

Blyth, R. H. *Zen and Zen Classics.* 5 vols. Tokyo: Hokuseido Press, 1955-1962.

Bryan, James. "Salinger and His Short Fiction," Unpubl. Diss. University of Virginia: Charlottesville, 1968.

Bühler, Georg, trans. *The Laws of Manu*. Sacred Books of the East Series, vol. 25. Oxford: Clarendon Press, 1882.

Bynner, Witter, trans. *The Way of Life According to Laotzu*. New York: Capricorn Books, 1944.

Chaitanya, Krishna. *Sanskrit Poetics*. Bombay: Asia Publishing House, 1971.

Coomaraswamy, Ananda. *The Dance of Shiva*. New York: Noonday Press, 1957.

—. *The Transformation of Nature in Art*. New York: Dover Publications, 1956.

Emerson, Ralph Waldo. *The Selected Writings of Ralph Waldo Emerson*, ed. Brooks Atkinson. New York: Modern Library, 1950.

Eppes, Betty. "What I Did Last Summer," *Paris Review*, 80 (August 1981), pp. 221-239.

Fosburgh, Lacey. "J. D. Salinger Speaks About His Silence," *New York Times*, November 3, 1974, pp. 1, 69.

French, R. M., trans. *The Way of a Pilgrim and The Pilgrim Continues His Way*. New York: Seabury Press, 1965.

Giles, Lionel, trans. *Musing of a Chinese Mystic: Selections from the Philosophy of Chuang-Tzu*, New York: Dutton, 1909.

—. *Taoist Teachings: Translated from the Book of Lieh-Tzu*. London: Murray, 1947.

Graetz, H. R. *The Symbolic Language of Vincent Van Gogh*. New York: McGraw-Hill, 1963.

Hamilton, Kenneth. "One Way to Use the Bible: The Example of J. D. Salinger," *Christian Scholar*, 47 (1964), 243-251.

Hyman, Stanley Edgar. "J. D. Salinger's House of Glass," in *Standards: A Chronicle of Books for Our Time*. New York: Horizon, 1966, pp. 123-127.

Kafka, Franz. *The Diaries of Franz Kafka,* ed. Max Brod. 2 vols. New York: Schocken Books, 1948.

—. *Dearest Father: Stories and Other Writings,* trans. Ernst Kaiser and Eithne Wilkins. New York: Schocken Books, 1954.

Kane, P. V. *History of Sanskrit Poetics.* Delhi: Motilal Banarsidass, 1971.

Kierkegaard, Soren. *The Point of View for My Work as an Author,* trans. Walter Lowrie. New York: Harper, 1962.

Lundquist, James. *J. D. Salinger.* New York: Ungar, 1979.

M [Mahendranath Gupta]. *The Gospel of Sri Ramakrishna,* trans. Swami Nikhilananda. New York: Ramakrishna-Vivekananda Center, 1942.

Nikhilananda, Swami, trans. *The Bhagavad Gita.* New York: Ramakrishna-Vivekananda Center, 1952.

—. *The Upanishads.* 4 vols. New York: Harper Brothers, 1949.

Pandey, Ray Bali. *Hindu Samskaras.* Delhi: Motilal Banarasidass, 1949.

Paniker, Sumitra. "The Influence of Eastern Thought on 'Teddy' and the Seymour Glass Stories of J. D. Salinger," Diss. University of Texas at Austin, 1971.

Plato. *The Dialogues of Plato,* trans. Benjamin Jowett. Chicago: Encyclopedia Britannica Corporation, 1952.

Prabhavananda, Swami and Christopher Isherwood, trans. *Shankara's Crest Jewel of Discrimination.* Hollywood: Vedanta Press, 1947.

—. *The Song of God: Bhagavad Gita.* Hollywood: Vedanta Press, 1944.

Shastri, Shakuntala Rao. *Women of the Vedic Age.* Bombay: Bharatiya Vidya Bhavan, 1952.

[Skow, John]. "Sonny: An Introduction," *Time*, September 15, 1961, pp. 84-90.

Stevenson, Sinclair. *The Rites of the Twice-Born.* London: Oxford University Press, 1922.

Suzuki, Deisetz Teitaro. *Essays in Zen Buddhism.* 3 vols. London: Rider, 1949, 1950, 1953.

—. *Manual of Zen Buddhism.* London: Rider, 1950.

—. *Mysticism: Christian and Buddhist.* London: Allen & Unwin, 1957.

—. *Studies in Zen.* New York: Philosophical Library, 1955.

Saraswati, Ramananda. *The Hindu Ideal.* Madras: Patanjali & Co., 1933.

Thoreau, Henry David. *Walden and Other Writings,* ed. Brooks Atkinson. New York: Modern Library, 1950.

Van Gogh, Vincent. *The Complete Letters of Vincent Van Gogh.* Greenwich, Connecticut: New York Graphic Society, 1959.

Vivekananda, Swami. *Inspired Talks.* New York: Ramakrishna-Vivekananda Center, 1958.

—. *Jnana Yoga.* New York: Ramakrishna-Vivekananda Center, 1955.

—. *Karma Yoga and Bhakti Yoga.* New York: Ramakrishna-Vivekananda Center, 1955.

—. *Raja Yoga.* New York: Ramakrishna-Vivekananda Center, 1955.

Watson, Burton, trans. *The Complete Works of Chuang Tzu.* New York: Columbia University Press, 1968.

Watts, Alan. *The Way of Zen.* New York: Random House, 1957.

Yutang, Lin, trans. *The Wisdom of Laotse.* New York: Random House, 1948.

INDEX